Praise For
The Key to the Quarter Pole

"Always a winner! Come along for the ride!"
Rita Mae Brown
Mystery writer and author of the Sister Jane foxhunting series

"A galloping good read! A thoroughly enjoyable story of Thorough-
bred racing that takes you behind the scenes from the backstretch
to the winner's circle with fast horses and fascinating characters."
Leeanne Ladin
Author of *Secretariat's Meadow – The Land, The Family, The Legend*
Secretariat Tourism Manager and Historian at The Meadow

"Every day at the racetrack, you hear the same thing and say the
same thing – 'You could write a book about this place.' Well, Robin
Traywick Williams has written the book, weaving the ups and
downs of the racetrack into a captivating and entertaining read for
a racetrack lifer or a racetrack neophyte. All the color and the character of racing leaps off each page. My favorite line? 'Oh, I'm fine,'
she said lightly. 'I don't have a broken heart or a broken collarbone.'
That's the racetrack – where a broken heart and a broken collarbone
can feel like the same thing."
Sean Clancy
Eclipse Award Winner
Writer/Editor, *The Saratoga Special*

"The stable area or 'backstretch' of an American racetrack is its
inner sanctum. Here, those who are allowed access will experience
a world of horses and the people who care for them which is like
no other. In *The Key to the Quarter Pole*, Robin Traywick Williams allows her readers to become racetrack insiders, giving them
a fascinating tour deep into the workings of the "Sport of Kings."
Her own involvement in, and first hand knowledge of, horse racing
makes this narrative come authentically alive."
D. G. Van Clief
Chairman, Virginia Racing Commission

"Tighten your girth for this exhilarating gallop around Virginia's own Colonial Downs. Colorful characters and a realistic portrait of life on the racetrack make Quarter Pole both highly entertaining and informative. Prepare yourself to be swept into the colorful tapestry of life on the backstretch…its hopes, disappointments, horseflesh, and passions. A fun read from start to finish! I hated for it to end!"
Polly Bance
Master of Fox Hounds, Deep Run Hunt

"*The Key to the Quarter Pole* is an engaging read about an independent woman with a weakness for hard-knocking racehorses. Williams maps the terrain of central Virginia and the motivations of her characters with equal aplomb."
Maya Smart
Judge for James River Writers' and *Richmond Magazine's*
Best Unpublished Novel contest

"The glories and worries of life are celebrated in *Key*, a novel of ambition and passion. The sharply drawn characters—rich and poor, young and old, sensual and salacious— race against and with one another as the reader turns the pages faster to see how it all turns out: love affairs, racetrack careers, and especially the delicate knee of fourteen-year-old sprinter, Alice's Restaurant, a horse you'll grow to love.

"*Quarter Pole* is a novel for any reader—not just racetrack lovers— who likes a fast-paced plot and fascinating characters all brought together by a strong protagonist: Sixty-year-old Louisa Ferncliff steps out of the novel's pages, drinks with you, rides with you, lures you into the passion of her quest in the arms of the track, which you never want to leave."
Patrick Smithwick
Author of the memoirs *Racing My Father* and *Flying Change*

"I have never met this character before. [Louisa Ferncliff] is an original… The language is gorgeous, clean and clear."
Bret Anthony Johnston
Award-winning author of
Remember Me Like This (soon to be a motion picture)

"Better than a day at the races, Robin William's debut novel is a guaranteed winner. With humor and expertise, *The Key to the Quarter Pole* shows us what makes Colonial Downs run, from the bad knees on an old, promising horse to the bruised heart of Louisa Ferncliff, who is willing to bet on everyone's happiness but her own… I fell in love with Louisa all over again!!!"
Mary Kay Zuravleff
Award-winning author of *Man Alive!*

"[Robin Williams] has a very Anne Tyler way with characters. If Anne Tyler knew as much about horses and Virginia horse racing as Robin Williams, she might have written *The Key to the Quarter Pole*. Williams has a loving touch that breathes life into human and equine equally, sinking us into their lives as completely as if we were breathing the same air. People and thoroughbreds, even a goat, are lucky to have found life in this story."
Tracy Dunham
Mystery writer and author of *Murder on the Mattaponi*

"From the opening of Colonial Downs, the highs have been really high and the lows very low. For stable area workers, it is a roller coaster that never ends. This is one compelling story."
Stanley K. Bowker
Former executive secretary, Virginia Racing Commission

Also by the author:

Chivalry, Thy Name Is Bubba
Bush Hogs and Other Swine
The Last Romantic War

THE KEY
TO THE
QUARTER POLE

By

Robin Traywick Williams

Author - Robin Traywick Williams

Publisher
Wayne Dementi
Dementi Milestone Publishing, Inc.
Manakin-Sabot, VA 23103
www.dementimilestonepublishing.com

Cataloging-in-publication data for this book is available from The Library of Congress.

ISBN: 978-1-7325179-8-1

Cover design: Todd Marks

Graphic design by Dianne Dementi

Printed in U.S.A.

The Key to the Quarter Pole is a work of fiction. Names, characters, places and incidents are the products of the author's imagination or are used fictitiously. Any resemblance to actual events, locales or persons is entirely coincidental. Colonial Downs is a real racetrack in Virginia with facilities largely as described; however, all events described herein are fictional.

Dedications

For Cricket, an unfailing supporter in my every endeavor,

Katie Bo, my best editor and my favorite racing buddy,

and

All the men and women on the backstretch who rub and ride that noblest of animals, the Thoroughbred horse.

Glossary

Quarter pole (eighth-pole, etc.) – a striped pole marking the point on a racetrack one-quarter of a mile (one-eighth of a mile, etc.) from the finish line, set as a guide for jockeys.

Furlong – one-eighth of a mile.

Track surfaces – grass (turf); dirt. "Off track" means "muddy" or anything other than "fast."

Backstretch – (1) the part of a racetrack away from the grandstand; the side opposite the stretch and the finish line; (2) the stable area of a racetrack.

Dark day – a day with no live racing.

Simulcasting – showing races over a closed-circuit tv network, usually to other racetracks or to off-track betting parlors, in connection with taking bets.

Exacta – a wager naming the first two finishers in order.

Exacta box – a wager naming multiple horses, two of which must finish in the top two for a payoff.

Trifecta – a wager naming the first three finishers in order.

Tri box – a wager naming multiple horses, three of which must finish in the top three for a payoff.

Win-place-show – first, second, third.

Straight bet – a wager on a horse to win, place or show.

Exotics – wagers other than straight bets, e.g., exactas, trifectas, boxes, etc.

PPs or past performances – published statistics describing the details of a horse's performance in previous races, used by handicappers to predict future races.

Handicapper – a professional who studies past performances and predicts the outcome of races.

Claiming race – a race in which each horse is available to be claimed, or bought, at the established price of the race; the lowest level of races.

Stakes – the highest level of races.

Bug boy – an apprentice or beginner jockey, so called because of the asterisk beside his name in the racing program. Bug riders are allowed to carry less weight in races.

Hot walker – an employee who leads a horse around to cool him off after exercise.

PART I

Chapter 1

As Louisa peered between the shoulders of men crowding the paddock rail at Calder Racecourse, she felt a little itch under her third rib. It always started this way, she reflected, that itch to find the next thing, whether she was looking for it or not. Stuffing a long strand of gray hair into her loose bun, she smiled and looked around the paddock, hoping to see the next thing, perhaps wearing yellow ribbons or leaning on a leather shooting stick. She craned her neck, and a drop of perspiration slid down her spine. She might dress it up in her imagination, but the next thing was usually a horse. Or a man holding a horse.

She had a good view of the horses parading around the oval in anticipation of the ninth race—not that any of them merited much inspection. They looked like the junk you find in the last race of the day at most tracks: a few young horses destined to retire as maidens, a few old campaigners patched together with molasses and steroids.

I could train these horses, she thought. *I could fix them up and win with them.*

Louisa Ferncliff was a fixer. She fixed horses so they could run and win, horses with bad ankles or scrambled eggs between their ears. She fixed people, too, or tried to, juicing up jellyfish to take hold of their lives and get out of that bad place. She even worked sporadically at fixing her own life, which, given the impulsiveness with which she lived it, called for a lot of fixing.

Whenever the itch came, smelling all mauve and magical, she was powerless, although now in her later years, she tried to fight back a little bit. Once upon a time, she had closed her eyes and let it pull her into the arms of attractive men without regard for their extreme unsuitability. Then later of course she would have to fix that.

Sometimes it pulled her to the stables, where she usually found heartbreak in an irresistible shade of bay. The only fix for that was to go away, far far away, some place where they played football instead of racing horses.

Jockey-sized, Louisa held her place at the paddock rail by laying her gnarled hands on the metal rim and leaning in. As she looked at the horses, she heard a replay of a phone call from Mike Lucci. "Come to Virginia for the summer," Mike had wheedled. "All that beautiful turf racing at Colonial Downs. Just one more season. I need your help with Alice."

Alice's Restaurant, she thought fondly. A chunky bay gelding with a big knee and an even bigger heart. It was probably a measure of Louisa's attachment to the horse that she gave Mike so much pushback: She had quit the track and she wasn't going back, no matter how much Mike Lucci begged. That part of her life was over. No more fixing horses with problems. No more sending out horses that didn't come back. If Alice was going to be one of those, she didn't want to be there. She'd stay here in Florida with her sister and go watch the Miami Dolphins.

Defiantly, she slapped her folded program on the paddock railing. The landscaped oval was nearly empty. The derby hats and fuchsia ties had left the paddock with the big horses a week ago. Louisa looked at the connections for these pitiful leftover horses—the jockey smacking his boot with his whip and the trainer giving too many instructions. Owners didn't bother to show up for horses running in the ninth race.

Louisa opened her program and compared the hieroglyphics below each number to the horses before her. The Four, she saw, was a hard-knocking racehorse, a horse who showed up for every race and brought home a piece of the check month in, month out, puffy ankles and sore hocks notwithstanding. Her kind of horse.

The trainer of the Four horse looked across the paddock just as Louisa ran her eye over him. Their eyes met and held as he gave a slow smile of recognition. Then, almost imperceptibly, he cut his eyes to the horse and back to her again. Louisa laughed, a sound like tinkling bells.

The trainer, she knew, wasn't above disguising a horse's ability in order to load up on him at the mutuel window and make a big score. There were worse things a trainer could do, she thought.

"Riders up!"

The trainer gave the blue and green jockey a leg up and the Four horse fell in line with the others, striding off to the track as the jock knotted his reins and tested his irons. As the horse reached the track, Louisa saw him jerk the reins and try to bolt. The rider on the lead pony beside him laughed and kept a tight hold. "Hold on, old man."

Louisa smiled to herself. How many times had Alice's Restaurant tried to bolt on the way to the starting gate? Dead quiet, those horses with fifty-sixty starts, until they went to the paddock. They knew where they were going. She pictured Alice trying to jerk the lead shank out of the groom's hand, ready to get past this paddock foolishness and get to the starting gate, put his hooves on the loamy racetrack. He did it because he loved his job. No whip was needed for horses like that, who would run on three legs if you'd let them and retire to the farm with sore ankles and a broken heart.

Louisa's phone tweedled. Tapping the screen, she said, "I'm not coming back. This time I mean it." As she walked to the track to watch the horses warm up, she held the phone off to the side, leaving Mike Lucci's tinny voice to beg the few remaining fans on the apron.

"We had to put Alice back in training," Mike said. "He was nothing but skin and bones. Being away from the track made him miserable. He wouldn't eat. Walked the fence." Louisa could easily imagine the horse pacing back and forth, galloping along the fence when the horse van went out the driveway. "I've got a new boy here and he's been jogging Alice for a month. The horse has put on a hundred pounds. You wouldn't believe how good he looks." Yes she would, thought Louisa. She knew what was coming next. "We're going to take him to Colonial for the summer meet but I need you to come take care of him."

She was ready for a new adventure, but surely the next thing would be more enticing than going back to the track. She let out an exasperated sigh. Mike kept talking about Alice's Restaurant until finally she said, "How's his knee?" Louisa could have kicked herself. She could almost hear Mike smile over the phone.

"Cool as an iceberg."

"Yeah, I bet," said Louisa, watching the Four horse canter to the gate. "You never could feel heat in a horse's leg anyway."

"I know, Louisa, you're the best. You have to come see for yourself. Tell me if we're doing the right thing."

"I don't want you breaking down my favorite horse, like you did the last one."

"Now Louisa, that's not fair. That mare passed the vet. We had no way of knowing."

Louisa didn't answer. Always lurking in the corner of her eye was the sickening image of that rangy black mare stumbling in the stretch and hobbling to the wire on three legs, reins loose, saddle empty. Mike was right. She couldn't blame him for that. It was the hazards of racing.

It was why she needed to stay in Florida, the itch be damned.

"I don't know how you ever got to be such a good trainer," she said, "but you'll have to do it without me this time." She clicked the tinny voice off.

The horses were approaching the starting gate. On impulse, she hurried to the line of mutuel tellers. Louisa seldom bet. Fooling with horses made for a hard enough life without pushing all your money through the mutuel windows. As she waited in line, she made a deal with herself. If the Four horse won, she'd go to Colonial Downs and take care of Alice. If the horse lost…

Hell, if the horse lost, she'd go to Colonial anyway.

Chapter 2

There were two kinds of people at the racetrack and Boyd Keswick was both of them. In the morning he was an optimist and by the end of the day, sometimes sooner, when all the problems he faced as president and general manager of Colonial Downs in New Kent, Virginia, had exploded into full-bore crises, he was a pessimist.

Keswick—"Wick" to his friends—knew a pretty racetrack when he saw one. He had worked at some real dogs in his day, and it made him proud now to manage Colonial Downs, one of the prettiest tracks in the country. The brick façade with thirty-five-foot-high white columns mimicked the architecture of nearby Colonial Williamsburg, a handsome departure from old wooden grandstands or modern steel-and-glass.

Every night, despite the cost, Wick insisted that floodlights wash over the imposing building to catch the eye of drivers on Interstate 64 in eastern Virginia. Every morning before light, as he arrived for work, Wick circled through the parking lot to admire the building. On this morning in June, Wick could see reassuring signs of activity as employees prepared for the opening day of the summer race meet.

In two days' time, eight thousand fans would fill the building from the exclusive club-level suites on the fourth floor to the fixed benches and beer stands in the cavernous ground floor room. Crowds would spill out onto the concrete apron that sloped down to the railing along the loamy dirt surface where the horses ran and winners were crowned. Off to one side of the building in a fenced paddock, grooms would parade the star athletes—the shiny sweaty horses—while handicappers spouted unintelligible commentary over the loudspeakers. Bettors would queue up at the windows, studying creased programs with stony faces or pointing out the silly names of horses to their friends.

Wick himself would roam the facility, making sure his staff provided VIPs the perks they expected, assessing the efficiency of the mutuel tellers on the ground floor, noting the crowd's response to his handicappers and asking fans what they needed to make the experience more enjoyable. He was, after all, in the entertainment business and he had a lot of competition out there.

The grandstand, the fans, the betting windows all existed to support the part of the track Wick truly loved, the backstretch. Far across Colonial Downs' enormous mile-and-a-quarter oval lay another world, the cinderblock city where a thousand horses and hundreds of people camped out and staged a summer of races. Wick often thought of the backstretch as backstage at the opera, where an extravagantly dressed cast, talented principals and invisible stagehands combined to produce brilliant entertainment for the paying public. There was a cast of characters of endless variety, all sharing one thing in common: racetrack fever. He knew he had the worst case.

This morning as usual, Wick poured a cup of coffee from the first pot made by Rodell, the proprietor of the track kitchen. At five a.m., the kitchen—a combination restaurant, bar and poolhall for the residents of the backstretch— was already filling up with unshaven grooms who had stumbled out of the low dormitories the track provided as temporary housing for backstretch workers. Down the hall from the kitchen, the lights flicked on in the racing secretary's office, center of all the administrative activity of the backstretch, from stabling to race entries. As he stepped outside into the cool morning twilight, two commercial horse vans idled in line at the backstretch gate while security officers shuffled health documents and registration papers. A man parked his car nearby and walked briskly towards the secretary's office.

Wick smiled at the racing secretary, the boss of the backstretch. He pointed his coffee cup at the vans. "The circus comes to town."

Jack Delaney laughed over his shoulder. "Hope we don't have too many orangutans this year."

The brakes on one of the vans sighed and the vehicle chugged through the gate, blowing little puffs of dust as it eased past the rows of long cinderblock stables.

Twelve more horses, Wick thought as he wandered towards the barn area. Keep 'em coming. He needed a thousand to fill nine races five days a week for the rest of the summer.

Each morning, Wick left the kitchen with his coffee and worked his way up and down the long barns. Walking a couple of miles around the backstretch wasn't as strenuous as the tennis game he no longer had time to play, but it kept him feeling good for a sixty-year-old. He inspected the activity at the two gaps in the track railing where horses came and went for their daily exercise routine, spoke to the outriders who patrolled the gaps during training hours and walked from barn to barn picking up gossip and complaints from the trainers in residence.

It was his favorite time of day.

Normally that stroll through the barn area made for a soothing escape from his personal problems, but this morning, just as he neared the first barn, his phone chirped. It was the night nurse from Norfolk. His heart jumped from zero to sixty, as it always did. Something had happened to Claire. The nurses never called with good news.

"Hello?" he barked.

"Mr. Keswick, I'm sorry to bother you so early. This is Jeannette deLong. I'm the third floor Family Liaison Consultant at the Norfolk Living Home Health Care Center and I'm responsible for liaison with the families of residents on this floor. I've been supervising Mrs. Keswick's care for the past six months."

Get on with it, Wick growled. *I know who the hell is calling.* "Yes, Jeannette. Tell me what's wrong."

The nurse launched into a long, tedious description of Claire's medication and diet and her response to various modifications, ending with, "What do you want us to do?"

He was vexed.

How the hell did he know what to do? They were the professionals, weren't they? Wasn't that why he was paying them?

As the Family Liaison Consultant elaborated on her report, Wick waved his hand in frustration, slopping coffee over his hand. The scalding sensation brought him back to the moment as guilt dripped off his fingers. There was a time when he would have gone straight to his wife's bedside and discussed the issue—whatever it might be—with the staff and made a decision…a decision, he thought wryly, that he imagined would make some difference in Claire's condition. This time, though, he was struck with the irony of the situation. *They* were asking *him* what to do about…some trivial matter, making a show of deference to his judgment, treating the whole issue as though it *mattered.* They knew it made no difference. How many times had they done that? Patronized him, promoting in him a false sense of comfort, staving off the day when his rational recognition of hopelessness and his emotional sense of denial collided. Well, now that day had come, and the collision had produced an explosion of guilt. He couldn't surrender to hopelessness. It was disloyal. But he couldn't leave work to drive to Norfolk…for what? To accomplish nothing! He tossed the coffee in the dust, crumpled the cup and scowled, angry at the Family Liaison Consultant for disturbing his emotional equilibrium.

"Just do whatever you think best, Jeannette."

Wick grumped along the horse path, a shady winding dirt road between the barns and the track that formed the commuter highway for horses going to and from work each morning.

"Keswick!"

Wick looked up to see Max Fox, a trainer from Florida who competed every summer with Mike Lucci for the title "Leading Trainer." Fox stopped his golf cart and said, "I'm not accustomed to complimenting track management, but you've got the place looking really good back here. The trees make a big difference. Just wish they'd planted them ten years ago."

Wick smiled. "It's a start. Wish we could do more."

"Yeah, I know. We put on the show, but we live in the ghetto back here. Everything's got to look good on the frontside."

Wick shrugged. It was tough to balance spending to improve the lives of backstretch workers and spending to entice fans to come watch and gamble. Horsemen put on the show, but fans paid the rent.

"The basketball court and the movies make my guys happy," Fox said.

Wick nodded. "Good."

"Makes me happy 'cause it gives them something to do after work besides drink."

As the trainer drove on to the gap to watch his horses train, Wick resumed his morning constitutional with more of his customary pleasure. He knew who, from habit, was settled in each of the fourteen barns with their high, ventilated ceilings and cool concrete walls, and he stopped to see a trainer here, an exercise rider there, the blacksmith, the track veterinarian.

As he strolled beside the shed row of Barn Six, where leading trainer Mike Lucci set up shop with forty horses each summer, he was pleased to see the man himself, directing grooms with short sharp gestures and barking commands. One of the vans Wick had seen by the gate idled at the end of the barn as grooms led a succession of horses down the ramp and into waiting stalls.

"How many you got coming?" Wick asked.

Mike did not turn to look at Wick but continued waving at grooms and pointing at stall doors. "Hey Wick. Nine more today. That's it till Louisa gets here."

"Louisa's coming back? No kidding?"

"Aw, Louisa can't quit the racetrack. It's in her blood," Mike said. "Gabriela! Get that filly out of that stall! Over here!"

"She swore last year she was through with racing," Wick said.

"She's been off watching football all winter. I'm betting she's ready to bandage some horses."

"Football?"

Mike shrugged. "She had to get over losing that mare."

Wick nodded. "That was ugly." The lowest low point of racing came with the catastrophic breakdown of a horse during a race. It didn't matter who you were, whether you trained the horse or bet the horse or just watched from the stands, it was a punch in the gut.

"I'll give you three-to-one she comes back. You want to see my hole card?" said Mike, still waving his arms and directing horse traffic.

"That filly you bought at Keeneland?"

"Nah," said Mike. "Here he comes now."

A groom led a solidly-built bay horse into the shed row. The horse's right knee sported an enormous red bandage, but Wick was drawn to the animal's face. Head up, ears pricked, the old horse beamed happiness from his bright eyes. He strode through the barn like he owned it. Wick whistled. "Alice's Restaurant? I thought you had retired him."

"We tried. He wouldn't eat. All his hair fell out. He was a damn bone rack. I figured I'd put him back in training and kill two birds with one stone."

Wick knew horses—and people, too—who couldn't leave the track. He left Barn Six picturing Mike's assistant carefully nursing the fourteen-year-old legs of a retired claimer as though the horse were a contender for the Breeders' Cup Classic. Louisa Ferncliff was one of the really good people who made Wick love the racing game. She was like a hard-knocking racehorse, always giving her best effort, thrilled

9

when she won, philosophical in defeat and so sick with racetrack fever that she would run her heart out on three legs rather than face retirement. The prospect of sitting in the Turf Club with Louisa and a couple of horsemen laughing over old times brought a genuine smile to his face. With his house empty and cold, Wick had come to substitute the Turf Club for his living room. He nodded with pleasure. "When will she be here?"

Mike laughed. "I don't think she knows she's coming yet."

Chapter 3

When you lived out of an RV, it didn't take long to pack. Louisa grabbed her nightie and a few things she kept in the spare room. Charlotte waited by the kitchen door as though preparing to block her exit. "Louisa..."

"Don't say 'Louisa' in that tone of voice."

"You can't drive off in the dark like this. You're being foolish."

"If I wait and go in the morning, you'll fix a big breakfast, then I'll be sleepy. Better to get on up the road a ways tonight."

Charlotte rolled her eyes. "I thought you had retired for good this time."

Louisa tried to squeeze past her sister with her bag. "Mike needs my help with a horse."

Charlotte grudgingly let her by, then trailed after her into the driveway. "Can't somebody else help him?"

"Not with this horse."

"Oh, Louisa." Charlotte's face took on a wistful expression. Shaking her head slightly, she said, barely loud enough for Louisa to hear, "You cried all winter over that other horse."

Louisa pushed her bag into the RV and turned to face her sister. "That's why I have to go back. I don't want to cry over this one." Charlotte was silent so long Louisa said, "What?"

"I worry about your being alone."

"I'm not alone at the track."

"You know what I mean."

Louisa shrugged. "You're alone."

"I had thirty-five years with Bryan and the girls come visit all the time. You saw how much they came.

"I had…Dean," Louisa said with an impish smile.

Charlotte snorted. "Well, at least you didn't say J. G. Lippin-cott."

"Oh right!"

Charlotte burst out laughing. "Louisa, you are impossible." She hugged her sister. "I do worry about you, though, hanging around with all those rough people, trying to help them with their messed-up lives. You're always looking out for everybody else. Who's going to look out for you?"

"I have my cat." She peered through the warm Florida night. "Here, kitty kitty kitteee!" she called in a falsetto. A calico emerged from under the vehicle and jumped into the old Winnebago. The two women hugged affectionately.

"Thank you for a wonderful visit," said Louisa. "I've loved being with you this winter."

Charlotte opened her hands helplessly. "What should I tell the man who's coming tomorrow to buy your RV?"

Louisa gave her an extravagant wave and climbed into the driver's seat. "Tell him it's gone!"

Louisa found a truck stop in Georgia about midnight and backed up next to the idling rigs to sleep a few hours. By five she was back on the road. It was her normal hour for rising anyway. She had a big mug of truck stop coffee and a full tank of gas, courtesy of the Four horse in the ninth race.

She drove through the Carolina sunshine making plans. First there was Alice's Restaurant. *I want to do right by the horse. He's miserable at the farm. But I don't want to run him if his knee isn't going to hold up.* Mike was a good horseman. Maybe she could get Mike to use Alice as a lead pony instead of racing him. The horse would be happy to be at the track and Mike could justify the cost of keeping him there. She wondered how many horses the trainer would bring. She would insist that Mike hire enough riders; if she was going to come out of retirement for Alice—it went unspoken that she would manage the rest of the barn, too—she would not, absolutely not, gallop any horses herself. She loved throwing a leg over a nice horse, but at her age, with her physical issues, it wouldn't take but one foolish two-year-old spooking at a leaf to plant her in the dirt. She'd already broken enough bones.

The more she thought about how she planned to run Mike's barn *this* year, the faster she pushed the RV up I-95. She pulled up to the backstretch gate just at sunset. The security guard gave her a big welcome.

"Ah, *la Madre*. Welcome back. Everyone is asking, when is she coming? We saved your parking place for you. The one in the back. Far away from the parties and the dorms," he said with a laugh. "The hookup is all ready."

Louisa smiled and let out a big sigh. "Oh Vinny, thank you. Am I glad to be here. It's a long way from Florida to Virginia."

The guard turned to his partner in the little building. "Go with *la Madre*. Hook up the RV for her."

Louisa waved. "No. No. I'm fine."

But the second guard was already opening the passenger door.

Colonial maintained a small RV park in the far corner of the backstretch, beyond the barns. Louisa and a few others who preferred quiet chose spots beyond the lights of the stable road. When she got the RV tucked under the trees by the back fence and all the hookups connected, she poured a glass of cranberry juice and sat in a lawn chair beside the RV. The lightning bugs and night sounds of Virginia danced gently around her. There was no moon, but she could see the end of the line of fourteen barns in the glow of the street lamps along the backstretch road. Horses bugled shrilly, asking where their stable mates from the last track had gone. Latin music and occasional laughter floated softly to her from the dorms. As she relaxed, Louisa knew that somewhere up the row of barns in a deep bed of straw, Alice's Restaurant rested contentedly, happy to be back where he belonged.

She let out her own contented sigh.

Later Louisa awoke to the wail of a siren. At first she thought it was a state trooper on the interstate, which ran along the north side of the track property. But then the cry became louder, closer, slowing down as it seemed to drive straight towards her camping spot. She heard shouts from the dorms and looked at the clock. It was about the right time for drunken fights. There was a time when Louisa would have investigated the fracas, but tonight she remained curled up with her cat. She chuckled to herself, lulled to sleep by the familiar, raucous sounds of the backstretch of a racetrack.

Chapter 4

Lawrence Hamner picked up two bobble-head dolls from the general manager's credenza and held them side by side. He rocked the cartoonish statues of a horse and a trainer, making the ceramic heads clack against the bodies in galloping rhythm. "They're at the top of the stretch, and it's Ferris Allen and Secretariat going head-to-head." He rattled the heads faster. "Now Allen puts a nose in front. Now Secretariat fights back." He began to shake the figures furiously, until the wire on one broke and the head popped off. "Oh! And it's Allen by a short head! But wait! Secretariat is claiming foul. The stewards are going to have a look at this one, folks, so hold your tickets. Wick, how about letting me be a placing judge?"

"No."

Boyd Keswick did not have time to fool with the clown prince of Colonial Downs. The Virginia Racing Commission was meeting in the morning and he had to produce a list of racing officials for the track's summer race meet for the commission's approval. Because horse racing involved gambling, the state's racing commission and their staff regulated everything pertaining to racing at Colonial Downs, which meant deciding, among other things, who could be licensed to work at the track.

At a time when many tracks struggled to survive, Wick felt the additional burden of making sure every day of the meet ran smoothly, a burden that began with hiring first-class staff. A week ago he'd felt good about this year's crew. All his best people were back, and he had upgraded some of the questionable ones from last year. But on Tuesday, Suzie, the horse identifier, called to say she was on probation and couldn't leave Maryland, and on Wednesday, George, the handicapper, fell over dead chopping wood.

Wick hired the new gal Suzie sent down from Maryland because he was desperate, not because he had any confidence in her. She seemed smart enough and knew about horses, but the application she filled out was almost illegible and he wondered if she were dyslexic or maybe illiterate. He'd have to keep an eye on her. It wasn't good to have a person who couldn't read in charge of verifying Jockey Club registration papers. On the other hand, over the years, he'd seen many people in the horse business work around what, at first glance, seemed like an insurmountable handicap, so he was willing to give her a chance.

That still left the handicapper slot to fill. Wick knew he needed someone who could pick winners but who could also relate to the crowd, most of whom didn't know an exacta box from an Exacto knife. A lot of tracks were using girls these days. Maybe he could find a girl who was good enough.

Out of the corner of his eye, Wick saw Lawrence pawing through his collection of Kentucky Derby shot glasses. He waited for the boy to break one so he could growl at him.

"Wick, I know my way around and I can do the drill now. How about letting me work in the paddock?"

"No."

Hank May, the track announcer, was a pretty fair handicapper, but Wick needed somebody else, somebody good to work with Hank on the pre-race commentary. He thought through all the heavy hitters who frequented the off-track betting parlors or staked out a regular seat in the simulcast center at the track. None of them would quite do. There was one guy who was good enough but he smelled bad. Wick knew fans couldn't smell him through the monitors around the grandstand, but he just drew the line at hiring somebody who didn't have enough pride to bathe.

Wick was pretty old school, and he liked handicappers who wore tweed coats and had some personality. George had an ersatz tweed jacket and was a decent handicapper but he put people to sleep explaining his picks. So Wick wasn't too sorry he was gone, even though it put him in a bind. This was his chance to upgrade.

He went through all the possible choices in his mind again while Lawrence Hamner ricocheted off the walls of his office. Lawrence came in every year looking for something to do during the meet to make a few bucks, anything to keep him at the track and supplement his income selling tout sheets. Wick liked the good-looking kid and always tried to find a place where Lawrence couldn't do too much damage.

The first year, Wick offered him a job running a camera in the first turn. Lawrence was grateful for the job. But the boy got so preoccupied with looking at the horses that sometimes he forgot to turn the camera on during a race, so the next year, Wick found a job for him in the racing secretary's office. He didn't contribute much to the productivity of the office, although morale there was high due to Lawrence's clowning around. While Wick and the racing secretary, Jack Delaney, both got annoyed the time Lawrence tried bungee-jumping off the grandstand, they never seriously thought of canning him. Lawrence, as annoying as he was sometimes, had become part of the racetrack family, and the family elders just kept looking for a suitable place to keep him.

Wick was thinking of all that history a week before Opening Day, the afternoon before the racing commission meeting, while Lawrence was strolling around his office, picking up all his racing mementos and looking at them while he talked and talked and grinned and made silly jokes and created so much static electricity with the friction of his personality against the air that Wick was afraid the whole room would go *crack!* if he tried to interrupt.

When Lawrence finally paused and smiled at him, Wick said, "Do you have a tweed coat?"

Wick was still in his office around eleven p.m., reviewing his notes for the racing commission meeting and second-guessing his decision to hire that goofy kid as a handicapper, when security called about a fire on the backstretch. *Fire.* He felt the blood drain from his face. Wick had visions of a thousand horses roasting in their stalls, and it was a second before he could ask where. He was at the Fairgrounds when the venerable New Orleans track had burned many years before. There was nothing more calamitous at a racetrack than a fire.

"Where?" he gasped. "How bad?" He ran down the steps of the grandstand as he listened to the answers and heard the first wail of sirens.

Six hours later, standing in front of the sodden dormitory while the New Kent County volunteer firefighters coiled up their hoses, a weary Wick asked the unanswerable question: "Why'd they build a fire *inside*? There's a brick grill right outside."

No one, not even the dorm residents who were standing around enjoying the spectacle, could explain why some of their fellow grooms had built a fire in a dorm room. Everyone professed such innocent amazement that Wick was sure they all built fires inside every night. He suspected it had to do with whatever they were cooking, which was either crack or one of chickens he heard squawking in the ravine next to the dormitory.

The backside of the racetrack was, at the height of the race meet, teeming with trainers and assistant trainers and lead pony riders and exercise riders and grooms and hot walkers. Those on the lower rung camped out in the dormitories provided gratis by the track, facilities they treated with the predictable level of respect.

When the track built some new dormitories, Wick insisted on low maintenance: Cinderblock walls on a concrete slab, with a drain in the floor of each room. That way, when the meet was over, all they had to do was bring in a power washer and hose down the cubicles.

After a long night of evacuating dorm residents and putting out secondary blazes, the volunteer firefighters headed home to clean up and go to their day jobs. Wick thanked them for their help and mentally decided on making a four-figure donation to the fire department.

"How much damage do you think?" Wick asked the maintenance superintendent.

The supe shifted his wad of chew, spit into a puddle and said, "It's cleaner now than it was before."

"How about the guys who started it?"

"They're long gone."

Wick ran both hands through his thinning blond hair and exhaled. It was almost five a.m. He'd go see if Rodell had any coffee going in the track kitchen, then go tell Mike Lucci one of his exercise boys wasn't going to be riding today.

Rodell, who ran the track kitchen, was a round little man of some indeterminate age between thirty-five and seventy. He had grown up in San Diego with his Chinese mother and learned to cook marvelous dishes for which, at the racetrack, there was little demand. Even if there had been any appreciation of his culinary skills out in the rural fastness of New Kent County, he was eternally unable to find the proper ingredients for his repertoire, at least until Wick drove him to the Asian market in Richmond one day. There, amidst the bins of packages with unintelligible labels and the baskets of strange but apparently edible plants, Rodell found brightly colored spices and mysterious, fleshy foods and crunchy roots with which to produce, in Wick's opinion, one of the most memorable meals he had ever eaten. Rodell had been so excited to have access to familiar cooking ingredients that he graciously compromised on the meat, which Wick insisted on selecting from a conventional American grocery store.

The influence of Rodell's Asian ancestry showed up mostly in his smooth round face, which had features applied to it like pepperoni on a pizza. He unconsciously enhanced the image by wearing a little brimless cap that made him look like he ought to be pulling a rickshaw. So it was always something of a surprise to his customers when he spoke to them with an accent heavily influenced by his Mexican father.

"*Buenos días, Señor* Wick. Is the fire done?" Rodell asked when the general manager came into the track kitchen.

"More mess than fire."

Rodell handed him a cup of coffee. "No one is hurt?"

Wick shook his head. "Couple trainers need to find new help."

"I am thinking it is Teg. He is *loco.*"

"You got any doughnuts yet?" Wick's thickening midriff did not yet extend beyond his barrel chest, allowing him to indulge in the cook's specialty.

17

Rodell pulled a tray of homemade doughnuts out of the oven and put some in a bag for *Señor* Wick.

Wick dropped a couple of bills on the counter. "Thanks." He headed out into the dark, sooty dawn, short on sleep, long on problems, and the meet hadn't even started. He squared his shoulders and strode bracingly towards Barn Six. As bad as it was, this was why Wick loved the racetrack: he never had time to think about Claire.

Chapter 5

As the sky turned pink, Alice's Restaurant stood patiently at the end of a lead shank, content to be back in the bustling shed row at Colonial Downs. Around the horse, the pungent odor of soiled straw rose from already-filled wheelbarrows, overpowering the sickly-sweet smell of molasses licked into the rims of the green feed tubs stacked nearby. Warning calls of "coming out!" mingled with cheerful Spanish expletives and the hard surge of water hosed into a bucket.

Trainer Mike Lucci held the stocky bay gelding while Louisa went over his legs like a blind woman reading Braille. First she squatted by Alice's right front leg and felt the grapefruit knee with both hands, pressing hard in several places, looking for the horse to flinch. Then she ran a hand down the back of each leg, her callused palm cupped around the tendon, her fingertips sliding along the flexor tendon as though searching for frets under a guitar string. There were lumps here and there, a popped splint that had set, an assortment of pimples that her fingers knew by heart.

Try as she might, though, Louisa could not feel any heat in Alice's knee. All four legs felt cool. His fourteen-year-old ankles were mushy, of course, but that wasn't where she feared a catastrophic breakdown would occur. It would be the knee or one of the long slender cannon bones that buckled under the concussion of a twelve-hundred-pound body pile-driving the legs into the dirt.

Mike spoke first. "What do you think? How 'bout that coat? Shining like a new penny. He looks good for his age, don't he?"

"He looks good for a lead pony," Louisa grunted and continued her examination. Mike did not respond to that notion.

When Louisa stopped and rubbed Alice's face, she said, "I was afraid you were conning me, just to get me up here, but he does seem to be okay."

"Ha! What'd I tell you?" Mike said. "Now how 'bout them legs? They cool? Like I said?"

Louisa finally laughed, a sound like wind chimes. "Yes, Mikey, you passed."

Mike stuck Alice back in his stall. "All right. Let's get down to business."

He went over his string of horses, so many here, so many yet to ship in from the farm or other tracks. Eventually horses trained by Mike Lucci and owned by people who lived up and down the East coast would fill thirty or forty stalls at Colonial Downs.

Louisa took that in stride but issued a stern warning. "We need another rider. Or two. You can't get all those horses on the track for morning exercise with three riders." Mike opened his mouth to speak but Louisa pointed a finger at him and said, "And I am not— Do you hear me?—not galloping any horses myself."

Mike held his hands up in surrender. "I've got this new boy at the farm, Jimmy Wiseman. I'll get him down here."

"Okay."

"He don't say much but he can ride."

"He doesn't have to talk. He just has to listen."

Mike laughed. "Yes ma'am, *Madre*."

Mike left for the farm at five-thirty and Louisa began wondering where in hell the third exercise boy was. Twenty minutes of happy-to-be-back burned off with the sunrise. She had threaded her way through the soggy piles of charred dorm furniture with surprise, learned that no one had been hurt in the fire and immediately turned her focus to Barn Six. Mike's crew knew Louisa's program and they had been ready when she appeared. The track opened for training at six, and she expected the first set of horses to be tacked up and walking around the shed row by quarter to six. Louisa frowned at the groom leading a bay horse with an ominously empty saddle.

Manny was on a small bay colt and Gabriela was leading a gray colt out of the stall. Louisa looked the gray over quickly and carefully with a skill honed by watching horses walk around the shed row every morning for more than thirty years. She checked automatically to see that the three-year-old was sound, something she was able to determine despite the fact he was pulling Gabriela this way and that, craning his neck to look at the other horses up and down the shed row.

When Gabriela presented the horse to her, Louisa rubbed the colt's face, murmuring to him as she looked into the dark pool of his eye. She believed looking horses in the eye was a way of establishing her authority over them. She had read somewhere about the Indians doing that and had immediately incorporated the practice into her morning inspection of each horse. In the seven years since she had been staring down fractious horses, her Indian trick had failed her only with gray horses and the occasional horse by Storm Cat they got in. Storm Cats tended to be nut cases and not even her eyeball-to-eyeball search of their souls was enough to settle them down.

But she was determined not to give up on the grays, and she fixed a keeper on this one's bridle as she gave him one last meaningful look.

Gabriela hopped on one leg beside the restive colt as Louisa grabbed her calf and gave her a leg up. "Next time make him stand still," she said. "He needs to learn the drill." *La Madre* had a program. You couldn't run a stable with thirty-five, forty horses in training without a high degree of organization.

With Gabriela and Manny up, two-thirds of the first set of colts were walking around the shed row. Louisa had seven more sets of horses to get out before the track closed at ten a.m. and the guy who was going to ride five or six of those horses was AWOL. She didn't waste energy being angry at an irresponsible employee; that was as much a part of the racetrack as saddle soap and sweat. Improvisation and getting the job done, that's what she had signed on for when she agreed to come back.

And Alice.

A piercing whinny caught her attention. She glanced up at the familiar voice and saw the plain bay head bobbing up and down over the webbing of his stall. "In a minute, boy. You'll get your turn."

When Wick walked into the end of Mike's barn, he smiled to see Louisa down the shed row giving some groom what-for. Her military posture gave her an aura of authority despite her short stature. Age had softened her looks instead of hardening them, and her heavy, gray-white hair, piled loosely on her head and starting to come down already, gave her a sort of dignified femininity. The word *elegant* came to Wick's mind, jeans and paddock boots notwithstanding.

By the time Wick reached the far end of the shed row, Louisa was sitting on a tack trunk buckling half-chaps around her lower leg. Her hand on the clasp was anything but elegant: brown, rough, the joints oversized from years of holding the reins at the barn.

"I see you've already heard the news," he said, as though they'd seen each other every day for weeks.

"Oh, hello, Wick. Yes, and we were already short-handed."

"Doughnut?"

She shook her head and zipped up her protective vest. "It's good for me to get on a couple. Keeps me young."

Wick smiled. "So how are the Miami Dolphins these days?"

"Missing me, I hope."

He chuckled. "Welcome back."

Louisa entered a stall with a tacked-up horse and began checking the keepers and the girth. "Yeah," she grunted as she pulled the girth tight. "I should have known better."

"I'm serious. Are you set up in your usual spot? The men taking care of you?"

At last Louisa looked directly at Wick, standing in the stall door. She exhaled and nodded. "Half the reason I keep coming back is because you're so good to me. Colonial feels like home."

Wick smiled.

Louisa was talented enough to be a jockey herself but she had come along too early, before women were readily accepted. Women had to fight for the right to race back then, and Louisa was too busy partying. Now, she retwisted her long gray hair into a tighter knot, clipped it, then stuffed it under her helmet and led the colt out of the stall.

21

"Manny? Gabriela? Are you ready?" Louisa called.

"*Si, Madre*," came the replies.

When Louisa had the colt standing properly, she picked up her left foot and let Wick grab her muscular calf and boost her up. Then her cell phone, lying on a bale of straw nearby, went off. Wick handed it to her. Mouthing thanks to Wick and signaling a groom to lead the horse, she talked as she walked the colt around the shed row.

Wick watched her admiringly and heard her tell Mike, "The boy might be good but he's gone now. Set fire to his dorm room last night… Who knows?… Yeah, well, bring him down if he wants to try it. We need some help."

The racetrack refrain, Wick thought. *We need some help.* No wonder Louisa wanted to retire. And no wonder Mike didn't want her to.

As the three horses walked to the track on the horse path, Louisa said, "All right, Manny, what do I need to know about this one?"

"Is *la Madre* galloping horses in Florida?" Manny asked.

Louisa snorted. "I haven't been on a horse since last season here."

Manny caught Gabriela's eye and they raised their eyebrows in unison. "My colt is good. Let me ride that one. He is strong."

"Are you telling me this colt is going to run off with me?"

Manny squirmed and Gabriela spoke up. "He is tough. I don't ride him."

She turned back to the barn so they could swap. Even the preceding season, when Louisa galloped one or two horses a day, she carefully selected the animals she would get on.

To her delight, the colt she switched to had a long swinging walk. She almost smiled out loud. It felt good to be back on a horse, especially a nice mover like this one. She anticipated standing over his neck, her hands lost in his blowing mane as his feet swished across the loamy track. Galloping was hard work and dangerous but it was the closest thing to racing, something everyone at the track dreamed about. When you saw a game horse thunder down the stretch and hold off a late charge from another horse, the thought always came: *Wouldn't it be amazing to know what that feels like?* That's why jockeys, despite their hard lives, were the envy of all who loved racing.

The three of them walked along the horse path to the gap in the railing that gave them access to the track. Trainers on cool Quarterhorses hung around the gap and watched their hot Thoroughbreds gallop past. A few rail birds sat on the fence, and the clocker's assistant stood nearby with a clipboard and a walkie-talkie to communicate with the clocker across the way in the grandstand.

"Hey, Louisa! I thought you were gone for good."

"There's always one more horse to gallop," she called back as the three of them jogged off the wrong way.

When her colt broke into a trot between Manny and Gabriela, her pleasure in the ride continued. You could almost set a tray of glasses on his back, he was that smooth. As the colt's long pasterns cushioned the shock of his gait, her own knees and ankles flexed in familiar symmetry. *Pat pat pat pat pat* they trotted under the streaky sky, under the long fingerling clouds that seemed to beckon her down the endless stretch. Despite her protests, Louisa never wanted to give up galloping entirely. And this was why: jogging down the track on a fresh summer morning and feeling between her calves, in the flexion of her ankles, in the tension of the reins, the rolling muscles of a good horse, a horse who might one day be a great horse, one she could watch bursting with grit and heart as he pinned his ears and stretched his stride and refused to let another horse come by him. It was magic. It was a disease. They all had it, she thought, without even looking at Manny and Gabriela.

But as soon as they turned around the right direction and cantered off, she realized she was in trouble. The colt stuck his nose out and dragged her around the track. Louisa stood up, crossed the reins and buried her hands in the colt's neck, popping the nine-month-soft muscles across her shoulders. The colt tucked his nose but did not let up on the pressure. As the burn crept up Louisa's thighs and across her lower back, she reminded herself, *First time back is hard.* She focused on keeping her back straight and her hands screwed to the colt's neck.

The pinky and ring fingers on Louisa's left hand had been broken badly that time a two-year-old had flung her into the corner post of the shed row. Even since, she had had to run the fat rubber-covered reins between her middle and ring fingers on that side, making it that much harder to hold a tough horse. When she was in shape—and younger—she compensated without much thought. But now her left hand began to throb along the old fault lines and the muscles in her back seemed to pull apart. *One more stride. One more stride. Do not let this horse get away from you.* Halfway around the oval, she went to Plan B, putting her feet in front of her for leverage and leaning back. Shifting her position was a signal to the horse to grab the bit and run, and Louisa felt the skin on her palms roll up and tear as she struggled to keep the colt even with his stable mates.

As they approached the gap after one circuit, Louisa could feel the horse getting away from her. The colt's neck bowed tighter and his haunches pushed him out of her hands, out of line with the other two horses. Louisa felt her fingers being ripped from their sockets. Beyond the pain, beyond the embarrassment of having a horse run away with her, Louisa the trainer worried about the horse. How long would it take to slow him down, once he reached full speed? Had he trained enough to blow out a half mile, a mile? What if he popped a splint or pulled a tendon? What if he were entered to race soon and she let him waste his race this morning? There was a reason horses had a prescribed training schedule. What a fine way to return to the track: wreck a horse's program.

Just as the horse leaped ahead of the others, she heard Manny call, "Okay. Mike say one lap for these ones."

The moment the riders slacked their reins the horses came back to them. Louisa's mount slowed with the others and Louisa half slumped on the colt's neck when he stopped pulling, unable to control the trembling muscles in her legs. *Thank God. Thank God.* She righted herself and turned to Manny, her face red as she breathed heavily. "That was close." No sense pretending otherwise. She did not express her opinion about what Mike had actually instructed Manny to do, she just wondered how she was going to risk galloping four or five more horses.

Even with vet wrap covering her hands, Louisa managed to ride only one other horse before her burned palms and sore back outvoted her dutiful determination to ride more. When Alice's Restaurant came back from a jog with a lead pony, Louisa sent her next mount out with the lead pony. Better for a horse to get a light gallop than to run off with his exercise rider. Annoyingly, with one hand swollen to a useless size, she couldn't tend to Alice's knee after the gelding's bath. When a groom brought her a sleeve of ice, she directed him to bandage it to Alice's big knee. Then she sat on a bucket beside the horse and tucked her hand inside the ice wrap. The horse leaned down and sniffed her hair. "Yeah, boy, I know what swollen joints feel like, too. Ice is good, isn't it?"

How could she have forgotten how hard it was to exercise a fit racehorse when you weren't fit yourself? There was nothing mauve and magical about a horse pulling your guts out. *I'll feel like hell tomorrow, but by the end of the week it'll be better,* she told herself. Then she could ride that smooth-striding colt again and bandage Alice herself. But even as she reveled in the memory of the streaky sky, the long stretch and the *pat pat pat* of light hooves, she felt a twinge of longing for Charlotte's porch.

Chapter 6

During her horse show career, Shannon Hill had shipped her horses in and out of Florida often enough to know that moving a horse around required the correct paperwork. So when she bribed the driver of a commercial horse van to put her three-year-old colt, Acky, in his one empty stall going to Virginia, she made sure he had enough paperwork to withstand any official inquiry into the horse's health, ownership or legal intended destination.

What she did not have was a stall at the other end to put the horse in. But that would just have to wait until she resolved a couple more issues. She was confident the van driver would unload the horse at Colonial Downs and not continue to drive all over the country with an unclaimed horse in the back, and she was equally confident that some nice person at Colonial Downs would put the horse in a stall and give him a bucket of water.

With Acky safely dispatched up I-95, she turned her attention to her two-year-old filly, Bread 'n Butter, who was stabled nearby at the training center.

"You'd better bring a pony," Shannon said as her friend, Richard, hitched up the trailer.

"A pony? What for?"

"I'm not sure how well she loads."

Richard looked at her skeptically.

"I mean because it's dark. If you have a buddy for her, I'm sure she'll walk right on."

As they approached the training center, Shannon directed him to the back gate. Once again, Richard eyed her suspiciously. As he turned the rig onto an unmarked sandy drive through the pines, he said, "Shannon, we're stealing your horse, aren't we?"

"How can we steal my horse? It's my horse, isn't it? I've got the papers right here. Now pull up a little further."

"If we're not stealing her, why don't we pick her up in the daytime, when there's somebody around to help us load her?"

"I wish you would quit talking about 'stealing' a horse. I'm exercising my right to move my horse somewhere else. Besides, I'm giving them another horse."

Richard snorted. "That old mare?" He himself had been given a worthless horse in lieu of the board bill one time and he knew what kind of reception this transaction would get, come morning.

Richard Sloan always thought Shannon Hill was the kind of girl he would like if he liked girls. She was adorable in a Jack Russell sort of way, cute and quick and feisty. He loved her energy and drive and her relentless optimism. That mare of hers was a real screwball but quite talented, and Richard was constantly amazed at how patiently Shannon worked to get the mare to perform. Shannon was a good rider and a good friend, and sometimes when Richard was feeling sorry for himself, he would call Shannon and she would cheer him up. He really loved Shannon. In fact, he loved her so much he went through a period of considering changing his ways for her. Thinking about Shannon like that made him wonder occasionally if he were bi, an exotic racy idea that he indulged himself in for sometimes hours at a time. But now that he had Gene, he was over that.

After Shannon's parents got divorced, she left the show circuit and drifted into racing, so he seldom saw her. She was always busy doing something to make money to support her horses. She didn't seem to have a regular job and he doubted her dad was supporting her, so he wondered how she survived.

Which sort of explained why he agreed to help Shannon move her two-year-old from the training center in Florida to the racetrack in Virginia. He was picking up a horse in Raleigh when Shannon begged to hitch a ride. He could hardly say no.

Shannon had picked Richard to help her with this project not only because he was her best friend and he had a horse trailer going towards Virginia, but also because he was a really good horseman. Now as she followed Richard's rig north through the Carolina night, she knew her confidence had been well-placed. Loading the stubborn filly had held them up a couple of hours and possibly cost her Richard's friendship, but she put that ordeal and Florida behind her and focused on Colonial Downs and the road ahead.

The truth was, she needed a fresh start. She felt as though she had been treading water in Miami. Her colt had raced several times and had little to show for it. She had begun to get a little worried about Acky. She had to figure out what would make the colt want to run before the stewards ruled him off. When she heard trainers talking about shipping to Colonial, which had the largest turf course in the country, she became convinced Acky must be a grass horse.

Plus her two-year-old filly, who was at the training center in Ocala, would be ready to start soon, and the soft dirt and resilient turf of Colonial would be good for a young horse, she decided. Moreover, at Colonial she could get away from the image she suspected she had of a rich horse show girl dabbling in racehorses— an image that persisted despite her immersion in the Hispanic culture that dominated the backstretch of the Florida racetracks. The 21-year-old pulled her hair back, wore old jeans and picked up the Spanish pastiche peculiar to *los caballos razas*, including a passable vocabulary of Puerto Rican and Cuban insults. Still, she couldn't completely hide her roots.

Shannon Hill had been raised to write handwritten thank-you notes and take her hostess a bottle of wine, a book or a *ballotin* of chocolates. Before she got hooked on racing, she had straightened her dirty blonde hair, experimented with highlights and worn more eye makeup than necessary. In high school, she showed hunters on the "A" circuit in Florida, an activity her father considered pointless.

"It's a sport," Shannon insisted, "like football."

"Horse racing is a sport," her father said. "The first horse across the line wins. Showing horses is an elaborate scam for gullible fathers with adolescent daughters."

When Shannon was a freshman at the University of Miami, Shannon's father left her mother for a younger woman with whom he promptly had a baby, which caused him to have post-nuptial amnesia, so that he lost all memory of his first marriage and the issue thereof. Occasionally he would have brief moments of lucidity, usually brought on by the shock of a phone call, during which he clearly recalled his firstborn child.

To assuage his guilt, Mr. Hill continued to provide tuition for Shannon to attend U. of Miami and to pay the board bill on her show horse, a Thoroughbred mare, now retired. Shannon's sophomore year at the university, which, technically, she never attended, provided the pattern for her junior and senior years. She simply pocketed the tuition money that her father put into her college account, investing it in her plan to be the breeder of expensive Thoroughbred racehorses. She had bred two young racehorses whose value was, so far, hypothetical.

Recently, her father had begun inquiring into her educational progress. The first few times, Shannon managed to string the conversation out without revealing the truth until he got bored and abandoned the topic. But she decided he was getting too interested on his latest phone call. The last thing she needed was for her father to find out where the tuition money had gone—at least not until she had converted that money into a profitable enterprise.

Grinding out the miles on I-95 as she followed the taillights of Richard's rig gave Shannon the leisure to refine her plan: Get both horses to Colonial Downs, then get them set up in their stalls and start galloping them. After that, the plan became mushy as a bowl of grits. She would enter the horses in some races, get a couple of wins for each horse and then either sell them or let them be claimed. Then somehow she would acquire more horses and do it again. She wasn't exactly sure how she was going to sell her two and acquire other horses, but she would cross that bridge when she got to it. In the meantime, she had to find Acky and arrange to get both horses into suitable races. She needed to go on and win a race with one of the horses pretty quick because she wasn't sure how long her stake from betting the rent money on the Four horse at Calder would last.

She had already paid Acky's trainer two grand and given her eternally broke mother some money. Hopefully, by the time her father called again… Okay, she didn't want to think about that.

Racing Secretary Jack Delaney stopped by the stall superintendent's desk and asked, "Luke, how many empty stalls we got?"

"Very few, Jack, very few."

"Did you ever find a home for that three-year-old colt?"

Luke grunted and shook his head.

"He still in the receiving barn?"

"Yeah. Freddy and Bones are looking after him."

"I reckon somebody will show up one of these days and claim him."

The two men shrugged in mutual amazement, and Jack said, "We'll give them till Sunday, then we'll raffle him off, okay?"

Luke brightened. "We could have a name-the-pony contest and give him away."

"Did you find out anything about the owner?"

"The owner's name on the papers is Shannon Hill. She's got an owner's license in Florida. The horse run five times down there and Sam Ben Fogle trained him, but he's not up here."

"What kind of horse is it?"

"It'll make somebody a nice show horse one day."

Jack nodded. "Can you get ahold of the trainer, ask him who he was sending the horse to?"

Luke consulted a Post-it note on his computer monitor and dialed a number. He had a short conversation, then hung up. "The trainer says he didn't ship the colt up here and he don't know what kind of deal the owner had. When I asked him what to expect, he just laughed and said for us to be ready when she got here because she was a piece of work."

Jack shook his head. "Okay, just keep tabs on the feed and bedding. We're not running a charity boarding barn." Jack went back to his office to work on the next condition book.

A guy who was working at the counter turned around and called to Luke, "Stall man? You got a customer."

When Shannon and Richard pulled into the receiving barn at Colonial Downs, the security guard sent her to the office. Luke, the stall man, seemed almost annoyed to see her.

"You got here just in time, girl, we're fixing to raffle that colt off this afternoon."

"Oh, I am *so* sorry. I was supposed to follow the van up here, but I had some trouble arranging transportation for my two-year-old, and I had to go to Ocala and take care of that, and it just took longer than I thought."

"Hmm," Luke said, his pen poised over the stabling sheet. "You got a trainer or you train them yourself?"

It was Shannon's turn to say, "Hmm." After the briefest pause, she said, "Yes, I train them myself."

Luke gave her a hard look but she didn't blink. Finally, he said, "You got a license?"

"I just got here. Is the licensing office open? I'll go get my license now."

"Nah, they'll be here at nine. Just wait here a minute." He left her at the counter and went into Jack Delaney's office and shut the door. She saw them talking earnestly back and forth. Then the racing secretary picked up the phone and made a short call. When he was done, Luke returned.

"All right, Missy No-license, here's the deal. We're going to put your two down in Barn Four, stalls twenty-eight and twenty-nine. You're going to be next to a trainer named Carl Starling. He's got four stalls. He said he'd put his name on the sheet till you can get squared away with your license. Does that work for you?"

"Oh, sir, I can't tell you how much I appreciate this. I knew y'all would take care of me."

Luke didn't crack a smile. "Go on and get that colt out of the receiving barn. Freddy and Bones are tired of taking care of him."

"How will I find them? I need to thank them and settle up."

"Don't worry. We'll send you a bill."

"I still want to thank the men," she said with a smile.

"You'll see them at the gap in the morning."

Carl Starling folded his cell phone and put it in his pocket. "Girls?" he called and his grooms gathered around. "The racing secretary has called and asked us to help a young lady from Florida who has just arrived with her two horses. They'll be stabled with us and they'll be under my name, so I know you'll see they get first-class treatment." He smiled.

"Will I be galloping the new horses?" asked Ashley.

"I don't know. We'll see when she gets here."

Carl had many of the same problems other horsemen had: a good horse who was lame at the wrong time, an owner who was three months late paying his training bill, a pickup he was trying to squeeze one more year out of. But the perennial plague for trainers—help—never seemed to bother Carl.

Most trainers had at least some Mexican help. They were good workers and they were cheap. But, except for Parson, an old black man who served as Carl's head groom, all of Carl's help were girls. Not just any girls, either. Somehow the seventy-nine-year-old trainer with three cheap claimers he had bred in the backyard attracted a bevy of pretty young single girls as grooms. He always had three girls for each horse. It was like summer training camp for the Dallas Cowboys' cheerleaders at the south end of Barn Four.

Carl's girls were eager to see the new horses and glad to have a larger string of horses in their care. If they couldn't have quality horses to confer status on them, they could at least have a little more quantity. It was hard to hang around the track kitchen and complain about how hard you were working when there were more grooms in your barn than horses.

Carl represented proof of Shannon's belief that somebody would be on the other end to take her horses in when they arrived.

His girls were making up a couple of stalls for her horses and he himself was smiling and welcoming her as if she were bringing in Grade I stakes winners. As the filly backed off the trailer and walked stiffly around, Shannon was glad she had Velcroed some shipping boots on her legs when they stopped for gas. They didn't provide much support, but it would have looked bad to unload the filly from a thirteen-hour trip with nothing on her legs.

Shannon offered the filly a drink and walked her in the grassy area between the barns while Richard unloaded her traps. The filly would walk briskly then stop suddenly to grab a few mouthfuls of grass before walking off again. Shannon let the filly tow her along, just as happy as the horse to be off the road and moving into her new home. She looked down the long barns that fenced them in, smiling dreamily at the parade of racehorses, bay, chestnut and gray, circling each shed row. Odd towels and ribbons of red bandages fluttered on the railing that ran along the outer edge of the shed row. Riders bantered with grooms and the melodious murmur of Spanish rolled behind the tinny sound of a radio playing salsa. Through a fringe of trees she could see the blur of horses galloping on the track. The dust in Virginia was different but the sweet smell of hay and sweaty horseflesh was the same. Shannon knew she would love this racetrack.

She thanked the girls who were making up the stalls and asked Carl where to find Acky.

"I'll go with you, honey. How long did you say he'd been in the receiving barn?"

"Four days, I guess. Can I borrow a chain shank?"

With the horses settled, Shannon and Richard went to look for a place for her to live. Shannon consulted Carl's exercise rider, who gave her directions to a couple of motels. The first one looked uninviting but the second one was worse. Richard tried to get her to drive on, but Shannon went back to check the rates at the Sta*light Motel.

"Sweetie, you can't stay here," said Richard. "If you don't get carried away by the roaches, you'll get a social disease."

"Ashley said a lot of exercise riders stay here. They call it the 'Staglight'," she said.

"Oh. Well. That makes me feel better."

"They've got a weekly rate—"

"I figured it was hourly."

"It's all I can afford."

Richard gave her a long look.

She gave him a big hug. "Thanks for helping me get my horse up here. And thank you for being such a good friend and putting up with all my…"

"Horse rustling? Fleeing across state lines? No problem. I have nerves of steel."

"I'm going to dedicate my first winner to you."

He got in the truck and rolled down the window. "Seriously, sweetie. Anything you win, you move to an apartment or something. That's the worst roach trap I've ever seen. You're not safe there."

"Bye, Richard. Have a safe trip." She blew him a kiss.

Shannon waved cheerfully as her friend drove off in a cloud of dust. When his rig disappeared, she found herself staring after it, following it in her mind's eye, a replay of the day years ago when her parents left her at summer camp. The camp in the North Carolina mountains was cool and green, not hot and dusty like the backstretch, but there was in the same distance a loud speaker making announcements and giving instructions that bore on her life. And directly in front of her the back end of a car with the only people she knew receded in a cloud of gravel dust. She was suddenly awash with loneliness.

Until she went to the stables.

From the moment she was assigned to care for a calf-kneed, sway-backed, brain-dead, fat little bay pony of indeterminate breeding, she was hooked. She had found in the summer camp stables a vessel in which to pour her previously unrequited affection and a screen on which to project her ambitions. By summer's end Shannon had learned to lean on horses, and when, in successive summers, her parents drove off and left her with a horse show trainer and a series of increasingly talented show animals, she readily transferred her trust and affection to the horse *du jour*.

The only difference now was she had no trainer to get her daddy to pay the bills.

Bread 'n Butter's crystal-shattering neigh pierced Shannon's reverie and she turned to see the worried filly pacing her stall. She walked briskly to the barn, ducked under the railing and began soothing the horse.

"It's all right, girl. I know it's a strange place but you'll get used to it," she said, stroking the chestnut neck. "You'll get to run and run and run here. You'll win lots of races, and then you'll be the queen of Colonial Downs."

Shannon fetched a bucket to sit on and Acky butted her with his head as she passed. "You too, boy. You're gonna love the grass here."

She sat down between the stall doors, caressing her horses with a steady stream of soft, desperate words. *This has got to work,* she thought.

Chapter 7

Track president Boyd Keswick entertained himself on the drive to the Norfolk Living Home Health Care Center by thinking of news to tell his wife. There was always plenty to tell about the track, but he tried to think of something to say about the house. He wanted her to know he was keeping things up while she was gone. He had a cleaning service but since he seldom used the front of the house, they got done in an hour. Recently, he had noticed the Christmas figurines on the living room mantel and he had wrapped them in newspaper and put them in a chest of drawers. The coffee maker had gotten pretty dirty. For some reason the maids didn't clean it. He pictured Claire dumping the soggy grounds, rinsing the carafe and wiping the machine briskly. Maybe he'd buy her one of those Keurig machines.

He pulled into the parking lot and wound through the undulating rows of crape myrtle, their bud-tipped branches arching over the curb. He smiled to see the shady spot on the end was empty. Leaving the windows cracked, he took a fat photo album off the front seat and walked to the front door. The doors slid open at his approach, and the receptionist smiled at him.

"Good morning, Mr. Keswick."

"How are you, Nicole?"

"Fine, thank you. Mrs. Keswick is waiting for you in the sun room."

When Claire Keswick began the descent into the physical and mental deterioration of Huntington's disease a decade ago, she and Wick had worked bravely together first to ignore, then to counter, and, finally, to cope with the effects. When she stumbled, they made a joke of it; when cooking became complicated, they went out; when she could no longer remember the proper sequence for washing clothes, he sorted the laundry and let her do it all on cold; and when her tremors caused her to fall out of bed, he put the mattress on the floor. She surrendered her car keys but not her willpower. When she became confused, belligerent and unable to speak intelligibly, he looked into her eyes and saw that she was still there and he held onto her.

He went through dozens of companions, aides and LPNs to keep her safe at home while he worked. The hours at the track during the live meet were long, bearable only because as a caregiver he needed the respite. Then, two years ago, at the end of the meet when he could focus on Claire again, Wick let the boys talk him into moving her to an institution. It almost killed him. He visited her daily at first. During the meet the next year, he could get away only on Wednesdays to see her. With no live racing on Wednesday, the usual crises of the race meet could be handled by Wick's underlings or they could wait. Wednesday became a sacred day. Visiting day.

When Wick entered the glowing golden room with picture windows framing a courtyard of orange daylilies, he found a person who used to be Claire Keswick belted to a wheelchair. Setting the photo album on a side table, he kissed her cheek, as he always did. "How's my girl today?" Pulling up a chair, he sat close to her, holding her hand and imagining that she held his in return. As he had done in the years before she became ill, he told her what was happening at work.

"I'm sorry I didn't get here last week. We're getting ready to open on Saturday and it's already crazy," he said, pausing to imagine her response.

Oh really? What happened?

"Some of the grooms built a campfire in the dormitories."

How awful! Was anybody hurt?

"Just my pocketbook. The dorms are nothing but cinderblock, I don't know why it costs so much to clean them up and put a few beds in there." With no place to stay, some grooms were sleeping in the barns, which was against regulations, but what could you do?

"Claire?" She raised her head slightly, like an old deaf dog struggling to respond to a distant call. "Look at this." He opened the photo album, loose pictures and news clippings sliding to the floor. Carefully, he turned the pages, pointing out Boyd Junior's fifth birthday party. David in a high chair. A tearful Jason wearing an alligator costume she had made. "Remember how the 'gator's tail kept falling off?" Claire clawed at the page and made vowel sounds. They were in Florida then, and their close friends, the Himmels, appeared in almost every photograph. "There's you and Karen beside the pool." Wick noticed how good Claire looked in that hot pink bathing suit, and he lingered over the old photo, remembering her soft curves when the suit came off. Then came Richmond and pages of pictures of graduations, a wedding in St. Paul's and Boyd Junior holding a baby. Claire turned her head in his direction and back to the album, her facial muscles slack, her eyes empty. She worked her mouth slowly.

Wick gathered the loose items that had fallen on the floor, carefully squaring them and arranging them in the front of the album and folding the cover shut. He slid the album onto a table and stared at it. That was their life. Their thirty-some years together, babies and grandbabies. No, it couldn't be. It was somebody else's life. Somebody he used to know.

At last he stood up. "Well, Sugar Pie, I've got to go. I love you," he said, kissing her cheek again.

Claire Keswick remained slumped to the side, exactly as he had found her an hour earlier. He studied her scalp, visible through her unfixed hair, then sank into the chair beside her again. Leaning forward, he hugged her awkwardly over the wheel of the chair, clutching her shoulders and pressing her head against his neck.

Let me go.

Wick released her, brushed the hair out of her face and left. When he reached his car, he realized with a guilty jolt that he was already rearranging tables and estimating the handle for Opening Day. Visiting day was over.

PART II

Chapter 8

Lawrence Hamner was having the time of his life. The twenty-five-year-old handicapper was standing in the middle of the paddock at Colonial Downs with a microphone in his hand, telling people what he thought about the horses in the next race. Thanks to the fact the horseracing network TVG had picked up Colonial Downs, thousands of people in the grandstand, at other racetracks and in betting parlors all over the country—*all over the world*—were watching him and listening to what he said. For a guy who liked to be the center of attention, it didn't get much better than this.

Hank May, the track announcer and Lawrence's running mate, stood beside him, and they made a good pair: Lawrence tall and dark, Hank tall and fair. Hank was in his early thirties, divorced and something of a ladies' man. Women were often beguiled into thinking they saw a streak of tender vulnerability in his boyish looks. Hank had a quick wit and he and Lawrence played off each other, throwing quips like a shortstop to first base.

In his first outing as the track's official handicapper, Lawrence had picked the daily double, including a thirty-two-dollar winner in the second race, thank you, ma'am. He anticipated bragging to Wick and milking him for information on the new girl in the racing secretary's office. As Lawrence and Hank waited in the paddock for the horses to be saddled for the eighth race, Lawrence told the announcer about target shooting with a friend.

"He had my .410 shotgun and he didn't know it would kick," Lawrence said, holding the microphone up to his cheek, mimicking sighting the weapon. "He fired that thing and—bam!—it jumped up and cracked him in the nose!" Lawrence illustrated by bashing himself in the face with the microphone. "Ow."

Hank laughed.

Lawrence bent over, holding his face. "Shid. By nose is breeding."

Hank pulled a handkerchief out of his pocket. "Jeez, Ham, even your nose breeds? Here." Lawrence's suffering was even funnier than the original story. "Hurry up," Hank said as the horses began parading around the paddock. "We're on in four minutes."

Lawrence mopped his face, but his nose wouldn't stop bleeding. Hank found a paper napkin somewhere and Lawrence stuffed it up one nostril, leaving a two-inch wick hanging out. Casting a glance over the walking racehorses, Lawrence said, "Okay, I'b ready."

Wick found himself enjoying Opening Day with more than his usual enthusiasm. Buttoning his navy blue blazer over a green horseracing tie, he toured Colonial Downs from the fourth floor Turf Club down through the clubhouse to the apron and the paddock with proprietary satisfaction, shaking friendly hands along the way. After a long dark winter, his living room was crowded with boisterous happy people.

The financial side of Wick's day was going well, too. He checked the handle after the fifth race and was pleasantly surprised at the number. Having Colonial on TVG was a godsend. As for Lawrence's contribution, Wick was more than satisfied with his new handicapper and not a little relieved. He had stood in the paddock to watch Lawrence and Hank describing the first two races for the cameras. Picking the daily double got Lawrence off to a good start and he looked like he was rolling confidently through the card. Whenever Wick caught a glimpse of him on one of the monitors that decorated every wall and table, Lawrence was giving a good analysis in terms people could understand. And on top of that, he and Hank were making little jokes and generally putting on a lively show. Wick was impressed.

By the end of the seventh race, Wick figured he had solved all the seating problems for racehorse owners and VIPs for the day. Surely folks could manage for three more races. He liked starting the summer meet with a soft opening on Friday because it gave him a day to make sure everything was running smoothly before the big day on Saturday. Of course, tomorrow he'd have seating nightmares all over again, as people showed up at the last minute expecting red carpet treatment. What he'd give for half a dozen more sky suites and any number of extra tables in the Turf Club. If the Breeders' Cup folks got serious about Colonial, the track owner would have to open his pocketbook and expand the luxury seating on the upper floors. That was a fight for another day.

Wick decided to go down to the paddock, see the horses in the feature race and maybe run into Louisa Ferncliff. He smiled at the thought of the veteran horsewoman's cheeky independence. It was hard to think of someone her age being impertinent, but that's what she reminded him of, a sassy impertinent teenager—albeit one with a rare gift of horsemanship. Her boss, Mike Lucci, put up with a lot, but it was worth it to the big-time trainer to have Louisa's skill in the barn.

Wick got to the paddock just as his two handicappers were giving their commentary.

"Lawrence, ChattahoochyCoochy is coming in off a two-month layoff after a successful winter at the Fairgrounds. She looks fresh and ready to run, but she might need a race to handle this distance. I'm going to use her in all my exotics. I'm going to box her with Gas Pump Girl and Pegaterrestrial."

"Hank, ChattahoochyCoochy is easily the glass of this raze," Lawrence said and went on to explain why Mike Lucci's filly should win.

Wick was looking for Louisa but Lawrence's voice sounded muffled and he turned to see why. He noticed Lawrence kept putting his fingers to his upper lip, which seemed to have sprouted an extra nose. A bright red nose.

"Unless she needs a raze – which I don't think she does, looking at her in the paddock here – she ought to gallop (snuffle, snuffle) past the rest of these fillies."

As soon as the camera light went out, Lawrence sprinted for the jockeys' locker room. Hank began making his way through the crowd to go upstairs to the announcer's booth to call the race. Wick stopped him. "What was that all about?"

"Lawrence got hit in the face with a shotgun," Hank said over his shoulder.

"*What?*" Wick shouted after him.

In the jocks' quarters, Wick found Lawrence bent over a sink spattered with blood.

"Are you all right?" Wick asked in alarm. "What happened? Hank said you got hit with a *shotgun*?"

Lawrence started laughing and spitting blood. "I'm all right. I'm all right."

Wick waited till he got cleaned up. Sitting outside the jocks' quarters with his head tilted back and another wad of tissue up his nose, Lawrence sheepishly told him the story. Why oh why, Wick thought, did he think this kid could be his handicapper?

Wick caught up with Louisa in the winner's circle with ChattahoochyCoochy and Mike. Most women trainers wore street clothes with the same sense of comfort as a farm hand in a Sunday suit, but Louisa's khaki skirt and polo shirt fit well and looked at home. A generous bosom softened her otherwise wiry frame. Her long grey hair, falling out of the loose knot on top of her head, gave her a comfortably casual look. The outlier was her hands, working hands with raised blue veins snaking under rough skin around prominent knuckles. Like an old campaigner, she showed the years of wear and tear. A dented copper bracelet hung from her wrist.

"Congratulations," Wick said. "She ran a nice race."

"The layoff did her good," Louisa said, gazing fondly at the sweaty filly. "I'm glad to have this filly back. She makes the whole barn happy."

ChattahoochyCoochy was one of those horses who found a way to win, whether she was supposed to or not. And her grateful owner often tipped Mike's staff when the filly won. As Mike's assistant, Louisa knew those tips meant a lot to the grooms who cared for the horse.

"Are you doing all right?" Wick asked.

"If you know any good riders, send them over," Louisa said, showing Wick her blistered palms.

He whistled.

"Mike says he's bringing a new boy down from the farm and hiring some freelancers, but I haven't seen any relief so far. And I want to retire from galloping."

"Just like you retired from the track."

Louisa laughed, charming Wick with the sound of wind chimes. "I'm getting good at retiring. Like a smoker: I've quit a million times."

"Come upstairs and let me buy you a drink," Wick said. Louisa took a breath and he thought she was going to turn him down. "I've got your special," he added. Louisa didn't socialize and seldom took a drink anymore but she liked cranberry juice. Wick had made sure the bar in the Turf Club was stocked.

"I can't refuse that," she said, letting the groom lead the victorious filly back to the barn.

Eager to continue the day-long party, Wick invited most of the people in the winner's circle to join him in the Turf Club for a late dinner as they watched the last two races: In addition to Louisa, he corralled Mike, Jack Delaney, the racing secretary, and his summer intern, Vicki Sullivan.

As they sat down, Vicki explained how a French major with a summer job in Paris ended up working for the racing secretary at Colonial Downs. When Muslim terrorists set off a bomb at the front gate of the U.S. Embassy in Paris, no one was killed and the damage looked worse on TV than in real life, but Vicki's parents immediately cancelled her summer plans. Her mother called Jack Delaney's wife and the next thing Vicki knew, instead of spending the summer immersed in French, she was working at a racetrack, where everyone spoke Spanish.

"It won't take you long to pick up racetrack Spanish," said Louisa. "I learned it in one summer."

"Have been in racing your whole life?" Vicki asked.

"Oh, I want to hear this," said Wick.

"I was with the New Orleans Saints for awhile," said Louisa, sipping her cranberry juice and ignoring Wick. "But other than that, yes. Since I got divorced. The first time."

Wick snorted and Vicki hesitated, but Louisa's blithe replies begged for more elucidation. Wick noticed Louisa's insouciant version of events skipped over her stint as leading trainer at the Fairgrounds. That was a fuzzy period she evidently didn't talk much about. He wondered if the Saints came before or after. Inevitably,

Louisa's life story got around to the years she spent working for New York trainer "Croaker" Norge. When it came to colorful racetrack characters, Norge led the pack. The whiskey—and the exploits that followed—made Wick wonder how he kept so many wealthy clients, but year after year, Norge trained a string of graded stakes winners.

"I've heard that name before," said Vicki.

"Everybody's worked for Croaker Norge at one time or another," Louisa said, including the rest of the table in her laughter.

Wick grinned, leaning back comfortably in his chair. They could stay up all night telling Norge stories. He had nothing to hurry home for.

When dinner arrived, the racing secretary and the trainer were talking shop.

"I see you brought Alice's Restaurant with you. You know we don't have a pool. How're you going to exercise him?" Jack said.

"Take him down to the James River," Mike said.

"It's been done," said Wick amidst the laughter. "When I was working for Norge, we had an old horse like Alice. He could run but he had bad ankles, so we had to exercise him in a pool to keep him fit. Well, the fella that owned him wanted to see him run at Saratoga. Always wanted to say he had a horse running at Saratoga. One time Norge saw they had a good race for him and he told the owner to go on over there for the week and watch his horse run. We had him at the Maryland Training Center where they have a pool but we had to take him up there three or four days early. He couldn't gallop and he couldn't stand in a stall the whole time, so every evening, we'd load that bugger up and take him out to this lake. Norge made me get in this canoe and paddle around while he held the horse's shank. The horse was used to swimming, so he walked on in the water to about his knees, but he didn't like the soft bottom and he'd paw the water every time before he'd go all the way in. Got both of us soaked every day. Damn near swamped the canoe."

"See what you've got to look forward to, Mike?" said Jack.

"Well, if you'd write him a race pretty quick, you might save me a swim. He can jog with a lead pony for awhile."

Mike and Jack negotiated conditions of a race that might suit the old horse, with Mike insisting the shorter the better. Jack, who kept a catalogue of the racing preferences of all nine hundred horses in residence in his head, did a mental search for other horses who ran short distances and compared their abilities based on purse winnings. He could probably make up a race at five furlongs but the purse wouldn't amount to much.

"How many times you think you can run him?"

"Coupla times. He's won ninety-some thousand. I'd like to see him get to a hundred."

"Ninety-some thousand is good enough," Louisa interjected.

"You're the one who let me bring him back," Mike shot back.

"Not to pound those old legs in a race," said Louisa. "I told you to bring him back as a lead pony."

"For God's sake, Louisa. Alice is the one who needs a lead pony. You know how he acts going to the gate."

"He's too fragile to race."

"We tried retiring him. He won't take it," Mike said. "Just like you."

"No, I mean it this time. When Alice goes, I'm going, too," she said, trying to look annoyed as the others laughed.

"You hear that, Jack? I got to keep that poor old crippled horse at the track just to keep my assistant. Ain't that a rub?"

Just then Lawrence and Hank appeared on the monitor at their table.

"Vicki, turn up the sound, would you please?"

The handicappers gave their analysis of the tenth race and they disagreed. Then Lawrence calmly pinched his nose and proceeded to explain why Hank's horse could not win.

"Is that an editorial comment? That's hilarious," Jack said.

Suddenly Lawrence disappeared from the screen and Hank, suppressing a chuckle, wrapped up. Wick shook his head.

Louisa saw Lawrence first and elbowed Wick. "There's your fair-haired child."

"The child part I agree with," Wick said out of the side of his mouth.

Louisa smiled. "He's growing up."

"I hope you're right," Wick said and waved to Lawrence. "Come join us."

Grinning and shedding electricity like a power line on a humid day, Lawrence pulled up a chair and starting talking a mile a minute. "So what do you think, Wick? Was that all right? I mean, six out of ten winners – seven if Neal's Boy wins – the daily double, two trifectas, parlay twenty bucks into two-hundred-fifty. That was so cool! Man, I had a blast! Can I do this again tomorrow?"

He had everybody at the table laughing.

Neal's Boy obligingly cantered home, capping off a spectacular day of handicapping for Lawrence. He was deservedly pumped up about his performance, the more so because he had an appreciative audience in the lovely Vicki.

"You picked almost every winner today?" she said.

"Yes ma'am," he said, grinning and taking her hand that held a mutuel ticket.

"How do you--" she began and stopped, distracted by the fact he was making lazy circles around her index finger knuckle with his finger. "If you tell everyone which horse is going to win, why doesn't everybody win some money?"

"Because, as hard as it is to believe, not everybody bets the way I tell them to." Lawrence explained that pari-mutuel wagering was not like casino gambling, where bettors played against the house. Instead, horse players bet against each other. "If everybody bet on the same horse, there would be no losers to win money from." He turned her hand over to reveal her winning mutuel ticket, now crumpled and damp. He took the wadded ticket, juggled it like a ball and said, "You want to gag the mutuel machine? This ticket's worth—" He glanced at the lighted display of odds and winning amounts on the tote board in the infield. "—Eight dollars and sixty cents, just enough for that drink you owe me."

The races were over for the evening and the last of the patrons were trickling out of the Turf Club and the hollow

46

grandstand. A dwindling line of people drained down the stairwells and escalators and flowed out the front doors. It was after nine, near the bedtime of regular horsemen. As the group said goodnight, the giant floodlights around the oval were doused. The blackness washed a hush over the track, drawing Wick's party to a close.

As Lawrence whisked Vicki away, Louisa leaned over to pat Wick's arm. "Thank you, Wick, for a nice dinner. I really enjoyed it."

"Let me say goodnight to the bar staff and I'll take you around in the golf cart," Wick offered.

"No, don't let me take you away from your work. I'll get a ride with Mike," she said.

Wick opened his mouth to argue, then sighed. The party was over.

Chapter 9

Louisa stood aside and let a groom toss her new exercise rider up on a colt. Her hand was still swollen and her thighs ached so she could hardly pick up her feet to walk. Ibuprofen knocked the edge off enough to let her shuffle around the shed row. By eight or nine, her taut muscles would loosen up and she could pretend to be all right. So when Mike showed up with Jimmy Wiseman at seven o'clock, she almost hugged the silent young man.

Sharing a golf cart, Mike and Louisa followed a trio of their horses to the gap in the rail where horses entered the track for morning exercise. Like Starbucks on a city street corner, the gap exuded buzz. Here trainers stood by the rail or sat on their lead ponies, watching their horses jog or gallop around the track, exchanging gossip and secretly studying the competition. Horses of all ages, abilities and experience jigged or pranced through the gap, jerking the reins, eager to blow off the energy accumulated in their stalls during the previous twenty-two hours. Passing them were horses who walked through the gap the other way, sweaty from blown energy, eager now for a bath and a long cooling walk. Exercise riders bantered with each other and the railbirds at the gap. Only the clocker's assistant, Dakota, who collected the names of horses taking an official workout, and the gap policemen, Freddy and Bones, riding well-broke Quarterhorses, remained businesslike.

Freddy nudged his horse over and challenged the new rider in Mike's stable with his favorite question: "You got a license?" As a racing official, Freddy was responsible for helping maintain security by checking to see that everyone on the backstretch had been fingerprinted and licensed by the regulatory agency, the Virginia Racing Commission. Freddy reported to the Commission stewards, who were both policemen and judges, issuing the licenses and suspending them—"giving days"—to ensure compliance with the rules.

Mike walked up and said, "Hey Freddy, how about letting him go? He's been galloping at the training center for years. We just drove in and I'm short-handed. I'll take him up and get him licensed after he does this set. Okay?"

The new boy hesitated but the colt he was riding carried him off with the others while Mike and Freddy argued. "Mike, you know that's flat out against the rules. It'd be my job to let that boy ride without a license."

"I know. I know. I don't want to get you in any trouble. I wouldn't ask you but I'm desperate."

"You are asking me to lie and I swore to my momma I wouldn't ever lie."

"Freddy, I'm really just asking you to approve this boy as an exercise rider. Because he is good. Here they come now. Look at him."

Mike's horses had jogged off and now they galloped past where the men sat on their horses and argued. Freddy and Mike paused and observed the set. The new rider sat quietly on the three-year-old, keeping him in line with the others. "I'll have to see him some more, but he looks okay to me," Freddy said. "Just get him a license as soon as he comes off the track."

"Will do. And thank you," Mike said.

Louisa had walked up the bank towards the track kitchen in order to see over the cluster of people at the gap. Out on the track she saw the new boy marry his hands to his horse's mouth and balance quietly over the galloping animal's center of gravity.

The young man's understated style made him seem a part of the horse, as the two moved in synchrony around the curve of the track. Louisa marveled at his skill. Simply by riding beautifully, he made the horse look talented and fast. She flexed her scarred hand gently and watched the pair recede smoothly down the backstretch.

Out on the track, Jimmy Wiseman snugged his hands in the three-year-old colt's mane and sat still. The colt galloped routinely. The horse had been to the track before but Jimmy had not. Jimmy had exercised the colt at the farm and knew his stride, but the horse felt entirely different here in the hallowed atmosphere of the racetrack.

Everything felt different.

Jimmy wanted things deeply but not deeply enough to say so, or to go after them. For instance, he had wanted to exercise horses at the racetrack for several years but he had never asked Mr. Lucci about it, nor had he spoken to any of the other trainers he knew. He had not even mentioned it to the farm manager at High Hill, Mr. Lucci's farm, where he was the top hand and the most sought-after rider in three counties. He got up every morning and went to the farm, mucked stalls, groomed horses, broke yearlings and thought about riding at the track. He was a good hand with a horse and a good employee, in the sense that he was never drunk on the job and he did not need to be bailed out of jail more than once or twice a year. He didn't talk much and no one knew how badly he wanted to go to the track.

Jimmy floated through life, reacting to stimuli and occasionally, painfully, being forced to make a decision. Like most people, sometimes he made good decisions and sometimes he made bad decisions. The memory of the bad decisions was what made him avoid having to make decisions at all, if he could help it.

The catalog of his bad decisions was printed on a rap sheet of misdemeanor fighting incidents. The most serious of these was an assault and battery that had been reduced to disorderly conduct following conflicting testimony from witnesses, including the waitress Jimmy was standing up for. Jimmy ended up with a broken nose, a dislocated shoulder and three broken ribs, plus the uncomfortable memory of the one hundred-eighty-pound guy he was fighting hitting the corner of a garbage dumpster with his head. The guy never could talk right after that. Although Jimmy stoutly defended himself when the subject came up—"Sumbitch shouldn't have grabbed that girl like that"—the sight of the injured man collecting grocery carts in the Wal-Mart parking lot always made him jerk his chin up, as though defying his conscience to trouble him. A man who abused women deserved whatever he got. Jimmy never did understand why they sent his cousin to prison after she stabbed that piece of shit she was married to. That, in his opinion, was an example of a good decision.

Jimmy had not made a bad decision in more than a year when Mr. Lucci told him he wanted him to go to Colonial Downs and help out with the horses. Jimmy liked working for Mr. Lucci because he was rarely required to make decisions. He had his routine at the barn, and he was left alone to work with the horses. In actuality, Jimmy had to make many decisions in dealing with the horses, but he viewed that interaction as more of an unspoken conversation. He had an easy rapport with the animals and was comfortable working out a daily agreement with them about their behavior. Making a decision, in his mind, meant telling a person that you were or were not going to do something. When Mr. Lucci brought up going to the racetrack, it was a decision so exciting that Jimmy would gladly have spoken up and said "yes." However, Mr. Lucci had, in his customary way, simply told him what he wanted him to do, requiring no decision-making on Jimmy's part at all. So Jimmy found himself galloping horses at the track, something he had dreamed of for years. He was grateful to Mr. Lucci for the opportunity and even more grateful that he hadn't had to make a decision about it.

Wick was beginning to sense another transition with regard to Claire. At the time, his recent visit hadn't seemed any different from the prior ones, but in the days since, he had felt a subtle tremor in his emotional equilibrium. There was just enough disruption that he had begun to feel queasy, a precursor to the nausea caused by the ground shifting under his emotional center. As he sought an antidote, he drifted towards Barn Six, subconsciously hoping Louisa was free despite the fact that it was the middle of training hours.

He didn't know what to think, or even what question to ask, he just sensed a change in the unresponsive woman who was his wife. Maybe Louisa would have some useful comment about the situation.

She was a woman, she understood that stuff. Didn't they call her "*la Madre*" on the backstretch? He walked faster, pleased that he had thought of a way to ease his discomfort.

The sight of his goofy young handicapper sitting in the golf cart with Louisa at the far end of the shed row deflated him, but Lawrence disappeared before he walked halfway down the barn.

"Oh Wick, hello," Louisa said, balancing an exercise saddle on her good arm. "How are things?"

Wick immediately relaxed at the sound of her voice. "You know how trainers are. They complain about everything. Then if you fix something, they complain because you changed it."

She laughed her tinkling laugh and put the tack away. "Some people are never happy."

Louisa filled him in on the news of Barn Six: three new horses and a talented new rider. Wick was less interested in the boy's talent than he was the possibility that Louisa might have coffee with him.

"Not this morning."

Even though Wick knew asking Louisa to take a break during training hours was unreasonable, he felt unaccountably disappointed. He needed to talk to her and she had turned him down, and it was all Lawrence's fault.

"I think Lawrence is a little nervous," she said.

"What's he got to be nervous about?"

"You've given him a big responsibility and he feels it. Can he repeat his success on Opening Day?" She opened her hands in question.

"You don't think he'd pull one of his stunts, do you?" Wick asked. "The last thing I need is for him to come out in an alligator costume or something."

Louisa laughed. "For goodness' sakes, Wick, what on earth makes you think he'd do something like that?"

"This is the guy who bungee-jumped off the grandstand, remember?"

"You hired him."

"Yeah, and I can fire him, too." Wick was annoyed with Lawrence for distracting Louisa. Clearly, he wasn't going to get the emotional relief he sought this morning. His consultation with *la Madre* would have to wait. "How many horses do you have running this evening?"

"We don't have but two in tonight. Second and third races."

"Come upstairs afterwards. I'll hold a table for you."

"Wick, you don't have to do that."

"I don't have to, but I'm going to. If the general manager can't hold a table for his friends, what good is he?" Wick said almost crossly. By God, there were some things in life he could control.

Louisa's cell phone rang, so she merely waved in response.

Wick grumped back to the secretary's office, the ground shifting slightly under his tasseled loafers.

Chapter 10

With the grandstand dark and the loudspeakers silent, the velvet night settled softly over the barns. A new moon showing a white rim like the eye of a fractious horse hung over the starting gate in the chute. A few lights shone here and there as horsemen finished cooling out the horses from the last race. A truck with a gooseneck trailer pulled out of the lot by the receiving barn, hauling a horse that had shipped in for the day to race. The shuttle van that Colonial ran between the Maryland tracks and New Kent took the shippers back up I-95. The activity, noise and lights gradually shifted to the dormitories. Some of the sensible grooms went to bed. Others gathered in small groups around the picnic tables to smoke and talk and drink; perhaps later they would fight. A few with their own transportation drove away, the exhaust systems of their large, ancient vehicles visually and audibly advertising their inefficiency.

After dinner with Wick in the Turf Club, Mike and Louisa stopped by Barn Six for one last look at the horses. A copper-colored gelding who had raced earlier in the evening stood with his head down, eating hay. Neat green bandages supported his legs, while wisps of straw in his mane and tail indicated the relaxed horse had rolled. He did not bother to raise his head to greet them.

"I wish they all knew their job like he does," said the trainer.

The comment made them both think of Ticket Taker, a gray colt who seemed to have talent but wouldn't fire in the afternoon. Alice wasn't the only horse Louisa worried about. Pretty much every horse in the barn had an issue, large or small, that kept Louisa studying. After all, that's what trainers did: They sorted out each animal's personality and individual prerequisites for learning the racing game. Ticket Taker was obedient enough but didn't seem to have the competitive drive for racing. He'd probably make a fine show horse, she thought, a good second career for the sound ones who couldn't run fast enough.

"Any ideas for Ticket Taker?" Louisa asked.

"Maybe your new jock will have one."

"I thought he looked good this morning."

"Oh, he's good. He's a real good hand with rough horses. I tell you, he's got guts," said Mike.

"But he has good hands, too," Louisa said. "Sometimes the ones who can handle rough horses are rough themselves."

"Not this boy. He's as cool as they come. He doesn't get mad. He doesn't even get excited. One time on the farm, I sent him out on a filly who wouldn't cross that little bridge on the way to the training track. You know, it's not but about four feet wide, she could step over it. She could step over the creek. And he came back about two hours later, both of them soaking wet, the saddle muddy, the bridle broken. I thought, what the hell…? The filly was just ambling along and he was sitting up there like he was driving a buggy to church. I was looking for blood and everything but he didn't seem upset, so I just said, 'Everything go okay?' And he said, 'Yeah.' Nothing else. Just 'yeah.' So finally I said, 'Did she go across?' And he said, 'Yeah.' That was it. He got off and put her up and didn't say another word. I never found out what happened, but by God that filly would walk across that bridge."

Louisa nodded. That was the kind of rider she liked to hear about. A quiet fellow who got the job done. "Has he been to the track before?"

"No, and I wasn't sure he would come."

"Really? Why? I never heard of a jock who didn't dream of going to the track."

"I don't know why. You're the *madre* of the backstretch. You figure him out."

Louisa smiled at the memory of the smooth-as-good-whiskey gaits of the colt who blistered her hands. She already had Jimmy Wiseman figured out. "Just take me home. I never should have gone upstairs for dinner."

"Yeah. You gotta watch out now, you might have some fun."

"I don't need fun. I need sleep so I can get up and take care of horses. And one more exercise rider," she added as she held up her left hand.

"I'm looking. I'm looking," said Mike. "How about Carl Starling's girl? He doesn't have but three horses. She ought to have time to get on a couple of ours."

Louisa brightened. "I'll walk over there tomorrow."

As they approached Louisa's RV, Mike said, "Looks like you got company."

The figure sitting on the portable steps beside her RV held a tiny dog on his lap and stroked it with little strokes that went from the dog's ears to the tip of its tail.

Louisa smiled wanly as she recognized one of her regular counselees. It was Rodell, proprietor and cook in the track kitchen.

"Rodell, what are you doing up here at this hour? Maria will be worried," she said.

"*Si, Madre*, but I need to talk to you," he said, putting the chihuahua in his pocket.

She sighed, invited him in and put a teakettle on to boil.

Louisa knew why Rodell was there. It was always the same issue. Rodell, a notoriously soft touch, especially where women were concerned, would "loan" twenty or fifty dollars out of the cash register to someone in need. And on the backstretch, there was always someone in need. Then Maria, who was a sharp businesswoman and ran a restaurant in town, would come in to balance the account and discover Rodell's generosity. Maria had been a good-looking woman in her youth and she knew the power of good looks, so when she found a shortage, she flew into a jealous rage. She backed Rodell up against the oven, snatched his brimless hat off his head and smacked him with it, all the time railing at him in rapid-fire Spanish and accusing him of humiliating her with his flagrant infidelity. These scenes, which occurred once or twice a month, were clearly audible and sometimes visible to any horsemen who happened to be in the track kitchen at the time, causing Rodell a mixture of pride and humiliation. The scenes provided an interesting diversion for the bored horsemen. Most people found the idea of the homely Rodell being unfaithful to the hot-blooded Maria somewhat far-fetched, but, as Louisa knew from Rodell's confessions, the unthinkable had occurred. Mostly, Rodell's loans were simply that, loans by a soft-hearted man to friends suffering from the vicissitudes of life—or their own poor decisions. But occasionally there was a recipient of Rodell's generosity who wanted to display her gratitude in a deeply personal way. Rodell's attractiveness to the opposite sex was a mystery to Louisa, but its existence was evident from Rodell's periodic consultations with her about his personal life.

"Rodell, you know Maria works hard to keep the restaurant going while you are working at the track during the meet?" Louisa would say.

"*Si, si,*" Rodell would nod.

"And she thinks the money at the restaurant and the money at the track kitchen belongs to both of you?"

"*Si, si,* she is right," Rodell would agree.

"So, don't you think it's unfair for you to give away money without talking to her about it first?"

"*Si, si,* you are right, *Madre,*" Rodell would say miserably. "I will never do it again."

Then Louisa would ask about the recipient in the current case. Was there a romantic connection there? Were Maria's jealous fears justified?

"No, *Madre,*" Rodell would insist. "I love Maria. I could never be with another woman."

"If you feel that way, Rodell, why don't you marry Maria? You've been together nine years."

Rodell would look at her sadly and say, "Ah, *Madre*, you know God would not let me marry another woman. In the eyes of God, I am already married."

"Rodell," Louisa would say sternly, "that was not a true marriage and it has been annulled. You are free to marry Maria. It would help solve your problems with her. I think she's insecure because you're not married. If you were married, she wouldn't be so jealous."

Rodell would nod. "Yes, that would be a good thing." He would nod some more, saying, "*Si*, I will go now and tell her. She will be so happy. Thank you, *Madre*. All my problems are gone. You are so wise, *Madre. Gracias.*"

But it never happened. By the next morning, his original mindset reasserted itself and he believed marriage to Maria to be religiously-proscribed because of his previous, now-annulled marriage. His understanding of Catholicism did not, apparently, include similar proscriptions against living conjugally with a woman for nine years without marriage or against periodic forays into other relationships of briefer duration.

With Rodell safely dispatched home to Maria, Louisa iced her hand and crawled wearily into bed. She had begun to tire of being *la madre*, the caring counselor who listened and wisely advised, who gave her free time and her heart over to helping solve unsolvable problems in human relationships, trying to bring peace and order to the lives around her; this, on top of her day job, where she strained to smooth the wrinkles out of the emotional psyche of horse after horse and tried to create happy, competitive athletes.

She hated to see people unhappy but she'd never understood why they clung to a bad relationship. She'd certainly made a bad decision or two herself, but she never let it ruin her life. You had to take control, fix things or move on if necessary, not float through life like a directionless jellyfish. But sometimes taking control meant being alone and most people couldn't handle being alone the way she did.

The horses, Alice, her cat, that was all she needed. And an occasional trip to the winner's circle.

Chapter 11

Paco Esteban approached Shannon Hill with an apologetic smile and the pages of the trainer's test that she had recently completed. Shannon knew she had failed. It crossed her mind to be glad she had asked Mr. Starling the day before to sign the entry form to enter Acky in a race. The old trainer didn't think the horse was ready but she overruled him, desperate for some purse money.

Racing steward Paco Esteban, an ex-jockey who was twenty years and forty pounds away from his old racing weight, projected an avuncular image to anyone who didn't know him back when. The young apprentice jocks learning the game, the assistant trainers trying to go out on their own, the eager teenaged girls exercising horses in the mornings, Paco tried to guide all of them around the potholes he had enthusiastically bounced through. He was so kindly, so interested, so patient, few of them could credit the stories they heard about him from the days when he rode first call for one of the big Arab owners. Paco had a habit of trading in wives for newer, more expensive models. He tried to scare one of them off with a little fire in the pool house, but it got away from him and burned down the garage with his Lexus and his Cadillac SUV in it. The wife's BMW was parked out front, and she calmly packed her stuff, loaded the car and drove away, calling 911 about the time the fumes in the half-filled gas tank of the Lexus reached a combustible level, making her phone call the first of several from that neighborhood.

"Miss Hill," he said, "did you have anybody to help you study for this?"

Shannon winced. Was it that bad? There were a lot of questions she didn't know, but she thought she had made up for it with her answers to the essay questions. Some of the short questions seemed more like they should be on an algebra test than a racetrack trainer's licensing exam: *What does 'nwx other than since September' mean?*

Shannon put on her best smile. "My trainer in Florida was getting me ready to take the trainer's test at Calder when the meet opened here at Colonial. I left before I had a chance to take it down there. I thought it would be pretty much the same in Virginia, but…" she shrugged, "…there were some things I wasn't ready for."

Paco nodded in a grandfatherly fashion. "You need someone to explain the condition book and the medication regulations to you. Aren't you stabled with Carl Starling? Why don't you ask him to help you?"

"Oh, he's already offered. I just hate to keep leaning on him." Truth was, she was embarrassed to let on that she didn't understand how to read the condition book. But she'd just have to get the old man to sit down and teach her. Studying was not her long suit. If she liked studying, she would have stayed at the University of Miami. What she liked—what she *loved*—was the racetrack.

Every morning Shannon leaped up, left her bug-infested room with hourly guests on one side and a family of screaming Pakistanis on the other and hurried to the magical land of racing, eager to splash around in the sparkling waters of training hours. She mucked her stalls, exercised her horses, cooled them out and cleaned her tack, each mundane, repetitive task carried out with hope and joy, hope for the future success of her horses and joy at being a part of the racetrack.

When she had done everything she could do with her little string, she roamed around the barn area talking to friends, getting a bag of Rodell's fresh doughnuts to share up and down the shed rows, stopping by the gap to hear the latest gossip.

Shannon gravitated to the gap because it was a conduit for information. A daily torrent of news flowed through the gap, sweeping horses and riders along like silt. She wanted to wash her hands in the current and sift out the golden flakes that would help her learn her way around this racetrack and make it her home.

But how could she make Colonial Downs her home when she couldn't even enter a horse in a race? She had to be a licensed trainer to enter her horses. And she had to train her own horses successfully so other people would pay her to train their horses. Having clients was the hedge, the alternate diploma to show her father she'd received for the three years' of college tuition she'd spent at the racetrack.

She recalled his voice on the phone. *So what are you getting out of this college education that I'm paying for?* Whether as owner or owner-trainer, she had to start running the horses soon. She needed the wins and she needed the purse money. She'd just have to run the horses in

Mr. Starling's name until she could figure out how to pass the damn test.

It occurred to Shannon that she might have to exercise a few horses on the side, just to make some money. She loved taking her own horse out in the rush hour traffic of morning training, hearing the swish of Acky's hooves in the sand, sensing the massive grandstand looming over them in the stretch, seeing the morning mist settle on his black mane like dew and feeling the smooth rhythmic churning of his haunches in three-beat time. Galloping horses as a freelance rider would help stretch her stake, but pride stood in the way at the moment. Her goal was a trainer's license, not an exercise rider's license.

As Shannon sat on the rail drinking in the flow of sweaty horses jogging and galloping before her, two trainers arrived with their charges, picking their way carefully down the slope. Shannon watched them with envious longing. The first one was riding a bay thoroughbred gelding who was very happy to be at the track in any capacity as long as he didn't have to run races. With him were two older horses, each sporting the same yellow saddle cloth with a fox's head embroidered in orange.

The racehorses jogged off the right way while the trainer nudged the bay over to the clocker's assistant, who was talking on a walkie-talkie and making notes on a clipboard.

"Hey, Dakota. Got two going a half mile."

The young man radioed to the clocker timing horses from the vantage point of the grandstand across the way. "Pair for Max Fox working a half." He released the talk button and held his pen poised over the clipboard without looking up. "Names?"

Shannon liked to hear the assistant feeding horses' names to the faceless voice in the grandstand. She did not know where, at Colonial, the clocker stood to time workouts. She pictured herself riding down to the gap on a lead pony to tell Dakota the names of a couple of horses in her string that were getting workouts. The image said *insider.*

Behind Fox rode Nicky Renfro, a fat red-faced man with a bandana around his head. He was riding a bony palomino and followed by a trio of three-year-old fillies. Slouched on the lead filly, Alvarez Montegro sported a battered green protective vest with no shirt underneath. Muscles like melons rolled over his shoulders and down his brown bare arms. He wore tight jeans, half-chaps and a casually confident expression. He legged the nervous filly forward with a mixture of loving and lewd urging. As they neared the gap, Freddy said, "Hey Teg, give that poor girl a break." Teg said something vulgar in Spanish and laughed. As he and the trainer rode past, Teg noticed Shannon, pursed his lips and blew her an exaggerated kiss. "*Mi chica*. I'll pick you up at eight." Not for nothing had Shannon spent her college years on the backstretch at Miami's Calder racetrack, where her ears rang with the dialects of Cuba, Mexico and Puerto Rico. She jerked her blonde, Anglo head up and blasted him in excellent street Spanish. He threw back his head and laughed in surprise, spooking his filly and the two others with him.

The exchange yanked Shannon out of her training reverie with an unpleasant jolt. No exercise rider would dare speak to a trainer that way, not even one of the perennially cheeky Hispanic guys.

Chapter 12

Carl Starling bent over an entry form and carefully wrote "Good Prospect" in seventy-nine-year-old handwriting. Then he listed the stakes race for Virginia-bred colts that was being offered on Sunday. As he wrote, Shannon approached his chair. "Mr. Starling?"

"What, honey?" he said without looking around.

"Mr. Starling, I hate to bother you, but I've got a problem."

She paused and Carl gave her a polite look of concern. "What's the matter?"

"Well, you know how the racing secretary asked you to put your name down as my trainer until I got my license?"

"They wouldn't take your entry for the race?"

"Oh no. That was fine. Acky's in the race. Thank you."

Carl waited.

Shannon plunged in. "I know you thought it wouldn't take but a day or so for me to get my license, and I thought so, too, and

I don't want to impose on you, especially since you were so nice to help me out in the first place, when I didn't know anybody here, but I didn't know they were going to ask all those questions about the condition book. I mean, I thought it would be the same as in Florida. Sam Ben always said the trainer's test was easy, as long as you knew what Isenglass was. Actually, I did really well. There were just a few things I didn't know. The stewards said I could try again whenever I get ready," Shannon said. When Carl nodded expectantly, she added, "But I have to wait three days." She sucked in through her teeth. "So, are you okay with that?"

Carl's smile was like a shower of silver. "Of course. Let me know if you need my help studying."

"Yes sir. Thank you. I will. I do."

A few hours later, Shannon and Carl sat silently in his box as Acky galloped across the finish line alone, the jockey's silks sparkling and Acky's white face blazing brightly, all untouched by dirt kicked up by the field racing twenty lengths ahead. Acky broke well from the outside post and ran hard throughout. He had a good trip but he came up short. Way short. Again. Shannon's heart sank down to her shoes as Acky struggled further and further behind. This wasn't how she imagined her debut at Colonial Downs. She was embarrassed in front of Mr. Starling. Her handsome colt with the eye-catching expression and the lovely way of going looked like he didn't even belong on the racetrack.

"I guess he lost more fitness than I thought," said Shannon.

"Even two or three days makes a difference," said Carl.

"I shouldn't have rushed him into a race. You were right."

"Don't feel bad."

"Maybe this will tighten him up," she said without conviction.

"Isn't your plan to try him on grass?"

She nodded as she picked up the halter and shank. "Thanks for saddling him for me. I'll go get him. You don't have to come down."

Carl patted her shoulder. "Let's go see what the jockey has to say."

As unhappy as she was in her embarrassment, Shannon appreciated having Carl at her side. As they worked their way through the crowd of horsemen watching the races from the apron, Shannon heard a familiar voice.

"Mi chica!"

She turned her head involuntarily and saw the swarthy leering face of Alvarez Montegro flanked by a clutch of grooms.

She looked away quickly, too miserable about her horse to work up the spit to banter with a smart-ass exercise rider. She could still hear his laughter and wolf calls as she and Carl passed through the gate to the track and she slipped the halter on Acky's elegant head. She stroked his sweaty neck. "I'm sorry, boy. That was my fault. I'll have you ready for the Turf Festival. Then we'll show 'em."

The Turf Festival was her plan all along. This was just a warm up.

Whatever Shannon's fears at night, her optimism reasserted itself in the morning. She sucked down her breakfast of Red Bull as the domino rows of stables came into view and parked her old Beamer alongside the other dusty vehicles at the end of Barn Four, eager to see her horses.

Racetracks run on hope and hope is strongest in the morning. Every horse is a potential winner, a work in progress, an interesting project that could one day come into his own and blast down the stretch demolishing the competition. In the magical mist of dawn on the racing oval, Acky's sixth consecutive loss did not seem as discouraging as it had in the oppressive darkness the night before. The horse was not fit, not a sprinter, not a dirt horse. What did she expect? The race was a tightener, not a yardstick of his progress.

She lingered over Acky, hand-walking him after the drain of racing, turning down help from one of Carl's grooms. She stroked his rich brown neck and muttered apologies for her training mistakes. His failure to be competitive on the track was her failure. Clearly, she was not a good enough trainer to figure out how to get him to perform. There had to be some secret she had yet to learn.

Carl had a three-year-old colt named Good Prospect, a colt who was unusually talented, given the average ability of Carl's other horses. Shannon pictured Carl as he occasionally sat on a bucket in front of Good Prospect's stall studying the horse. He saw through the horsehide and bone to the horse's heart. He *knew* that horse.

How do you learn how to do that? she wondered as she put Acky away and walked to the gap to watch the end of training hours. She debated sitting on a bucket in front of Acky's stall and staring at him as Carl had done, but she had a sense this would accomplish nothing except to make her look foolish.

Carl seemed to understand horses. She would have to follow him around, ask questions, suck him dry if that's what it took to figure this horse out. She just had to find a way to make sure he paid attention to Acky every day.

Chapter 13

Wick promised himself he wouldn't stay at the track but an hour, even though he knew this early in the meet crazy things happened and he would get caught up and probably never get away. Wednesday was supposed to be Claire's day, the day he paid homage to his marriage, to his love, to the mother of his children. But Wednesday was crazy, and then Thursday was crazy and now here it was Friday, and he was determined to take care of just one little piece of business, maybe swing by Mike Lucci's for a minute, then be gone. He already had the flowers in the car.

He drove down to the lower barns, back to the dormitories, to meet with the maintenance superintendent and the building inspector. The previous week's fire had damaged the wiring—about the only flammable part of the building, aside from the residents' belongings—and the building inspector insisted on an upgrade.

After the meeting, during which Wick failed to keep his temper, he drove away trying to remember feeling good about the opening week of the meet.

Attendance was up slightly from the year before and the betting handle was up a healthy six percent. Keep that up and the TVG folks would be happy. That Hamner boy had done a good job as handicapper, surprisingly good. Wick knew he could pick winners, but putting him on camera had been something of a gamble. Lawrence and Hank seemed to work well together, but Wick still worried the boy was too youthful for his older patrons.

Although Wick paid lip-service to the National Thoroughbred Racing Association's mantra that racing must attract a younger audience, he knew the core of racing's business came from men who were middle-aged and up, and that's who he catered to. That demographic had not changed since he was a boy in short pants.

Wick glanced at the dashboard clock and decided he could spare ten minutes. To his delight, when he showed up at Barn Six, Louisa immediately invited him into her office-slash-tack room while she made notes on the horses.

"Everything all right so far this morning?" he asked, looking at the big American flag tacked to the back wall.

She frowned briefly. "I'm worried about Chat. She had some filling and heat in her right front this morning. Doc's coming down to ultrasound it."

"I hope it's nothing."

"She's walking sound on it, so maybe it'll be all right."

Louisa bent to her task, her lips pressed together.

"Something wrong?"

Louisa sighed. "I was up late with a visitor."

A weird wave of jealousy swept over Wick, imagining Louisa with a lover. "Who?"

"That little girl who gallops for Noel Twyman, Erin?"

Wick relaxed.

"She lives with one of Max Fox's owners. Has a baby by him. He's not a nice person. Last night he slapped her around again and she knocked on my door about midnight. She was mad and crying, but I couldn't get her to go to the police about that SOB. She says he'll take the baby away from her."

"With all your counseling clients, how do you have time to train horses, *Madre*?"

"It's sad that people, good people, don't know how to manage their lives."

Wick snorted. "They don't try."

"Wick, that's not fair."

"Louisa, have you ever seen anyone around here think for even a minute before doing something stupid? No. They do what occurs to them at the moment."

Louisa didn't contradict him.

Wick stared out the door at the hot walkers leading horses past. It would take an hour of plodding around the shed row— up one side of the long barn, left turn, down the other, left turn, repeat—for the freshly-washed horses to dry in the thick humid air. Hot walking was the lowest of entry-level jobs, but even so, it was the highest-level job some employees could aspire to. As Louisa made notations on charts, Wick wondered what she was doing here. She had to be sixty, camping out for the summer in an RV behind the barns, galloping horses and counseling people utterly lacking in life skills. That wasn't much of a life for someone like her, someone who was…what? He wanted to say "refined" but her blistering take down of a careless groom the day before still rang in his ears.

She seemed out of place, in a way, but when he tried to imagine her in a kitchen, all he could conjure was a woman in jeans cleaning tack over the sink while a couple of muddy dogs lay underfoot. He wondered, did she even have a kitchen? Where did Louisa live? She stayed in a cottage on Mike's farm sometimes, he knew. She had apparently spent the winter with her sister in Florida. When she talked about retiring, though, she always joked about buying a condo in Green Bay, Wisconsin. He realized with a slight shock that Louisa was, essentially, homeless. The image of his empty kitchen, once the bustling center of a noisy family of boys, flashed through his mind. He remembered the flowers wilting in the car. He was homeless, too.

Chapter 14

Darcy's Dream was a train wreck looking to happen, even with a good jock like Alvarez Montegro in the saddle. A three-year-old filly whose breeding might best be described as "junk", Darcy's Dream had, throughout her life, been handled, broken and trained by people who were well-meaning but remarkably ignorant of the sensitivity of horses. Accordingly, she hated the racetrack, she hated galloping and she especially hated galloping with the two fillies alongside her this morning.

Teg, on the other hand, loved the racetrack, loved galloping and loved horses, even a rank, nasty filly like Darcy's Dream. Teg was a gifted rider cursed with the same large rawboned frame that made Darcy's Dream look like she might be a racehorse. Good for a racehorse. Bad for a jockey. He rode races at sixteen, but Mother Nature began leaning on him almost immediately. At seventeen, he took up cocaine—for purely professional reasons, of course—made the weight and rode another year. But by the time he reached eighteen, not even a heroin habit could have kept him under 120, much less 110. So he retired to exercising horses in the morning, keeping the coke habit for consolation.

Darcy's Dream, never a happy camper, was feeling especially cross this morning. She was coming into season and her sides were tender and she just wasn't in the mood to work. Although her owner paid the trainer for a regular shot of hormones to prevent her coming into season, her trainer used the money to pay the feed man, reasoning that Darcy's Dream was such a witch that it was hard to tell the difference anyway.

Teg was also having a bad morning. He misjudged his timing of the end of the party and the beginning of the workday, so he tried to compensate by having a beer before making his way from the dormitory to Barn Twelve. It seemed like once before, when his Uncle Pablo was pounding the steel drums in his stomach and the mariachi band was tooting in his head, that a beer had calmed things down. Or maybe it was a joint, but he didn't have a joint, so he drank a beer.

To make things worse, Teg had to borrow a saddle from the trainer he was riding for. Recently he had run up a tab with his supplier and he had sold his saddle. Now he was trying to find a tight seat on this piece of crap he found in the tack room and the mariachi band was whooping it up in his eyeballs and this filly who couldn't outrun a fat man in rubber boots was throwing her head around, trying to bust his face.

Darcy's Dream recognized the guy on her back: He had nice hands and a soothing way of crooning to her, but today, instead of sitting still, he kept hitching his knees forward and shifting his weight in the stirrup irons, causing the saddle to dig into her back just behind her withers. After jogging half a mile, she felt a raw hole growing in her back and a ragged edge on her temper. When the guy punched her into a gallop, the gouging in her back became sharper and she threw up her head, trying to twist away from the pain.

As the three horses galloped around the clubhouse turn, Darcy's Dream saw ahead of her across the track, beyond dozens of horses coming and going and walking and cantering, the gap. The gap was the opening in the rail that led to the horse path back to the barn, back to the comfort of her stall. It was the escape route for fillies in torture and she took it. First she propped with her front legs, putting her head down and jerking the guy forward. Then she threw her head up as high as she could, bashing the guy in the face. As he loosened his grip on the reins, she bolted across the track, leaving the guy behind.

Directly between the filly and the gap was a lead pony alongside Alice's Restaurant. Both horses stopped short at the sight of Darcy's bucking fit. In the moment that it took for Darcy to stop galloping, buck and bolt for the gap, Alice's Restaurant assessed the situation and decided to flee from the horse-eating monster that was obviously chasing the filly. But Darcy was already in full flight, and before Alice could take a step, the filly slammed into him broadside, knocking him down with a sharp crack. The gelding hit the ground hard and rolled over into the lead pony, who stumbled and threw his rider.

Frightened by the horse's flailing legs, Darcy leaped sideways then charged forward again, her anger changed to panic. The guy was no longer on her back but the stirrup irons swung wildly, bouncing on her sweaty sides, urging her to run as though a cougar were on her back raking her sides. In her terrified flight, she saw other horses wheel and rear and scatter, some kicking at her as she brushed past. Their panic fed her own, driving her to greater madness as she galloped single-mindedly towards the gap.

By now the gap was clogged with horses and riders pausing in the face of chaos. Darcy's Dream's exit was closed when she got there. Never slowing, never flicking her ears to signal that she saw the obstacles in her path, Darcy's Dream drove towards the eye of a needle, a sliver of air between the corner post and another horse. The rider waved and hollered vainly to turn her. At the last moment, the filly shifted slightly to the right. When her shoulder hit the rail, Darcy's Dream was going thirty miles an hour. The rail stopped her body momentarily, long enough for her hind end to flip over her back, driving her head into the clay ramp and snapping her neck.

Out on the track, Alice's Restaurant righted himself, organized his legs and climbed to his feet. As he became panicked by the turmoil around him—loose horses and shouting humans, an off-key siren, not to mention, somewhere, a horse-eating monster—he did what his ancestors had done in the face of danger for thousands of years: *fly*. No broken neck, no cougar, no monster for *him*. He could outrun the wind—at least for five-eighths of a mile.

Horses are creatures of habit, so as Alice fled, he worked his way through other galloping horses until he could hug the rail. Free of a leadline, free of a rider's hand on the reins, Alice indulged in the flight he was built for. Nostrils wide and sucking the humid air, he churned his hooves in the dirt and barreled down the backstretch towards the turn. But as the rail bent away from him on the left, he coasted across the track to the outer rail. He was still running hard about twenty feet from the rail and he gathered himself to jump when a voice hollered *Whoa! Whoa!* Flicking his ears, he processed the *Whoa* and hit the brakes about six inches too late. Turning sharply in a half-rear and dragging his haunches, he threw up a rooster tail of dirt like a downhill skier. His right front leg two inches above the knee that Louisa tended so carefully took the brunt of his weight as he slammed into the metal railing, which buckled but held. Alice scrambled a few steps and paused to let his windblown sides heave. When Bones, still hollering *Whoa*, reached the horse, Alice's Restaurant was waiting curiously for someone to lead him back to the barn. He'd had enough for the day and looked forward to his post-workout bath. And maybe some ice for his knee, which hurt like a sonofabitch.

Louisa and Wick were talking in the Barn Six tack room when they were interrupted by a siren twisting through the backstretch. Louisa felt her heart sink. At ten a.m., a blast from the horn meant training hours were over and the track was closed. It was a sound that, oddly enough, gave many horsemen a feeling of relief. Training hours were over. Another morning's work done. All the horses safely back in the barn.

But when the off-key sound blasted forth at an odd moment, barely seven a.m., it meant danger: *loose horse*. Some horse had spooked at another one coming up behind, tossed his rider and taken off like a drunk driving the wrong way down I-95, demolishing innocent passers-by along the way.

Louisa always pictured a pack of thousand-dollar bills tossed above a bonfire, separating and wafting down around the flames. A loose horse was like that, thousands of dollars on the hoof heading blindly into danger and taking other horses with him.

She and Wick jumped up and went outside. Through the fringe of trees, they could see the strobe lights blinking at each furlong pole. Wick's predecessor had installed the strobe lights because, amazing as it sounded, exercise riders couldn't always hear the siren. Wick and Louisa could see Bones and Freddy trying to round up loose animals. The track was crowded with horses and riders, most of them seeking shelter from the storm. Young riders on young horses hugged the outer rail and trotted their nervous mounts away from the loose horses. A few old riders on old horses coolly continued their gallops but kept a wary eye.

The siren continued its eerie cry, and a rumble of voices from riders trying to calm their mounts and the outriders calling instructions wafted ominously through the trees. Whatever it was, it wasn't over yet. As they stood on the horse path and watched through the trees, a riderless bay colt came tearing down the path, stirrups banging his sweaty sides as he dodged in and out of other horses. Wick and Louisa held up their arms and attempted to stop him, but he ducked past them and continued his mad search for the safety of his stall.

Wick set off towards the gap. Louisa forced herself to stay in the barn and wait for Mike, who was at the gap on his lead pony watching his horses train. *Please keep my horses safe. Please. Please. Please.* She ticked off the list of horses who were at the track at that moment and quickly got to Alice's Restaurant. Gabriela and Jimmy were schooling two fillies out of the starting gate, while Manny and Wendy galloped two older horses. That left her favorite. She had dispatched Alice for a jog with a lead pony. Alice was such an old pro, Louisa could just about lead him to the gap, tell him to jog around one time and turn him loose. But now he was out there somewhere in danger, a target for any panicked horse running blindly around the crowded racetrack.

Shannon was sitting on the rail sloping down to the gap when Darcy's Dream turned a cartwheel and landed practically in her lap. Darcy had tried to thread the needle between the post and Carl's prized three-year-old, Good Prospect, who had just arrived at the gap with his exercise rider, Ashley. When the filly crashed into Carl's colt, Ashley was knocked out of the saddle and the colt took off across the track.

Shannon threw herself backwards off the fence to escape the stampede in the confined chute, rolled instinctively and jumped up, standing on the grassy slope above the swirling cloud of horses. At first she was agog at the heap of dead horse just a few yards in front of her. Even as loose horses were flying in all directions and people were shouting in several languages, she couldn't take her eyes off the corpse. The filly lay on her back pointing downhill. Her hind end canted to the side opposite her head and neck, which were entwined in the buckled post and pieces of the railing. Her mouth was open, exposing her teeth, and her tongue lolled in the sand. As Shannon stared at the one-graceful creature dumped in the dirt, she was struck by how awkward and clunky the horse's shod hooves looked stuck on the ends of its slender legs.

Carl Starling's voice, hoarse from running, yanked her attention back to the action. "Shannon, did they catch Good Prospect yet?"

Shannon scanned the track guiltily, just in time to see the sweaty horse cornered. "Freddy's got him," she announced with satisfaction, as though she had done nothing but worry about her mentor's prized horse throughout the chaotic episode. She vaulted the rail and hurried to where Ashley sat in the dirt holding her wrist, oblivious to the horses that milled around her. "Ashley, don't move. Are you hurt? Here, let me see your eyes." Shannon peered under the brim of the exercise rider's helmet.

An ambulance manned by the New Kent Volunteer Rescue Squad followed the jockeys around the track for every race, but exercise riders were on their own during training hours in the morning. A paramedic appeared with Carl just as Shannon said, "She's moving but she has a concussion. Her pupils are dilated."

Carl looked from Ashley towards the groom leading Good Prospect and back again. Shannon could tell it was difficult for him to decide what to do. "Do you want me to stay with Ashley or go back with the horse?" she asked.

It was as though he couldn't hear her, torn as he was between two responsibilities. In the end he waited for the ambulance to drive away with Ashley, but Shannon was struck by the pain in his face as he glanced repeatedly towards Barn Four.

When Wick arrived at the gap, he found the track a shambles. People were leading sweaty horses with broken reins, there was a crowd around a downed horse in the gap and there were still at least two loose horses. Freddy, Bones and a couple of the guys on lead ponies were trying to corner the loose horses. One horse was trotting the wrong way up the backstretch towards the gap, broken reins floating in the froth of his lathered neck. The colt stopped and stared suspiciously at the cordon of riders tightening around him. Suddenly, he dove for an opening between Freddy and the rail. Freddy leaned over, grabbed the cheek of the bridle and nearly got yanked out of the saddle. His Quarterhorse, who had been through this drill before, backed up like an old cow pony to put some slack in the line between Freddy's shoulder and the escapee. A groom with a halter and shank materialized and collared the sweaty colt.

As horses were led away, the siren was silenced, the strobe lights doused. The ambulance left with Carl's exercise rider, but without flashing lights or a siren. Gradually, the rhythm of the morning workouts picked up again, like members of an orchestra joining a musical number one by one, until all the instruments were playing their parts, the slow ones and the fast ones, the trots and the canters, in a euphonic score.

The music continued in a minor key, though, the mood somber as the riders passed the awkward heap of horseflesh by the rail. Wick stood upwind of the dead body, which was already attracting flies in the heat. It seemed strange to think that such a graceful creature could, in an instant, become an ungainly heap of carrion.

As Wick stood by the gap and watched the guys with the horse ambulance winch the carcass of Darcy's Dream into the trailer, he flipped open his cell phone and hit speed dial. "Third floor, west, please… This is Boyd Keswick. Please tell my wife I'm running a little late."

Manny returned to Barn Six with a report of multiple loose horses ricocheting off each other and a dead horse at the gap. He didn't know whether Jimmy and Gabriela were involved in the wreck or not. Wendy rode in and said she had avoided trouble, too. It drove Louisa mad to stay at the barn and do her duty, so she was almost wordless with relief when the other two fillies strolled into the barn. The siren had been silenced by then. Jimmy had little to say. She listened to Gabriela's account of the disaster, saw that the horses were bathed and walked, and sent the exercise riders out on the next set before she remembered Alice's Restaurant.

How could she forget Alice? Alice, who had replaced the black mare as her favorite horse in Mike's string? That amazing big coal-black mare, strong-willed, demanding, a horse with a host of minor problems but, oh, she had a heart full of run.

Before Louisa could stop it, the memory of the black mare in her last race flashed through her mind. Louisa saw the horse stumble at the top of the stretch as a jillion undetected stress fractures in her left front leg became one catastrophic explosion of bone. The mare pitched forward, hurling the jockey over her head. Heart and shock kept the mare hobbling towards the finish line, oblivious for a few seconds to the pain. It was an image that lurked in the corner of Louisa's brain, minimized but ready to fill the screen whenever something clicked it. She squeezed her eyes shut, slamming the image back into the corner. Just as quickly, she opened her eyes and sought a healthy walking horse to replace the image. Focusing on a hot walker leading a wet filly down the shed row, Louisa let herself think about Alice. Where was Alice?

Mike was sitting on his brain-dead buckskin Quarterhorse in the chute watching Jimmy Wiseman work miracles with the Rondo filly, persuading the gate-shy three-year-old to walk through the open starting gate, when the commotion at the gap caught his attention. He whistled when he saw Darcy's Dream flip over the rail and crash in a broken-necked heap. Then he saw the chain reaction as one loose horse begat three more loose horses who in turn begat four more loose horses. Even as he recognized the first loose horse as Alice's Restaurant, he had kicked the Quarterhorse into a gallop. But Bones was way ahead of him, and the outrider was leading Alice with his sandy sides heaving up the backstretch by the time Mike reached them.

"What happened?" Mike asked, eying the sand stuck to Alice's sweaty coat.

"That filly knocked him down. Then he took off. He was fixing to jump the rail when I hollered at him. So he slammed into it instead."

Mike whistled. Louisa would have a conniption fit if that horse got hurt. He looked the gelding over. The horse was still blowing from his sprint but he seemed to be standing firmly on all four legs. Mike motioned to Bones to move off with the horse. Alice walked normally. Mike waved Bones on and he jogged Alice a few strides. Mike studied the horse's stride keenly. "Okay."

The horse would be body sore tomorrow and it would be a miracle if his knee didn't blow up, but for the moment he was more or less okay. Not that he'd be able to sell that to Louisa, he thought, as he led Alice through the gap and along the horse path to Barn Six.

When they reached the barn, Louisa rushed up and took the lead shank herself. "*There* he is! Did he get loose? Is he all right?" she blurted, stepping back to run her eyes down the chunky bay's lumpy legs. Alice turned his head and Louisa saw that it was caked with sand.

"He got knocked down but he seems—"

"Knocked down? *Knocked down?*"

"—he jogged sound—"

The diminutive assistant trainer blew her gray stack like an insistent teakettle. "Here I've been pacing the shed row, wondering where the hell he was, worried to death he was galloping around the track, ripping up what's left of his knee! And it's worse than that. He got run over by some damned loose horse! What do you mean by letting Alice get mixed up in a mess like that?" she ended furiously.

If a horse had sat up on his haunches and barked at him, Mike could not have been more surprised. "I…uh…" he began.

"He shouldn't have been out there when all that mess was going on. After all the time I've spent nursing that knee." The top had boiled off Louisa's anger and now it just sizzled on the stovetop as she squatted beside Alice, feeling his enormous knee and muttering about damn fools. "It's fragile, you know. He doesn't have a whole lot more strides left in it. And then what? How're you going to get him to retire at a hundred if you break him down first?"

Mike was relieved that Louisa had finally said something he could respond to. He uttered a short sharp laugh. "He doesn't want to retire. He wants to run. He'd run if you put him on crutches."

Louisa blazed up again. "I'll be damned if I'm going to let you put this horse on crutches!"

Now it was Mike's turn to be angry. "Louisa, what the hell's got into you? The horse ain't hurt. Stick him in the hole. We've got three more sets to get out."

The entire shed row had fallen quiet as the help busied themselves out of sight—but not earshot—of the argument. *La Madre* and the big boss fighting was something they had never seen and they didn't want to miss a single curse word.

Louisa had been dismissed. Without another word, she led Alice's Restaurant away.

Gradually, grooms and hot walkers crept out of stalls and tack rooms to resume their duties.

While Mike directed training for the remaining horses and felt their legs after they cooled out, Louisa stayed in the wash rack with Alice. She bathed him thoroughly, rinsing all the sand off his face and sponging his whole body with liniment. She ran her own scarred hands over all the old lumps and bumps on the stout black legs, feeling for heat, for a dent or ripple that didn't belong, starting over again when she found nothing. Then she hosed his knee with cold water for twenty minutes and squirted a double dose of bute paste in his mouth to ease the soreness. Finally, she left the horse standing in ice boots on his front legs before turning her attention to the five horses Mike had running that afternoon. She directed grooms with short words served on a sharp tongue. With Saturday post time for the first race at one p.m. instead of the weeknight post of six p.m., the daily schedule was as tightly compressed as Louisa's lips. Louisa checked off her supervisory tasks automatically while her heart pounded and her mind pictured the dead horse at the gap.

Someone in some barn had tacked up a horse and sent him out to gallop and the horse didn't come back. Every day with every horse it was a gamble. Some piece of tack reached the end of its useful life, some young horse spooked at a plastic bag, some undetectable stress point in a ligament tore, causing a chain reaction of catastrophe.

If by the grace of God Alice survived the knock-down and running around loose and whatever else happened to him out there, Louisa could not, would not let Alice go to the track again. No more training. If Mike wanted to run the horse, she would feel his legs and let him go. Racing alongside a handful of horses was the norm. But training with fifty others was too dangerous. She'd have to find another way to keep him fit.

Louisa banished the Xs and Os of an option play that began to form in her head. It was too soon to go back to football.

PART III

Chapter 15

On top of a trying morning, Wick had had a busy afternoon with the usual complications of weekend racing: not enough tables, not enough mutuel tellers, too many wacko patrons. One woman had brought her dog, a sort of golden retriever-looking thing, and when she was refused entry, she tied knots in the leash to form a harness and claimed the mutt was a seeing-eye dog.

On the other hand, the Himmels, good friends from Florida, where he worked as general manager of Calder before he came to Colonial, were passing through, and he spent some time with them. The reunion was happy until they began to reminisce about Claire.

"We had some good times then, when the children were small, didn't we?"

Wick had to agree. He found himself nodding at their far-away voices.

Claire and I had our babies together and everything. I was miserable when you all moved to Virginia...Yeah, Karen moped around like she'd lost her sister.

The couple prattled on, oblivious to the guilt Wick felt over failing, for the third day in a row, to leave work and pay a ten-minute visit to his wife. Finally he interrupted them. "Are you being taken care of?" He signaled a waiter. "I'm sorry but I have to get to the paddock. Michael, please get Mr. and Mrs. Himmel a drink and put it on my tab."

"Tell Claire... Give her a hug for us."

"I will."

The memories of laughing with friends at dinner or the children's birthday parties depressed Wick. It reminded him of the day two weeks earlier when he had taken a photo album to the

Norfolk Living Home Health Care Center. He and Claire loved to talk about the old days, friends in Florida, all the funny things the boys did when they were small. He had tried to engage her, coax a smile from that vacant face, anything to fan a spark of the Claire he used to know. At home, loneliness pervaded every room, but at the institution, it was the feeling of helplessness that enveloped him. There was nothing he could do. He couldn't make her better. He couldn't make her comfortable. He couldn't even make her smile. He was useless.

When Wick got to the paddock, he saw Louisa watching Lawrence give his handicapping analysis. After exchanging pleasantries with the principals in Six Saints Stable, he joined her, hoping to offload some of his despair. Just standing next to her helped take his mind off the Himmels and Claire. When Lawrence and Hank finished their commentary, Louisa laid her hand on his arm and said, "Wick, I need your help. It's important."

I need your help. There was hardly anything Louisa could have said at that moment to make Wick feel better. He puffed up and smiled. "What?"

"I need to find a swimming pool." She told him about Alice's being slammed to the ground by Darcy's Dream that morning. If his knee was cool the next day, she would hand walk him, but after that, even if he hadn't injured his leg, the old horse would need to swim to get over being body sore, not to mention getting racing fit.

"All right," Wick said. Despite his easy acquiescence, Wick did not know, right off, how he was going construct an equine exercise pool nearby in the next twenty-four hours. It seemed just as challenging as showing photo albums to Claire and getting her to smile. Still, Louisa needed him and he leaped at the prospect of being helpful.

Although now, as they drove out of the racetrack, Wick did not know which way to turn when he got to the highway.

"How far is the river?" Louisa asked, and Wick turned south, towards the James River.

"Route 5 runs along the river. It's ten or fifteen miles over there," he said.

"We need a boat landing," she said.

"And a boat."

They crossed a small bridge over a rivulet with a sign announcing this was the Chickahominy River.

"You could walk along the banks of the Chickahominy and lead him," Wick said.

"Don't think that would cover his ankles."

Wick laughed and kept going. At Route 5, he turned west and drove parallel to the James River, which was screened from view—and accessibility—by acres of corn and hardwood forests. Signs indicated the waterfront was laced together in the privately-owned colonial plantations: Evelynton, Shirley, Berkeley. They did not see anything resembling a public boat ramp.

The drive along the scenic highway was pleasant and Wick relaxed. It crossed his mind, now that he finally had Louisa to himself, that this was his chance to talk to her about Claire. Somehow though, the issue didn't seem as pressing. He struggled to think what it was that he wanted to say to Louisa about his wife. Louisa, *la madre* of the backstretch, lifeline to all the lost and misguided little people floundering through the flooded streams of life. Had he become one of those?

"Let's see what's back here," Wick said. He turned the car into a dirt road by a sign for Riverside Park. The road skirted a field and entered a small woods with signs for a nature trail on either side. As they emerged from the woods into a gravel parking lot, they saw the river spread out before them, three hundred yards wide and forty-five feet deep there, a few miles below the fall line at Richmond. "That'll cover his ankles," said Wick.

"I wonder if it's always this crowded?" Louisa asked.

A middle-aged man was using the boat ramp to load a jon boat onto his trailer, and a young couple waited nearby to ship their canoe. Another car with a boat and trailer was parked on the side, and a couple of men sat on a picnic table drinking something next to a cooler. On the dock several people were fishing. Prominent signs posted on the dock and by the boat ramp read, "No Swimming."

They stared at the scene in silence.

"Let's go back and explore the Chickahominy," Louisa suggested. "Maybe it gets deeper if you go east."

"Louisa."

"Now Wick, don't say 'Louisa' to me in that tone of voice."

Back on the highway, Wick glanced at his friend, who sat forward scanning the landscape as though she believed a suitable body of water lurked behind the pine brush. He wanted to find something that would work, just to make her happy, but the whole thing seemed impossible to him. Finding some water they could get the horse into. Getting permission to use the body of water. Getting the horse to swim around. Trailering him back and forth. It was overwhelming. "This isn't the old days and I'm not Croaker Norge," he said.

"Thank goodness for that!" said Louisa without taking her eyes off the passing view.

"And Alice ain't Seabiscuit."

"Look. There's a sign for a public boat ramp."

They turned off the highway and followed a narrow road that wound between small farms and old gingerbread houses set close to the road. Other small roads intersected but, in the way of rural areas, where locals know where they are going and strangers are unexpected, there was little in the way of directional signage. Periodically they saw yet another small brown sign announcing the existence of a public boat ramp some undisclosed distance ahead.

"This damn boat ramp must be on the Atlantic Ocean."

Louisa laughed.

At the next intersection, he turned around.

"Here. Turn down this little road."

They drove a mile or so between cultivated fields, passing a white frame house with several outbuildings and farm equipment neatly parked around it. Then the pavement ended. "Louisa," he said, in that tone of voice, "this is somebody's farm. We might get shot for trespassing."

"No it isn't. Look. There's a state route sign."

They followed the gravel road through some woods and emerged in a clearing. Directly ahead was a large body of water, large enough to swim most of the racehorses in Virginia in. They had found a place where the Chickahominy languorously spreads over the flat coastal plain and loops back on itself. Fringed with marine grasses and dotted with floating islands of lily pads, the marshy area contained secret channels for the river that were easily deep enough for a horse to swim and a man to drown.

"That looks perfect!" Louisa said.

Wick drove as near to the water as he dared. Louisa got out and began exploring the shoreline for a firm place to lead a horse into the water. Wick followed, wondering why he had not anticipated hiking through a marsh and worn something more suitable than the tasseled loafers of his Turf Club attire. The ground was soft and the bank poorly-defined, but Louisa pressed on, pushing tall marsh grass aside and searching optimistically in the fading light for a paved ramp at a thirty-degree angle into the water.

"Louisa, I don't think this is the place."

She walked a few more yards then stopped. "I guess you're right."

"You're damn straight I'm right. It's nothing but a bog. You've got about as much business leading a horse through here as a kitten in Sunday school."

Louisa returned to the car dejected.

As it turned out, driving a car along the bank made as much sense as a kitten in Sunday school, too. Wick tried forward and reverse, but the wheels spun in deeper. It was nearly dark as they gathered some pine branches and laid them behind the wheels to provide traction.

"All right, see if you can back it out easy. I'll push," said Wick. "If it gets moving, don't stop till you're on the road, even if I fall down and have a heart attack."

"Oh Wick, I'm so sorry. You're such a good sport. You were so nice to take me on this wild goose chase and now I've ruined your shoes and gotten your car stuck. I feel terrible."

"Well, you ought to."

They both laughed.

The pine boughs failed to provide enough traction.

"Come on," Wick said after Louisa spun mud on his trousers. "Let's go see if that farmer back there wants to fire up his tractor tonight. I don't think triple-A covers this situation."

The farmer was surprised to find a muddy, middle-aged couple knocking at the door seeking assistance. He had, on occasion, been approached by worried teenagers who had parked too close to the marsh on a Friday night, but these folks seemed a little old for that sort of thing. For twenty bucks, though, he was happy to get the tractor and pull their car out of the marsh. Besides, he sort of liked showing off his shiny new Massey Ferguson with the enclosed cab, air conditioning and CD player. With the car on firm ground, the axle chain stowed in the tractor's toolbox and a fresh Andy Jackson in his billfold, the farmer couldn't resist asking what they were doing.

"We're trying to find a place to swim a horse," Wick said, feeling foolish.

"Alice is handicapped and needs the exercise," Louisa said.

"Alice? Your horse's name is 'Alice'?" the farmer said.

"Alice's Restaurant."

"Oh," said the farmer, "like that Arlo Guthrie song: 'You can get anything you want at Alice's Restaurant.'"

"You know Arlo Guthrie?" Louisa asked with delight.

"Well, not personally," said the farmer. "I've got a CD of old folksongs that I play a lot in the tractor. I really like 'The City of New Orleans.'"

"That is a great song," said Louisa.

"Thank you for helping us," Wick said, taking Louisa's arm and guiding her towards the car.

"What about your horse?" the farmer asked.

"We'll figure out something."

"What are you trying to do?"

"It's a racehorse," Wick said, "and he's got a bad knee. Back home they have a pool they swim him in to keep him fit between races. We've got to find a place to swim him around here." He shrugged. "We thought maybe we could swim him in the river. Sorry to bother you."

"He's got a regular pool he swims in back home?"

"It's a pool for horses. It's got a ramp to walk down and it's got a walkway around the edge for a man to lead the horse. You know somebody who's got one like that?" Wick said with a smile.

The farmer looked thoughtful. "I don't know if it's still there or not, but there used to be a pool like that down there." He nodded towards the east.

Wick and Louisa looked at each other.

"They used to have this camp for handicapped children. It's seven or eight miles from here. My wife used to work there. They had a ramp in the pool because some of the kids were in wheelchairs and it was easier to get them in the water that way. That what you need?"

Later that night, after a clandestine tour of the defunct handicapped children's camp and the discovery of a small but serviceable swimming pool with a ramp, the two explorers stopped at a country store for beer and nabs.

"Oh Wick, isn't it great we've found a pool for Alice? You are such a good friend. Thank you."

"I just hope it'll work. You've got a few more hurdles to get over."

"The pool was the hardest. You found me a pool, I can make the rest work."

Wick was certain Alice's Restaurant would never get anywhere near that pool, but Louisa's gratitude for his help gave him a satisfied glow. As they drove through the barn area to the camper park, they were enveloped in the aroma of drying marsh mud.

"Sorry about your shoes," she said.

"I've been thinking of setting up a shoeshine stand in the grandstand," he said. "In the old days, all the tracks had them."

"You said this wasn't the old days."

He smiled.

"Bring them to me in the morning and I'll soap them for you."

"I've got saddle soap at the house."

"Yes, but it's the least I can do for you."

He sat a moment, contemplating the thought of a woman doing something for him. "I hate to go home," he said at last. "The house is so empty."

Louisa nodded. "It's hard, I'm sure."

"The boys don't… I was…mad for awhile because they don't go see her, but Boyd Junior said he wanted to remember her the way she was. I guess it's better for them to go on with their lives. They have children of their own to look after."

"If they are trying to be good parents, isn't that a tribute to Claire and you?"

He shrugged.

"Maybe that's the best thing they can do for her now."

"I guess."

"But what about you?"

"What about me?"

"You've been very loyal."

He looked surprised. "I love her."

"I know."

Wick stared through the windshield. "I need her."

Louisa nodded. After awhile she said, "It's hard to let go."

"Is that what I'm supposed to do?"

"One day," she said and opened the car door.

"Gracias, Madre."

"Buenas noches, Señor Wick."

Chapter 16

Louisa went over Alice with her customary thoroughness, examining everything from his eyeballs to his hind fetlocks. He was stiff but amazingly there was no heat in his knee. She handed him over to a groom for thirty minutes of walking around the shed row. Reluctantly, she moved on to her other problem horses.

Jimmy Wiseman was cleaning tack, rubbing golden glycerin over the supple bridle leather with a damp sponge, when Louisa approached him.

"You did a nice job with the Rondo filly yesterday—before the mess and afterwards, too. Mike says she walked through the gate."

He gave her a quick smile in thanks. Louisa was used to communicating with employees who didn't speak much, usually because they didn't speak much English, so she accepted Jimmy's smile as a fully-conceived and uttered reply, even though she was pretty sure in this case English was the employee's first language.

She nodded encouragingly and Jimmy took a deep breath.

"At first she didn't want to, but I talked to her a little bit and she finally said, hey, I'm going on through."

Louisa tried to picture that, but all she could see was the Rondo filly's belly as she reared up and fell over backwards, fighting Gabriela in back of the starting gate. The filly never was real good in the gate, then she got banged up before a race in March when a horse fell under the gate, thrashed around and pawed the caged filly's slender ankles. The next race, she wouldn't load into the starting gate and the stewards scratched her. She was on the gate list, consigned to remedial starting gate lessons, which so far had done no good because neither Manny nor Gabriela nor the gate crew could get the filly within fifty feet of a starting gate. Mike decided to give the filly a break from the track, so she went to the farm for a month and Jimmy galloped her. Now, at Colonial, Mike was hoping the bad incident was behind her. But horses never forget the bad things that happen to them. When Gabriela took her for a schooling session, the Rondo filly stood up on her hind legs and fell over backwards rather than submit to the metallic clutches of the gate.

"And so you walked through the gate…?" she prompted.

"Right when we come out, we sorta trotted off, and when we get to the main track, these three boys come busting around the turn, working them horses, and blam! One of them stopped and propped. The boy he went rolling. The horse, he ducked out for the gap. Took out about five other horses. Knocked Alice plumb flat down on the track. Hit some chestnut colt at the railing. Looked like the girl riding him ought to be killed."

"Ashley's kind of beat up, broke her wrist, but she's going to be all right."

"Whew. I thought she…" He shook his head. "Me'n Gabriela, we pulled up, looking for a place to hide." He chuckled nervously.

Louisa smiled. "If you kept that filly quiet through all that, you really are a miracle-worker, Jimmy."

"Oh, me and her get along fine."

Louisa liked his understated confidence. "Ashley won't be able to ride for awhile, and her trainer needs some help. How would you feel about exercising her horses?"

Jimmy's face lit up. "The chestnut colt, too? He's not hurt?"

Yep, thought Louisa. He's like all the rest. He lives to ride a good horse. "Especially him. He's running in a Virginia-bred stakes tomorrow and the trainer wants him on the track in the morning to make sure he's okay."

"I can take care of him," Jimmy said.

"Great. I told Carl I thought you would. He's worried the colt'll be spooked from the accident."

"I can take care of him."

Louisa was impressed by Jimmy's intensity, not to mention the veritable torrent of words that flowed from his mouth. "Thank you for doing that. Carl Starling is a good guy. I'm glad we can help him out."

Jimmy, exhausted from his volubility, just nodded.

As much as Jimmy liked working for Mr. Lucci, he loved working for Louisa Ferncliff. Being with her was almost as easy as being with the horses. There was the same sort of elemental communication that did not require spoken words. She told him what to do, of course, which horse to ride and what kind of workout the trainer wanted, but it was in the post-workout conversations where they communicated so easily. Jimmy had an intuitive ability to understand the horses he rode and Louisa had a similar ability to understand him. Information about each horse flowed smoothly from the animal through Jimmy to Louisa in a sort of emotional continuum.

Louisa seldom came out and asked him directly about a horse. She would perhaps take the bridle of a colt she was curious about that day, and when Jimmy slid off and she caught his eye, he would say something as simple as, "He's learning," and Louisa would understand that, although the colt had been fighting the bit and wandering around the racetrack in his gallops, he had that day begun to tuck his head and move on a line for a few strides at a time.

Jimmy appreciated this aspect of his job because the farm manager at High Hill was always asking him to explain how some horse worked, and Jimmy couldn't understand why the man couldn't understand his simple explanations.

Jimmy was not terribly introspective, but he realized that he was probably as happy as he had ever been in his twenty-eight years. That feeling lasted for about a week, until he realized there was something he wanted even more than galloping horses in the morning: racing in the afternoon.

Chapter 17

After Shannon ran her colt in Florida the first two or three times, her trainer suggested it might help the horse run faster if he carried a little less weight. So Shannon had him gelded. The colt did beat a couple of horses one time after that, encouraging Shannon to believe she had done the smart thing. The trainer knew the colt was destined to be the prettiest horse that never broke his maiden, of course, and he was just helping Shannon get him ready for his second career.

Shannon didn't view her horse as a lead pony but she knew he was a steady-eddie work partner.

After Darcy's Dream crashed into Carl's prized colt, Good Prospect, the horse refused to go anywhere near the gap, rearing up and throwing himself on the ground. Jimmy Wiseman came over from Mike Lucci's barn to ride the horse until Ashley recovered, but even he couldn't get the horse to the track. Carl scratched the horse from the Virginia-bred stakes race, which, Shannon could tell, about broke his heart. She figured she had the solution: Put Acky alongside Good Prospect every morning. Good Prospect just needed a familiar work partner and he'd probably go straight to the track. Then, with the two horses galloping together, Carl couldn't help but watch her horse and, maybe, solve the mystery of Acky's slow times.

So Shannon was ready when Carl asked for Acky's help. "Sure, Mr. Starling, I'd be happy to help. After all you've done for me."

She had a few qualms though when Carl told her he intended to jog the horse up and down the horse path on the backstretch. For safety reasons, walking was the speed limit on the horse path, where hundreds of horses commuted to work each morning. "Isn't that, like, illegal?" she said.

Carl said, "I think we'll be all right."

Shannon gave a passing thought to the trainer's license she didn't even have yet. At this point, getting Mr. Starling's help with Acky far outweighed the risk of sanctions for breaking the rules. If Acky didn't start winning soon, she'd have no use for a trainer's license.

Lawrence Hamner first noticed Carl's horse the day Darcy's Dream decided to play bumper cars on the track. Lawrence had been sitting on top of the tote board in the infield when Good Prospect got loose. Then he watched the chestnut colt flee the horse-eating dragon on his tail, racing the wrong way around the track with freakish speed. As a handicapper, he was curious to see the horse in a race, but when he saw Carl scratched the horse from his next race, Lawrence went to Barn Four to investigate.

Carl introduced him to Shannon, a girl who galloped her own horses in Carl's barn. As Lawrence and Shannon appraised each other, Carl outlined his plan to rebuild the colt's trust through a series of exercises to be carried out on the horse path and throughout the barn area. Although Lawrence did not have a long history of studying training methods, he recognized Carl's proposal as bizarre. He tore his eyes away from Shannon.

"How are you going to keep him fit walking and trotting around the barns?" Lawrence wanted to know.

"Hopefully, this won't take too long," said Carl. "But if it does, he can get in a decent amount of work up and down the horse path."

Lawrence was incredulous. The horse path was possibly more dangerous than the track itself, as hundreds of horses passed up and down the path between the barns and the track; walking on the horse path was the sacred rule. The outriders supervising morning workouts were quick to police traffic on the horse path as well as on the track itself. "You think Freddy and Bones are going to let you train on the horse path?"

"Sometimes it's better to ask forgiveness than to ask permission," said Carl.

Shannon burst out laughing. "That's me all over."

Lawrence found himself in the unaccustomed role of being the cautious one. "Carl, this is not going to work."

"We'll have to take it a day at a time. That boy Jimmy is a good rider."

"No. I mean you'll never get away with it. They'll shut you down the first day."

Shannon broke in. "Maybe we could have some kind of diversion."

"Yeah. I could run around the track in an alligator costume."

Shannon laughed. "I was thinking of firecrackers in the bathhouse, but the alligator thing would probably work, too."

Lawrence ignored her. "No, Carl, you gotta get Wick or Jack Delaney to sign off on this. You'll lose your license."

"Lawrence, this is not your problem. Good Prospect is my colt and I'll take the responsibility for him. I don't know if he'll even jog on the horse path. You let me worry about it."

Lawrence turned to Shannon in frustration. "You're going to lose your license, too, you know."

Shannon gave him an elaborate shrug and spoke to Carl. "I'll go tack up Acky."

Shannon and Jimmy did a couple of turns around the shed row, then walked out to the horse path and down towards the lower gap. Just before they reached Barn Nine, they turned and jogged up the path through the trees parallel to the track. When they neared the receiving barn, a few dozen yards shy of the upper gap, they stopped and turned around. The pair walked down to Barn Nine and repeated the jog uphill. Good Prospect tucked his head and jogged like an old horse. Shannon nervously scanned the path ahead but the outriders were nowhere to be seen. On the second pass, though, Freddy caught them as he rode off the track at the end of training hours.

"Whoa, here! What're y'all doing jogging on the horse path?"

Jimmy took his characteristically thoughtful approach to the outrider's question, which allowed Shannon to leap in.

"Freddy! Thank you for approving my exercise license. Look! Now I get to ride with one of the best riders on the backstretch."

Freddy relaxed but he still wasn't smiling. "You look good there, Shannon. Yeah, Jimmy can teach you a lot. Like there ain't no jogging on the horse path."

"Yessir. We were just in a hurry to get to the track before it closed."

Freddy laughed then. "You musta started in Richmond. The track's done been closed fifteen minutes."

Meanwhile, to Jimmy's private delight, Good Prospect had been standing quietly with Shannon's colt not ten yards from where he had his first panic attack.

Shannon suddenly turned to Jimmy and said, "Jimmy, I'm sorry. I should have listened to you when you told me we were too late." Jimmy looked at her in puzzlement. "Thanks, Freddy!" She jerked her horse around and Jimmy followed, just as Carl and Lawrence arrived. "Carl," she said, "we have to go back to the barn right now. Freddy says training hours are over. We're too late."

Carl opened his mouth but Lawrence spoke first. "Yeah, I told y'all Freddy wasn't going to let you on the track this late." He turned Carl around and nudged him towards the barn.

Freddy sat on his horse, watching them retreat. "If everybody knowed it was so late, why in hell were they hustling up the horse path?" he grumbled. "Everybody thinks they can make their own rules around here."

Chapter 18

By six o'clock, Louisa had made up the day's work schedule according to Mike's instructions, sucked down a mug of thick black coffee and started inspecting the horses in need of special attention, which was most of them. Louisa began with Ticket Taker, looking him in the eye, calling on every drop of Indian blood that she thought she possessed, determined to find the fleet colt's heart and goose it up. Ticket Taker needed to continue on his path to maturity a little more quickly than he might like because his owners were running out of patience, not to mention money. The gray colt had an alert, intelligent eye and Louisa peered deeply into it as though searching for a label with instructions. *Use delicate care cycle only.*

"You want me to take him first?" Jimmy asked.

Louisa looked around in surprise. "Are you done at Carl's already?"

Jimmy rubbed his face. "Mr. Starling said to get done here first."

"Really?"

Jimmy did not want to tell Louisa about the old trainer's plan of jogging on the horse path at the end of training hours but he didn't want to lie, either, so he just grunted.

Louisa sighed. "I hope that colt is going to come right. That's the first really good horse that man's ever had."

Jimmy just nodded.

"All right. Take this colt now. The Rondo filly's going out after the break. Mike wants to school her in the gate again. Let's see if she'll stand this time. If she'll stand, maybe they can close the front."

With the first set on the track, Louisa pulled Alice's Restaurant out and undid his bandage. Amazingly, after a few days of icing and hand walking, Alice had come out of the trauma of Saturday morning all right. She felt the bulging knee, running her hand over it on all sides, feeling carefully for any heat. The knee was cool so she moved on to the other legs. As she ran her hand down his hind leg, Alice whickered. Louisa looked up to see a dusty rider in a western saddle waiting to take the gelding for a jog. While Louisa had reservations about sending Alice to the track during training hours, having the swimming pool in her back pocket cheered her enough to let him go until the camp was ready.

"He's getting to know me, Louisa."

"Not much gets by this old boy," she said, slapping his rump.

"What are we doing today?"

"Jog him one turn. He's in tonight."

The horseman took Alice's shank and led him off towards the horse path.

"Watch out for loose horses!" Louisa called after him.

"You really should find a place to swim that horse," said Wick, coming up behind her.

She turned around with a laugh. "Now why didn't I think of that?"

"How's he doing? Is he going to hold up long enough to go to camp?"

They watched the stocky bay jigging alongside the pony. "As Mike said, he'd try to run on crutches. I just don't want it to come to that."

"When do you want to move him?"

"He's running tonight, of course, and I still have a few things to work out…" Louisa said, picking up Alice's bandages.

"Like getting Mike to go along? Or are you going to tell him?"

She hummed under her breath as she hung the bandages on the railing.

"Louisa?" When she didn't answer, he laughed. "I seem to remember you learned a thing or two from Croaker Norge about keeping people in the dark."

She went on with her work. "We've got a round pen, but we'll have to get stall mats for the ramp, and do you think you could find me a goat?"

Wick ran his hand through what was left of his hair. "I'll get you some rubber mats, but I'm not goat shopping. I thought you hired that old man at the end of the road to babysit."

"Alice might need a four-footed friend."

"Get him a pony. I never did like goats."

"It's not for you. It's for Alice."

"I'm already in pretty deep with all this stuff that's supposed to be for Alice, so don't talk to me about goats."

"Really, Wick. You're taking the goat way too personally."

"You mark my words: that goat'll be nothing but trouble."

Louisa glanced around guiltily. "Come in the office…There," she said, closing the door. "It's not Mike I need to keep in the dark, it's the help. If we do this, Mike won't want anybody—and I mean anybody—to know about it. You know how secretive he is about his training."

Wick nodded. "He doesn't want anybody laughing at him about Alice vacationing at the crippled children's camp. I guess that's a good place for a crippled old horse."

"Alice is *not* crippled."

"Yeah, and I'm Santa Claus. You want to ride over there in the daylight and see if we need to build a barn while we're at it?"

Louisa looked at her clipboard and sighed. "No time today. We've got four in tonight. But tomorrow's a dark day. I'll be done early. Ten o'clock?" she asked as she looked up.

Wick dropped his eyes and looked uncomfortable. After a pause, he said, "No. It's Wednesday." Wednesday. The sacred day.

When he didn't say anything more, Louisa shuffled some papers, stood up and said, "You know, Wednesday's really not a good day for me, either. Let's go later in the week. All right?"

Wick met her eyes again, and she matched him look for look, trying to peer inside the way she looked inside Ticket Taker's eye.

Wick's mouth softened slightly. "All right."

He moved towards the door, and Louisa followed him. As he held the door for her, she looked up at him again. "It'll be all right," she said.

Wick nodded without conviction.

They walked up the shed row just as Jimmy and Manny came in on a pair of sweat-soaked bays, steaming even in the summer warmth. "I heard your boy's been helping Carl."

"Just what I needed to do: loan out one of my exercise riders."

"How's that Good Prospect colt?"

"Hard to tell. The colt wouldn't go to the track after the accident. Carl had to scratch him out of that Virginia-bred stakes race."

Wick shook his head. "That might be a nice horse, if he isn't ruined."

"He could be."

"I need to check on his stablemate."

Louisa raised her eyebrows in a question.

"Some wacko girl from Florida. Sent one of her horses up here by himself a couple weeks ago. Nobody to meet him. Then she comes waltzing in four days later with another horse. Says she trains them herself. No license. But Jack Delaney says she'll talk the shirt right off a clothes rack."

Louisa laughed. "And Jack asked Carl to keep an eye on her? Poor Carl. Doesn't he have enough to do?"

"What else does he have to do? Those girls of his have about rubbed the hide off those three horses."

Louisa seized on the notion of extra help. "I wonder if she'd like to gallop a couple of horses for us. I'll have to ask Jimmy if she can ride."

Wick laughed. "You'll be getting the short end of the stick if you trade Jimmy for that gal."

"I was born with the short end of the stick," Louisa said.

The sun was getting low when Louisa led Alice's Restaurant to the paddock for the fifth race on Tuesday evening. Those among the seven or eight hundred fans in attendance who noticed saw a crescent of horses, nine in all, walking evenly along the outside rail, the sun burning the outline of backs and legs. The walk from Barn Six to the paddock was half a mile, allowing Alice time to loosen up before the post parade and the warm-up gallop.

Alice was jigging but not pulling the shank. He flicked his ears and glanced at the grandstand when the loudspeaker came on.

"That's right, boy. Take it all in." Louisa smiled indulgently at the old campaigner. He knew his job and he loved it. He'd give Jesus, his regular jockey, everything he had for five-eighths of a mile, running his heart out because that's who he was. He was so eager he would even try to grab the bit during the post parade, so Mike always sent a lead pony with him.

Louisa let one of the grooms lead Alice around the paddock while she stood with Mike and Raphine Steele, the jockey who was riding Alice tonight. Jesus had been suspended by the stewards for three days for "careless riding." Jesus had gotten a little aggressive when that smart mouth apprentice jock tried to come through a hole on the inside, with the result that the apprentice went over the rail. Jesus thought it was the apprentice who was careless and told the stewards as much. In any event, he now had three days to go home and see his family and play a little golf.

Raphine was a hard-knocking female jock who was pushing forty. She was unusually tall but light-boned enough to ride at 109 pounds. Against her weathered skin, exotic dark eyes and perfect teeth made her face striking; she had a voice like liquid cashmere that went with her eyes. Years of galloping in the mornings and racing in the afternoons had given her physique the distinctive features of a jockey. In grotesque contrast to her slender build, she had heavily muscled shoulders and upper arms. Her hands looked too big for her body, and her fingers were gnarled and bent with oversized knuckles at each joint, the residue of countless breaks and sprains. She was tough and professional. Over the years, the men in the jocks' room had pretty much come to accept her, and she drank with them, played pool with them and got tattooed with them. Few people knew that she had a life outside of racing: she had been married for twelve years to a brick mason with whom she had two small children.

"Anything special I need to know about this one?" Raphine asked Mike.

"Just don't fall off and you've got a ticket to the winner's circle."

"I like these old boys who know their job."

"If he don't know his job by now, it's too late to train him. He's got more starts than you do."

The race pitted an undistinguished group of three- and four-year-olds who might well retire as maidens and a few older horses who had lost so many steps over the years that it was a safe bet nobody would claim them, even at the modest tag Jack Delaney had set for this race. On paper, Alice's Restaurant would seem to be ripe for claiming, despite his age, but the big knee made an effective Keep Out sign.

On the monitors and the big screen in the infield, handicappers Lawrence Hamner and Hank May pointed out the obvious to the fans, Alice's Restaurant was the class of the race. One of Carl Starling's fillies was in the race but the handicappers did not think she rated a mention.

"The best pick of the card is the number Two horse, Alice's Restaurant. He's been around a long time – 116 starts – but one of the most consistent horses you'll find," said Hank.

"That's right, Hank. He's owned by trainer Mike Lucci's farm manager. They tried to retire him when he was twelve, but the horse was so unhappy they put him back in training. This is his first start back, but those old fellas don't forget what to do," said Lawrence as the horses circled them in the paddock.

"You have to go back a few years, but this horse set a new track record at three different tracks at this distance. Lawrence, even with all the candles on his birthday cake, Alice's Restaurant ought to make chop suey out of this bunch," said Hank.

"I'm going to box Two, Seven and Four for the trifecta," said Lawrence.

Shannon had put on a clean shirt and some earrings and had come to support Carl. It seemed like a good opportunity to show Lawrence she didn't always have a bandana and a hard hat on. She sidled over to the handicapper when he finished his analysis. "You coming to watch Carl's colt again tomorrow?"

Lawrence nodded. "Yeah. I hope you and Jimmy can get him fixed before Freddy takes your license away."

"Another close call tomorrow and…" She shivered in mock fear.

"Just get that horse to the gap."

"What horse? What's happening tomorrow?" asked Vicki from Lawrence's other side.

Shannon stepped away from Lawrence's ear and mustered a professional attitude. "I've got a horse I want him to watch in the morning."

Vicki looked down from her tall, strappy sandals. "Who do you ride for?"

"I have my own stable," Shannon began in a tone of voice that Lawrence had heard women use before, not in a good way.

"Uh, Vicki, we'd better get up to the box or we're going to miss this race," said Lawrence. "See you tomorrow, Shannon." They ducked between the parading horses and left the paddock. Shannon stayed to watch Carl's filly.

The paddock judge called "Riders up!"

Mike gave Raphine Steele a leg up on Alice as he jigged around the walking ring. "I'm serious about falling off at the start. He breaks fast."

"Thanks, boss."

The outrider slipped a leather line through Alice's bit and trotted out onto the sandy track. Raphine posted a few strides then stood up and felt the horse's stride. As they cantered off from the post parade, Alice tried to bolt, but the guy on the lead pony laughed and said, "Whoa here, fella. Not yet."

Louisa and Mike hurried up the steps to Mike's box in the grandstand. At the gate, Alice became all business, loading promptly, standing alertly and breaking so fast Louisa thought for sure he out-broke the bell. By the time she and Mike got their binoculars focused, Alice had blazed down the backstretch and into the turn, his huge haunches churning, his lumpy legs a blur. Louisa's heart was in her throat as the horses came around the turn and Alice neared the spot where the black mare had broken down. Please let him get to the quarter pole, she prayed. Over and over the image of the mare lunging forward on her broken leg replayed itself as Louisa closed her eyes.

She opened them to find Alice's green blinkers bobbing in between two other horses. The three horses ran head to head, pulling away from the rest of the field as they passed the quarter pole safely. Now please let him finish, she thought. The outside horse fell away, leaving Alice and the rail horse dueling down the stretch. Alice pinned his ears back and barreled forward as hard as he could go. As they neared the finish, Louisa joined the rest of the crowd in shouting for her favorite. She could let go now and revel in the race. All those hours of icing and bandaging, hand-walking and jogging, worrying, running her hands down those solid legs, gazing into the old horse's bright shiny eyes—this was what it came down to: Letting him run until his nine-pound heart nearly burst. Letting him look another horse in the eye as they neared the wire, letting him break the heart of any challenger. She often imagined Alice growling at the horse running beside him. As she watched, Louisa felt her own heart might burst. Down in the sand, Alice ran with every fiber and sinew of his being, mysteriously imposing his will on the other horse, refusing to let him come by. The old horse held on for a neck at the wire as Raphine stood and waved her stick in triumph.

In the win picture, Alice, still on the muscle, looked the part of the winner, Raphine's exotic face beamed from her helmet, Mike and the groom stood to the side, and Louisa proudly held the bridle. It was a picture of pure happiness.

Raphine hopped off and uncinched her saddle to weigh in. "Hey Mike, you were right. Easy winner. Thanks."

"What'd I tell you?"

"Call me if you got any more like this."

"Will do."

Louisa relinquished the horse to the groom and turned to see Wick smiling at her. She gave him a quick hug. "Isn't he wonderful?"

"All heart."

"It makes you want to do anything for him, doesn't it?"

Wick glowed from Louisa's hug. "I'll find you a goat," he promised.

Shannon watched the race with Ashley and the groomettes but they fluttered after Carl when he went to meet his filly after the race. She had no protective coloration then when Teg approached her.

"*Mi chica.*"

"Stop calling me that."

"Then tell me your name, pretty lady."

"Marilyn Monroe."

"Oh, *Guapa*. You are angry because your horse runs bad."

Shannon knew from her years at Calder that the Hispanic exercise riders were incorrigible womanizers. Teg fit the profile with his boldness and bad reputation. But he was hot, she conceded as he strutted around in his wife-beater and tight jeans. Raw hotness on the hoof. She didn't respond but she didn't walk away either.

He smiled with almost comical confidence at her and finally she said, "I'm angry because you won't leave me alone."

Teg took that as acceptance and said, "This horse, he is good-looking like his owner, but he no run fast. *Por qué*? He bleeds?"

"No," she said wearily, "he's not a bleeder." I wish he were, she thought, wondering if the bleeder medication Lasix would improve his performance.

"You should let me ride him."

They drifted towards the paddock and Teg stopped at a drink stand where he bought two beers. Shannon took one. "Why should I let you ride him?"

"Because he needs a *man* to talk to him."

Shannon laughed shortly. "A man who is full of crap."

Teg put his hand on her cheek. "I can make him run for you, *Guapa*."

"I don't juice."

Teg shrugged elaborately, sending quick ripples up his muscular arms. He looked past her to the horses parading in the paddock and said, "Do you see that horse, Seven? He wins tonight."

She noticed that the horse, who was nervous and washed down with sweat, was trained by Nicky Renfro. "Is that a tip?"

He bared his teeth like a cat with a chipmunk. "No, *Corazon*, it is the fact."

Wouldn't that be a relief, Shannon thought. She wondered how many horses went to the post with some illegal stimulant in their systems. With all the post-race drug testing done by the Racing Commission, she wondered how a trainer got away with it. Some of them didn't, she knew, and paid for it with big fines and suspended licenses. She studied the sweat-soaked horse as he jigged around the walking ring, white rims showing around his eyes. Jogging illegally on the horse path was nothing compared to juicing a horse. No way she could handle that kind of risk.

Chapter 19

For a dark day, Louisa thought, Wednesday had been especially hectic. She barely had time to run her hands down Alice's legs after his hard-won race the night before. Mike was in Delaware with the rest of the string, and he had called numerous times with changes in training instructions for various horses. On top of that she had to deal with injured horses and unexpected visits from owners. Then after dinner she drove the golf cart back to the barn to check on a filly who had tied up with muscle cramps after galloping. Fortunately, she was resting quietly. When Louisa crawled into bed at last, her body was aching for rest but her mind was too busy to sleep.

She tried not to let on to anyone, but it was getting harder and harder for her to hold the fat, rubber-covered racing reins with her arthritic hands. The lingering soreness in her hands and legs bothered her in a way she had never felt before. She knew after an injury—or a lot of birthdays—riders sometimes lost their nerve, but she wasn't there yet. She couldn't bear the thought of hanging up her tack, missing out on the feel of a young horse muscling up and getting ready to unleash his unknown potential on the track. She would just be careful about which horses she got on.

Thank the Lord for Jimmy. Not only could he ride the toughest screwball in the barn, he had recruited this gal Shannon to ride a couple. Now Louisa could run the barn without being distracted by her personal issues. The physical ones, anyway.

As she waited for the ibuprofen to take effect, she tried to soothe her mind with sweet images of Alice's Restaurant: jerking the shank in the paddock, posing proudly in the winner's circle, nuzzling her hand for a piece of grapefruit. But her mind, instead of melting over horses, kept pulling up people, flipping scenes like cards in a Rolodex: Lawrence and Vicki flirting the first night, Jimmy communicating with a word and a nod, Rodell and Maria's endless squabbles, Erin and her abusive boyfriend, Wick lonely and loyal to Claire.

The mystery of human relationships. How did people learn to stay together? Most of them didn't, in her experience. But what about the ones who did? They started out with a physical attraction and the ability to make each other laugh and then, somehow, they kneaded all that sweet sweat and laughter until it puffed up like yeast bread into a warm lifetime of love. Somehow. How? It was the kneading—or was it needing?—that she didn't know how to do.

Look at Wick and Claire. *I love her*, he had said. *I need her.* What did Claire have that he needed? Was it just the memory of his wife that he clutched? While Claire's body still breathed, her life, her personality, even her consciousness of Wick, all were gone. Yet Wick visited her regularly, took her flowers, talked to her and talked about her. She wondered what it would be like to have somebody love you for so many years. To love you after the sex. For a moment Louisa envied Wick and Claire.

She turned her thoughts, as she always did in moods like this, to Dean. Despite having been married to several other people over the years, Louisa considered Dean the love of her life. They met when she was working for Croaker Norge after her first divorce. Oh, what a summer that was. The memory of that happy love had kept her warm on many a night since. Tonight however, the memory of Dean, instead of filling a void, emphasized the emptiness.

She wondered what would have happened if she hadn't left to work in New Orleans. One of Norge's rivals had offered her his second string to train at the Fairgrounds. Assistant trainer in New Orleans? Let the good times roll! The deal had everything but Dean. They had an explosive fight about it, their blazing affair cracking like hot glass in icy water. Dean disappeared and Louisa told herself she didn't need him.

But what if she did? What if that was how you kept a relationship going? –Needing each other for something besides sex and a good laugh. She thought again of Wick and Claire. Even if "need" was the key to a long relationship, how would she get there? She didn't need anybody. She had never needed anybody. Except the horses.

Louisa walked to work in a steady rain the next morning, her mood no brighter than the weather. Reliving her life at the track inevitably led to the Fairgrounds and her wildly successful year of training horses for J. G. Lippincott. Despite her professional achievements, that was not a year she wanted to recall. It was twenty-some years ago and the wounds still had not healed. As she plodded along, she wondered whether there was a scar somewhere on her body.

Let go of it, she told herself. Her one shot at being a trainer hadn't panned out. So what? She'd had a good life. After the debacle at the Fairgrounds, she had taken refuge in the Superdome, where she wrapped ankles for the New Orleans Saints and distracted herself by watching the precise execution of Xs and Os. Moving through the trainer's room among giant sweaty athletes, patching here, bandaging there, Louisa discovered there was little difference between professional athletes human and equine. They pushed their bodies beyond all known levels of endurance, driven by some inner will to finish first. She grew to love the football players for their stoic dismissal of sore ankles, bad knees and broken fingers, seeing in them the old claimers who had won her heart at the track. At the end of the season, she had crept back to racing with a renewed reverence for the horses. After all, it was the horses who made her love racing, not the people.

She pushed J. G. Lippincott back in a box and shut the lid.

The problems at the barn on Wednesday carried over into Thursday, complicated by the weather. Louisa could hardly make her voice heard over the thrumming of the rain on the tin roof. She kept several horses in the barn, including Alice, restricting them to being hand-walked around the shed row instead of galloping on the muddy track. Sore horses, loose shoes, pouting grooms and a late feed delivery completed a crummy morning.

Just before the track closed at ten, though, the rain stopped, the clouds loosened up and Wick arrived. He often stopped by in the morning and tried to get her to break for coffee. She always dismissed him as she dealt with some minor crisis, but this morning he came in like the sunshine and she warmed herself in his smile.

When Wick insisted they go look at Alice's camp, the idea immediately refreshed her after a sleepless night of brooding. The barn problems somehow resolved themselves or seemed less urgent and she left, indulging herself in the delightfully irresponsible feeling of playing hooky.

"Your horse ran a good race on Tuesday," Wick said as he drove.

"Hard-knocking race horse," Louisa said.

"You ever miss training them yourself?"

Louisa laughed. "That was a bad experiment."

"I thought you led the standings for awhile at the Fairgrounds."

"The horses were good. The owners were bad."

Wick nodded. Handling owners often made for more of a challenge than conditioning the horses. As soon as an owner learned a little bit about the business, he wanted to tell the trainer how to do his job. The owner paid the bills, after all.

As they pulled into the camp, Wick's cell phone rang. He looked at the number and answered it. Louisa got out while he talked and waded through the waist-high weeds to the pool and studied the cavity full of leaves and deadfall.

"Problems?" she asked when Wick joined her.

"Somebody setting off firecrackers in the bathhouse. Where do they come up with this crap?"

The immaturity of most residents of the backstretch was a never-ending source of problems for track management because no sane person could anticipate every bizarre thing they might think of to do. Who would think you'd need a sign prohibiting firecrackers in the bathhouse?

Wick surveyed the camp property. Here in daylight, the prospects for converting the place into an equine spa were laughable. You'd have to get a bushhog in here, clean all that trash out of the pool *and* fill it, set up a round pen under the trees – and pray the horse would be fooled into thinking this was the Maryland Training Center. What were they thinking?

"You know," said Louisa, who was picking up broken chunks of concrete from around the pool and making a pile, "I think we could clean this up in a couple of hours. Maybe our farmer friend will bring his Massey-Ferguson with the CD player over here and mow for us. We've got stall mats for the ramp. And have you found me a goat yet?"

While Louisa prattled on, Wick listened in amazement. Finally, he chuckled, down in his solar plexus. "Louisa Ferncliff, you are something else."

She looked at him in curious surprise. "What?"

"Nothing."

Later, driving back to the track, Wick said, "It looks like that boy Jimmy is working out all right for you. I haven't seen you galloping any yourself lately.

"Not only is he sober, he's really good. You know that Rondo filly who got beat up in the starting gate when the horse next to her flipped? He's got her standing in the gate again. Gabriela couldn't even get her to go in the chute."

"How's he doing with Carl's colt?"

"I don't think they can get him to the track."

"Yeah, I heard that."

"They must be walking him under saddle, because Jimmy goes down there when he gets done with ours."

"What does he say?"

Louisa shrugged. "Alice talks to me more than he does. You'd think words cost a dollar apiece."

"Maybe you'll have to pay up."

"No, I'll just ask Shannon what they're doing. You know, the gal from Florida."

Wick rolled his eyes.

"Jimmy, bless his heart, brought her over and I hired her to ride a couple for us."

Wick shook his head. "You just can't resist taking on problems, can you?"

"She's all right. Rides well and always brings doughnuts to the barn."

Wick drove through the backstretch gate. "You want to stop and get a sandwich?"

"No thanks. I've seen enough of Rodell lately."

"Another fight with Maria?"

She shrugged. "Yes. I told him if he would just marry her, it would relieve some of her jealousy, but he keeps telling me the Church won't let him. What am I going to do about his fixation?"

"It's the glory of it. He still talks about his *esposa.*"

"But it wasn't a real marriage. It was a marriage of convenience, for God's sake, so he'd have health insurance."

"If you can't explain it to him, no one can," said Wick as he stopped at the end of Barn Six. Watching Louisa walk down the shed row, he thought about how much of herself she gave away to the needy people around her, that exercise girl with the abusive boyfriend, Rodell. Even Lawrence depended on her for encouragement. He wondered if she kept anything for herself. Maybe she didn't need to. Louisa seemed comfortably independent, unattached to anyone except her horses. In contrast, his dependence on Claire came to mind. It was irrational, he knew, but he played a little game with himself where he treated Claire's stay in the institution as temporary. That way he could think about their happy life together as something that would resume shortly. The truth was, lately he was finding it harder to maintain that illusion. The ground shifting made him uneasy. What would he do if he didn't have Claire to love? Louisa was right, he'd have to let go one day, but he doubted he could be self-sufficient like Louisa. Then what?

Chapter 20

Louisa did not say anything to Mike about taking Alice to live in a round pen in the woods of a defunct camp for handicapped children so he could swim in the camp swimming pool until she had worked out all the answers to all the questions he was sure to ask. She and Mike were outside the track kitchen sitting on picnic tables overlooking the gap one morning waiting for a trio of colts to go out and work when she presented the idea. Mike was skeptical.

"Louisa, have you lost your mind? You can't leave a racehorse in a round pen out there in the woods by himself like that!"

"He's not going to be by himself. There's an old man living near the entrance who used to have a couple of mules he did logging work with."

"He's going to keep the horse in his barn?"

"Oh, heavens no. That little shed fell down sometime in the last century. He's going to come over and babysit Alice."

Mike snorted. "Alice ain't going to be there long. He's going to jump out and head for the track."

"Well, we have arranged an animal babysitter for him, too, in case Mr. Johnson is not up to the task by himself. We found a nice goat to keep Alice company in the round pen or tied nearby or whatever it takes."

Just then, Jimmy, Gabriela and Manny approached the gap on the colts. Louisa walked down to where the clocker's assistant was sitting. "Dakota, these three are going to work a half mile."

"Names?"

Louisa gave him the names.

"Maggot?"

"No, B-A-G-U-E-T-T-E."

Manny, Gabriela and Jimmy jogged onto the track on their fresh colts.

"You all know what you're doing?"

"*Si, Madre.*"

She returned to the picnic table. The colts jogged the wrong way along the outside rail around to the finish line, disappearing behind the long low tote board that blocked their view across the infield.

"A 'nice' goat, huh? Ain't no such thing."

Louisa just nodded.

When the colts reappeared, now cantering under wraps the right direction, Louisa said, "If he's swimming every day, he'll be satisfied that he's in training to race."

Ticket Taker, who normally was in the bridle and pulled hard every morning, appeared relaxed under Jimmy's smooth handling, even as the three horses gradually built up speed approaching the half-mile pole. The gray colt's head was encased in a red mask with a cup beside each eye.

"Think the blinkers will fool him?"

"We'll see, I guess."

The horses broke off into a run and moved smoothly over to the rail as a unit, rapidly receding down the backstretch and rolling around the rim of the rail like a roulette ball. The trainer and his assistant could see the blinkered head of Ticket Taker pulling ahead of the other two as the trio disappeared behind the tote board. Mike made a guesstimate and punched his stopwatch, glancing at the face. Tilting the watch so Louisa could see it, Mike nodded at Jimmy and Ticket Taker as they galloped around the turn. "That boy's good, isn't he?"

"He's good with every horse he gets on," Louisa said.

"Are you thinking what I'm thinking?" Mike said.

Louisa nodded.

"You think he can make the weight?"

"He would if you asked him to."

The colts trotted back to them along the outside rail.

"Who else knows about Alice?" Mike asked.

"Wick."

"Wick? How the hell'd he get in on this?"

"He found the pool."

Mike sucked in his upper lip.

"And the goat."

Mike got down from the picnic table and walked to the fence as the horses came off at the gap. He scanned the gray colt closely and looked Jimmy in the eye. "How'd he feel?"

"Like a different horse."

Mike nodded.

He and Louisa followed the horses in the golf cart. "I wish I knew how blinkers worked. Sometimes they fix things that don't seem to be related."

Louisa nodded. "You think he's ready to run again?"

"You gotta get your new jock on the scales, first."

Louisa smiled.

They drove to the barn in silence until Mike said, without looking at her, "I don't want to know any more about Alice. Don't even tell me where he is. Just tell me when he's ready to run. Hey! Gabriela! Go get that black colt. Let's blow him out."

Louisa was wrapping Alice's knee when Mike called from Delaware. Louisa knew what his first question would be.

"How's the Rondo filly doing?"

"She stood in the gate again with the doors closed."

"Tell Jimmy to break her without the bell next time. You talk to him about riding races?"

"I'll catch him today." Louisa smiled, imagining what Jimmy would say to the idea. Mike saw Jimmy-the-jockey as a way to get the Rondo filly to the races again, but Louisa saw it the other way around: the Rondo filly's problem gave Jimmy the opportunity to broaden his career. Louisa wanted to fix the filly, of course, but she had become increasingly interested in what would happen to the laconic young man who rode her. Over the years, several of Mike's exercise riders had been licensed as jockeys, but their race-riding had mostly supplemented their income from galloping in the morning. Jimmy, though, Jimmy had talent. He had the touch.

"He'll have to lose some weight," Louisa said, almost to herself.

"He ain't nothing but a beanpole now. Where's he going to lose it from?"

The eternal question facing would-be jockeys. "It's better not to ask." Thanks to Louisa, there were numerous unpleasant details of racetrack life that Mike didn't have to think too much about.

"Well, tell him to get on with it, 'cause there's a race for that filly next week."

Louisa gathered the bandages and tape from doing up Alice's knee and wiped the sweat off her chin on her sleeve. Nodding to the groom to put Alice away, Louisa called Jimmy over to talk.

"Mike and I have been watching you with the Rondo filly," she said as she threw the used tape into a fifty-five gallon drum full of baler twine. Jimmy watched her anxiously. "Tomorrow we want you to try to break her out of the gate without the bell." Jimmy nodded. "If she'll do that a couple times, then we'll add the bell." Jimmy nodded again.

Finally, Louisa smiled at him and said, "And if she's okay, Mike wants to send her back to the races next week." Watching the growing light in Jimmy's face, Louisa smiled and said, "Mike wants you to ride her. Would you like to ride races?"

Jimmy's bedroom eyes opened wide, giving her an unexpected look at the intensity inside. All the emotions roiling inside this quiet young man flashed a vivid swirl of primary colors. Although she had been eager to bestow this gift on him, there was something unsettling in Jimmy's reaction. Instead of pleased, she felt distressed. What had she started? What skein of events would unravel from her pulling on this one thread?

His words were simple enough, belying the passion she glimpsed in his eyes. "Yes ma'am. Thank you. What do I need to do?"

What do they all need to do? Guilt pinched her brow as she heard herself slap the innocent smile off the boy's face. "How much do you weigh?"

It was like yanking a Christmas pony away from a six-year-old. The bedroom eyes drooped.

"You don't have to lose it all at once. Mike just wants to get the filly back to the races." Yes, but then what? Then this talented, soft-spoken young man was consigned to a life of bingeing and purging, drugs and home remedies, sweat boxes real and improvised. Louisa worried about the intensity she had glimpsed. Jimmy was tough, she knew, with the small town street smarts of a man who spent an occasional Saturday night in jail. But his ability to communicate with horses bespoke sensitivity. How would he fare in the alluring, punishing world of the track? Was the rush of racing, the joy of being first under the wire, enough return on the down-payment of pain, on the daily struggle to get the ride on a good horse? Was the racing connection to a horse with heart, a fighter, a grinder, a winner, worth the endless sacrifice to get there? Would Jimmy pay the price?

Louisa recalled a moment in the New Orleans Saints's locker room when she was untaping and retaping a rookie's wrist, one of many body parts that had been bruised, sprained or broken. The young 300-pound tackle had worked as hard in practice as he would in a game, if the coach ever played him. Beyond sacrificing his body in the exhibition season to earn a place on the roster, he had yet to make his debut as a professional player. He had driven himself in the offseason, since draft day, running, lifting weights, doing endless reps of torturous exercises in the gym, then icing, stretching, massaging muscles and tendons and old college injuries, all for the chance to walk on the big stage. That day in the locker room, the coach walked past, hardly pausing, just tossing her some instructions: "Tape him good, Ferncliff, he's playing tomorrow."

The boy's face lit up like sunrise over the Caribbean. "You mean it, Coach?" he said breathlessly, pulling his hand away to follow the coach. In that young man's unshaven face, below the dreadlocks, shining out of his glowing eyes Louisa suddenly saw herself. In that moment, she understood horse racing. Physical suffering was merely a mortal experience. Stretching oneself to the limit in all-out competition was a spiritual experience that lifted men and horses into a rarified realm of ecstasy. Of course Jimmy would pay the price.

Who could resist the siren call that lured otherwise sensible people to dash themselves to pieces on the rocks hidden beneath the glamorous silks? Louisa looked down the long tunnel of the shed row, smiling at the horses' heads' nodding or dozing or alertly scanning their world, ears pricked or flickering at the music of the backstretch: the trailer rumbles, the loud speaker voice and squealing, bugling horses.

Resistance was futile, once you heard the call. She knew that much. She had felt the rocks.

Chapter 21

"Croaker Norge had one that wouldn't go to the track at Keeneland," said Wick. He was sitting in the racing secretary's office, looking at the list of colts nominated to the Virginia Derby. It was a nice list. Half of the horses had started in at least one of the Triple Crown races. Five graded stakes winners. Now that the Breeders' Cup had a three-year-old turf division, Colonial Downs' marquee race, the Virginia Derby, was an important stop for any horse seeking the year-end divisional title. It was Colonial's day to shine in the national spotlight. The "big horses" and their famous trainers flew in from all over the country, attracted by the million-dollar purse. Among the dozens of horses nominated in the spring, only the top fourteen money-winning horses would go to the starting gate. Local horses seldom made the cut.

"Horse would gallop on the training track but wouldn't go to the main track," Wick continued. "Ol' Croak tried using a different gap, tried using a pony, blindfolded the horse, twitched him. Finally one day he tacked him up and loaded that bugger in the trailer. Drove him halfway to Louisville and back. When he got back, Croaker got the track superintendent to take down part of the outside rail and he drove through the front of the property and right out onto the track. He had the horse all tacked up, and he led him out of the trailer, threw this boy up on him and away they went. Two minute lick. Straight out the trailer. Next thing that horse knew, he's galloping two miles on the main track."

"That cure him?"

"Three days later Croak put him in a race and he run like a thief in the night."

The men contemplated Croaker Norge and his problem-solving techniques.

"Not quite Horatio Luro," Jack Delaney ventured.

"Where was it Northern Dancer wouldn't go to the track? Had to be Hialeah."

Wick nodded. "Luro jogged him in the barn area for a week."

"Can you see trainers today putting up with that? They'd raise some kinda hell."

"You think Sabatini is really going to send this horse to the Virginia Derby?" Wick asked, studying the nominations list again.

"Well, you know, Wick, for a million-dollar purse, it's worth taking a chance."

"What about Carl's colt?"

"He won't have enough earnings to qualify."

Since Jimmy didn't waste much of his time talking, he had a lot of time to spend absorbing what was going on around him. He spent most of his time in the energy field around various horses and he focused on sensing the explosions that blew off their bodies. It was interesting how the energy field around horses at the track was so much more intense than what he felt around the horses at the farm. That was particularly true of Good Prospect.

Every morning when he got done riding Mike's horses, he walked to Barn Four. He walked a little faster than usual, looking ahead for the barn itself and then when it came into view, looking down the long shed row, trying to pick out stall thirty-two to see if a chestnut head was hanging over the webbing. He looked for the horse every morning and the horse seemed to look for him.

Although Jimmy had yet to canter a single stride on the horse, he could tell Good Prospect was an animal of unusual talent. The energy field around Good Prospect was so charged that Jimmy could feel the hair on his arms and the back of his neck prickle when he picked up the bit and jogged off a few steps.

Just think what it'd be like to gallop this sumbitch, he thought over and over.

It was a good thing for Carl that Jimmy was enamored of his colt because the ramifications of getting caught for breaking the rules were making him sick to his stomach. The intoxication of riding Good Prospect was just barely strong enough to drown the misery that Jimmy felt from jogging the colt illegally. The uncertainties that he felt the first day had blossomed into parched-mouth fear.

He worried about betraying Louisa, who trusted him to ride the colt in the first place. And he worried about the penalties for doing something that was clearly out of bounds on the racetrack. Would he lose his license and be banished to the farm? If he couldn't stay at the track and ride the Rondo filly, would she be able to go to the races again? Would Mike fire him? Every day as he trotted up and down the shaded horse path, he reveled in the marvelous feel of the talented horse and grew nauseated at the prospects for personal disaster. And every day as he alternated between pleasure and pain, he debated telling *la madre* what he was doing. Part of him felt like she would understand and assure him it was all right, but part of him feared she would quite understandably make him quit. And he did not want to quit riding this horse. So he agonized about the situation but in the end made no decision.

As she did every day, Shannon marveled at Jimmy's connection to the horse. His talent was natural, like the color of his eyes, and his execution almost careless. Today he exuded an especially powerful magnetism based on this unconscious skill. Over the years, Shannon had noticed there was something sexy about a man doing the thing he was good at, whether it was laying brick or riding a horse. She loved how a man could live in the moment and shut her out. Jimmy was engrossed in riding that colt, not thinking about what the trainer said yesterday or the fact that a girl rode alongside watching him. In a perverse way, his exclusion of her made him even more attractive. She would have to find out what he was like when he wasn't riding.

"So what finally brought you to the track?" Shannon asked as they jogged through the trees.

"I was working on the farm for Mr. Lucci and he said he needed me here. So I came."

"Nobody to hold you back?"

Jimmy shook his head.

"No girlfriend saying, 'Jimmy, I'll die if you leave me.'?"

Jimmy looked at her and laughed.

Good, she thought. Got that settled. "Did Mr. Lucci say you could ride in the afternoon?"

Jimmy paused. "Yes."

He thought back to when Louisa took him aside and asked him did he want to ride races? His heart almost stopped beating. Mr. Lucci, Louisa said, wanted him to ride the Rondo filly in her next race, if he could make the weight. She told him he could be a couple of pounds over the first time, because Mr. Lucci just wanted to get a race in her after all the problems she'd had.

He didn't hear a word after "ride races".

"Oh, Jimmy, that is so cool. When? Does he have a race for you?"

"Next week." *Next week.* Eight more days.

"Wow. Are you ready?"

"I have to lose some more weight."

"What are you doing? Putting on a garbage bag and running around the track in the heat of the day? You're not doing drugs are you?"

Jimmy looked startled. "No."

"Be careful. I'm friends with a lot of the jocks in Florida and some of those guys do horrible things to themselves. Like flipping. I know it's easy but the gastric acid from your stomach will rot your teeth and corrode your pipes. And coke. They get hooked on coke. It's— Oh, shit!"

Jimmy was surprised by her vehemence.

"Hey! What do you think you're doing?" Freddy the gap master was standing on the horse path in front of them, a hot doughnut in his hand. They jerked the horses up.

Jimmy was unfortunately familiar with what it felt like to be slugged in the gut and that was exactly how he felt when Freddy stopped them. He had that breathless feeling when everything stopped and you were helpless and unable to move. It was a scary moment and if you didn't force yourself to respond quickly, the next thing you felt was usually a painful crack to your face. Jimmy forced himself to take rapid shallow breaths to clear his head and be prepared to dodge the fist coming at his face. He heard Shannon's voice in the distance.

"Freddy! Hi! We were—"

"Don't even say it, Missy. Then I'll have to give you a ticket for lying to a track official, too. Give them nags to a groom and get your butts up to the stewards' office in four minutes, 'cause in five minutes I'm yanking both your licenses."

"Freddy, listen. Really—"

Freddy held up his arm and looked at his wrist. "Ten, nine, eight…"

Jimmy had been stroking his colt's neck to keep him calm. Now he nudged him along towards Barn Four. "Come on, Shannon, do what the man says." Let's get on with the funeral, he thought.

A phone call from chief steward Paco Esteban diverted Wick from his pleasant anticipation of taking Louisa to see Alice at the camp. They had spent the previous afternoon getting the horse settled and introduced to the pool. Despite the labor involved in setting up the round pen, dragging the damned goat around and hauling water to the trough, Wick mostly recalled the laughter as he and Louisa made jokes about their secret "training center."

Now some problem in the racing secretary's office was going to delay his return to the woods. Paco hadn't given him any details but he was a capable steward. He wouldn't call Wick unless it was something out of the ordinary.

As Wick approached the secretary's office, he could hear voices from inside and he thought he could see the batten board walls of the building bulging as though an explosion had gone off inside. Nevertheless, he was unprepared for the commotion he found. It seemed as though every racing official, every commission employee and half the backstretch were crowded into the room, all shouting at once. Wick paused inside the door and stared at the crowded scene, which resolved itself into several clusters of arm-waving people. Four trainers were ganged up around Jack Delaney, the racing secretary. Outrider and gap master Freddy was squared off against that new exercise rider of Mike Lucci's, Jimmy something, in front of one of the stewards, who held the two angry men apart. Wick was distressed to note that his handicapper was arguing with another steward while Carl Starling stood by looking unhappy. The only person who looked remotely calm was that kooky gal from Florida, who was earnestly talking to Paco Esteban. Somehow he was not surprised to find her mixed up in this. Passers-by stopped and studied the action as though they were handicapping horses in the paddock. The employees in the secretary's office made no pretense of minding their own business; they sipped coffee and watched with interest.

Wick decided to confer with the chief steward first, but just as he stepped forward, he heard a scuffle and looked over to see Jimmy fling the secretary's "pill bottle," full of colored cubes with post position numbers, across the room. There was a fifth of a second of silence as heads turned and watched the missile fly through the air then shatter a computer monitor with a crackling explosion followed by a small mushroom-shaped cloud.

More and more, Wick thought, this job reminded him of that dreadful period when he and Claire had three children under five. He gave a piercing whistle that silenced the room. Then he waded through the crowd to Paco and they herded the key players into a conference room.

The racing secretary went first. "Freddy caught those two jogging horses on the horse path," Jack said, gazing ominously at Shannon and Jimmy.

"What a stupid goddam—" Wick blurted, suddenly angry.

Paco interrupted, waving his hand gently. "Let's hear what they say."

Wick looked sharply at the chief steward who was making peaceful motions with his hands. Then, uncertain whether he was more upset by the breach of rules or by the interruption of his plans, Wick exhaled sharply and nodded. After a moment, he realized that he was still nodding, remembering how Alice had confounded him by walking into the pool with little hesitation. Louisa had enchanted him with her girlish pleasure at the improbable success of their project, leaving him as soft and warm as a bucket of hot mash.

Now, as he turned to the outrider, he tried to restrain his annoyance. "Freddy?"

The outrider, still in his shabby body vest and dusty half-chaps, demonstrated the gravity of his report by standing at attention. "It was after training hours, at least fifteen-twenty minutes. Rodell came out with a tray of them doughnuts of his, so I had one of them, and I seen these two come jogging up through the trees. I seen them once before, last week, and it looked kind of suspectful then, but Missy Florida, she done told me the first time they was late getting to the track, and she was reared back fixing to give me the same story again, I reckon."

Lawrence rolled his eyes and Shannon started sputtering. Wick glanced over and cut her off. "Hold it." He turned back to Freddy. "What did they say?"

"Didn't say nothing," said Freddy. "I told them to hand them horses off and beat it to the office, and I come up here straight away. They can't be jogging on the horse path every morning with a thousand horses coming and going."

"You did the right thing." He turned to Shannon, fumbling for her name. He tried to remember Louisa saying the girl's name, which just made him angry again. Finally he just nodded and said, "What about it?"

Shannon faced him earnestly. "Mr. Keswick, I don't blame you and Mr. Delaney and Freddy and Bones for being upset. This is a serious safety issue, and I just want you to know that I understand the importance of having rules to keep everyone from getting hurt out there and I feel sure Jimmy does, too, because he's told me so. That's why we're being real careful, staying away from any other horses or people and mostly just walking around, maybe jogging a few steps here and there, you know, because this is a good horse, he's not foolish, he's just working through some issues due to being in such a terrible, frightening accident. Mr. Starling has figured out where his head's at and Jimmy's done such a good job with him that I think he's going to be fine. I hope you will take into account that Mr. Starling has a lot at stake here, and nobody has been hurt. No harm, no foul."

As Wick digested this speech, Carl stepped forward. "Boyd, this is my doing. You can't penalize Jimmy and Shannon. I took advantage of their good nature and their eagerness to help me get my colt to the track after the accident last week."

Wick remembered the sick feeling in the bottom of his stomach at the sight of so many loose horses that morning and his dismay that one of them was Carl's colt. Not only was it Carl's colt, it was the first decent horse Carl ever had. "Yeah, Carl, I heard he had a problem."

Paco somehow lowered the temperature in the room, asking calmly, "How much longer do you think he needs?"

Carl took a deep breath. "He's a very intelligent horse. I think he's sorting it out."

Shannon started selling again. "He's getting better every day. He's more relaxed. I thought he might walk out on the track today."

Jimmy had been staring at Shannon in disbelief since her speech. He was awash in guilt for breaking Louisa Ferncliff's trust as well as at least fourteen rules of the backstretch, so he was amazed to hear Shannon talking to the president and the racing secretary— who were pretty much like God and Jesus in his book, only more powerful—as though they ought to excuse her and him.

"Jimmy, what do you think? You're riding the colt, aren't you?" asked Paco.

All eyes turned on the exercise rider. Jimmy flushed. "He's… He's…doing good. Feels good."

Lawrence stepped in. "Wick," he began seriously, "I know nobody's going to like this—" He glanced around the room. "—but you've got to give this horse a chance. This might be the best horse that's ever been on this track." It occurred to Wick what a mellifluous voice Lawrence had. He was usually focused on some goofy thing the kid did. "Wick, you and Paco and Freddy need to find a way to make this work. This horse runs like Rembrandt's Paint. Carl knows what he's doing and Jimmy, Jimmy's amazing with the horse. He can talk to him. I've watched them every day. He's gonna fix this horse. You've got to give him a chance. Please. I have to see him run again."

Wick was inclined to let the stewards sanction them and get on with his day, but Lawrence's impassioned plea gave him pause.

Jimmy was impressed by Lawrence's speech, too. Lawrence had clearly gone out on a limb for them and had specifically said that he, Jimmy, could save the day. Jimmy had never heard anyone speak with such assurance about his skills and had certainly never in his life been viewed by anybody in any situation as a hero. He stared at the handicapper in awe.

As the little group in the conference room mulled Lawrence's speech, Shannon wondered if anyone would make the connection between jogging on the horse path and diversions like firecrackers in the bathhouse.

Jack was the first to comment. "Bullshit. The horse hasn't even run through his conditions. How can you say he's the best horse you've ever seen?"

Paco, who, as chief steward, was technically the one empowered to deal with the situation, said, "The horse's record doesn't have anything to do with it, Jack."

Lawrence stuck to his pitch. "He was entered in a stakes when he got run over. That wasn't his fault. It seems to me the least you could do is give him a chance. What do you think, Jimmy? Couple more days? Week?"

Jimmy nodded.

Jack snorted derisively. "You get horses working on the horse path, I'm going to have fifty trainers on my neck—"

"Come on, Jack," said Paco. "Since when do you let trainers tell you what to do?"

While Jack, Paco and Lawrence argued, Carl stood serenely by, confident that matters would take their course and he would continue training his horse. Jimmy watched in agony, awed by having Lawrence as his champion, worried that Mr. Keswick would side with the racing secretary, fearful of losing his job.

Shannon kept quiet.

As Wick listened to the debate, he felt his frustration returning. He just wanted to leave and go to Alice's camp with Louisa. "Paco, give 'em some days and let's get back to racing," he growled.

Paco pulled Wick into a corner and spoke to him softly. "Wick. It's not a big deal. We can make this work, give the old man a break with his horse."

"Then what? Every time some trainer has a problem, we'll have horses jogging in the paddock or working on the turf track." Wick's voice rose and his face went red. "What about the goddamn rule book?"

Paco made a soothing little sound, an unconscious habit left over from his long gone racing days. It worked. Wick relaxed enough to hear what the old jockey said: "Sometimes you gotta forget the rules and look at the people. Who's getting hurt?"

Obediently, Wick looked over Paco's head at the old trainer waiting patiently for permission to train his talented horse, just as he had waited patiently for the horse to appear in the first place. He glanced at Paco and back at Carl. At last he exhaled and waved at the little group of guilty horsemen. "All right. Everybody out. Paco, Jack, wait here. The rest of you, don't go far."

The group filed out into the hall and wandered around in front of the licensing desk. Shannon and Lawrence went to the track kitchen. They brought drinks back to Jimmy and Carl. The four of them had finished their drinks and were sucking on the ice when the door to the conference room opened. Wick jerked his head and they filed in.

As he shut the door behind them, he said, "Now this is how it's going to be."

PART IV

Chapter 22

Alice's Restaurant stood on the faded blue concrete apron and surveyed the pool. Louisa waited patiently for the horse to decide he was ready. After a moment, he inched down the steep ramp until the water reached his chest. At that point he stopped and played, taking a drink, splashing with his muzzle and then burying his face up to his eyes. Finally, he blasted the water as he exhaled through both nostrils. Then he looked at Louisa who clucked him on. He eased himself deeper into the pool, moving off with symmetrical strokes, propelling his twelve hundred pounds through the resistant water. Louisa walked around the edge of the pool, a long pole holding the shank while the horse swam.

Wick looked at the scene and shook his head. He could not have imagined that they would ever get Alice into the pool the first time and certainly not the second time. But if you had a good relationship with a horse and he trusted you, you could get him to do unbelievable things. Wick always thought that about trailers, which rattled and were loud and beset by frightening experiences on the highway. When an eighteen-wheeler blew by a horse trailer, the trailer fish-tailed and the noise was deafening. Scary stuff for a horse.

"It's amazing what you can get horses to do," Wick said as Louisa came around the near side of the pool.

She laughed. "You mean this?"

"Yeah," he said.

"It's amazing what you can get people to do."

Now it was his turn to laugh. "You mean this?" He held up the lead rope to the goat, which was browsing in the prickly brush beside the pool fence.

The sun was beating down on them like a hammer on a gong, and Wick tried to stay in the shade of a bouquet of scrawny trees of paradise that had grown up in the ten-year absence of lawn mowers and weed eaters. The goat, of course, was determined to graze under the broiling sun. As the goat tugged on the rope to reach some mysteriously delectable patch of weeds, Wick reluctantly stepped out of the shade. "Damn," he said, "I meant to bring a lunge line with me this time." At least he had on old shoes instead of his tasseled loafers.

"There's one in the back of my truck," Louisa called, "but you insisted on driving your car."

"I guess I need to stop being such a gentleman," said Wick.

"Please don't," she said and the last wisp of Wick's anger from the scene in the racing secretary's office wafted away.

Just as he had a routine for entering the swimming pool, Alice had a ritual for leaving the pool. When Louisa turned him to the ramp and he touched bottom again, he simply stopped and let his tail float and spread around his muscular haunches. He played in the water with his muzzle again and took one last dive until his face was submerged up to his eyelashes. Then, with a snort, he climbed up the ramp, pulling a wave of water with him as he emerged like a breaching bay whale. He shuffled carefully across the slick concrete apron around the pool. Gallons of water streamed down his sides and met under his belly to fall like a curtain from the centerline. As soon as he reached the secure footing of the grass, he stopped and shook. Louisa rewarded him with some grapefruit sections and stroked his face. Alice's wet brown coat was almost black. The sun reflected off it in blue patches. His wet tail hung in two points like shiny black stalactites.

"He looks good for an old claimer, doesn't he?"

"He looks happy," said Wick. There was no way the horse was ever going to look good. Although he had a powerful engine in his hind end that propelled him to forty miles an hour a few strides out of the starting gate, he had a skinny neck and legs that looked as though they'd been through a meat grinder. His head was ordinary when viewed from the side, but he had a pretty face and a kind eye.

"He ought to be happy," Louisa said. "We're giving him everything he wants, the racetrack, a swimming pool and plenty of grapefruit." She let the horse graze alongside the goat as they talked.

Wick examined his sticky shirt, peeling it away from his chest and letting it cling again. He never did anything to sweat anymore. "When are you going to run him again?"

"I told Mike this morning to find a race for him." Louisa smiled a dreamy smile. "You know most people love the big horses – Cigar, Zenyatta – but I love these guys. These old campaigners love to run just as much as Cigar."

"That's the way horsemen are too, aren't they?"

Louisa shared her dreamy smile with him, beaming a soft caress from her face to his until Alice pulled her around the back side of the pool.

Wick watched the diminutive horsewoman, her clouds of gray hair gracefully piled on her head and coming undone, as always. She had a contented air today. Though he knew she had a hard life, he had never heard her complain. He dismissed her talk about retiring and moving to some football town as a long-running joke. She'd found a niche for herself in the racetrack community and she had the serenity that went with that. He envied her that serenity. Lately he had felt restless at the racetrack. If all the clowns on the backstretch would quit acting up and the horses would quit getting loose and running into each other, then maybe he could remember what it was like to enjoy a horse with a lot of heart like Alice's Restaurant. The goat gave a tug on the line and Wick followed, in no hurry to put the animals away and return to work. He felt pretty serene himself, out here in the woods with Louisa and the animals. Maybe he'd move out here when…when he had to let go, as Louisa said.

Louisa stroked Alice's neck. "It's so peaceful here. I hate to go back."

"I suppose now you want me to clean up the lodge." He nodded at the dilapidated remains of the bunkhouse.

She laughed like tinkling bells. "No fear of that. I like my creature comforts."

A line of big white thunderheads reaching thousands of feet into the air crept across the western sky, blocking the brutal sun, giving them welcome shade. They grazed the two animals across the ratty lawn of the camp.

"Thank you for giving those kids a break today."

Wick's annoyance over the scene in Jack's office had dissolved in the calm of the woods. But he wondered about his unaccountable decision to allow Shannon and Jimmy to jog on the horse path for another week. It made him uncomfortable to bend the rules. Rules were important. The backstretch was a big messy world where the outriders and stewards struggled to maintain order. Even if the system seemed arbitrary at times, there was security in knowing what was allowed. And yet for some reason he had agreed with Paco Esteban, stood up to Jack Delaney and waived a rule. Wick bent down to untangle the line from the goat's legs. "It was about Carl, really."

Louisa waited.

Wick recalled how the young folks seemed more intent on helping Carl than saving their own hides. "Lawrence said Carl's colt was the best horse he'd ever seen. And that girl Shannon made quite a sales pitch herself." What a con artist. He smiled in spite of himself. "Even Jimmy said a few words."

"What did Jack D think?"

"Oh, he was hot," said Wick. "He thinks I've lost my mind. Maybe he's right."

"There's more to life than following the rules," said Louisa.

"They'll carve that on your tombstone, but I didn't expect to hear it from Paco," said Wick, ducking when she flipped the end of the lead rope at him.

"Even Paco knows that people's lives are more important than the rulebook, Wick. You gave Carl a chance to maybe do something with the only horse he's ever had that has any talent. And you left me my exercise boy that I desperately need."

"Oh, so it's really all about you."

"If it's not, it ought to be," she said, flashing him a saucy smile.

Just as Wick felt himself sliding from serenity into another, equally pleasant emotion, Alice's Restaurant snorted loudly, threw up his head and tried to bolt.

"Bees!" shouted Wick as Louisa spun around with the horse, letting him trot away under a tight hold. The goat scampered off with

Wick doing his best to keep up. Louisa got Alice to stop near the woods and they regrouped.

"Alice stepped in a nest of ground bees," said Wick when they had the animals quieted down. "I'll come back at dusk and throw some gasoline on the hole. You think the horse will be okay in the pen?"

"I think the pen is far enough away. Did you get stung?"

Wick was rubbing his ear and his neck. "Not but four or five times. You owe me, *Madre*."

"I owe you a lot, Wick."

Chapter 23

Shannon found jogging on the horse path with Wick's blessing even more worrisome than when it was a secret. The fear of getting caught had conveniently diverted her attention from her own problems. Acky's training was stuck on hold until Good Prospect came around, and with it, her career as a trainer. Even though she galloped a horse for Max Fox and two for Mike Lucci and made a dime turn around twice before she spent it, money had become an issue. Before she left Florida, she put aside a hundred-dollar bill for an emergency, but the way she was going, in a few days breakfast would qualify as an emergency. She had begun slipping a few scoops of grain out of Carl's feed bin into her own when no one was around. She worried about running Acky again before he was ready, but she had to get one of her horses in a race and win some money.

To make matters worse, her mother called. This was not quite as bad as if her father called, but it brought her up short nonetheless.

Shannon had called her mother in the beginning to let her know she had arrived safely and that everything was going well. She planned to call her again after she had a win under her belt. Then she could tell her mother she would send her some money.

But Mrs. Hill called first. Her dad's check was late and the condo fee was due. Shannon wished her dad would just pay the fee and take it out of the money he sent her mom each month. Mrs. Hill never managed to have money left over for things like monthly bills.

Shannon told her mom she couldn't swing the whole fee, but she would send a couple hundred dollars.

She'd have to run Bread 'n Butter. The filly had taken to the racetrack like a duck on a June bug and was quite cheerful about grabbing the bit, sticking her nose out and running for all she was worth. She seemed to have heart. "Heart's won more races than talent," she heard an old racetracker say one time.

On a muggy morning four days after their reprieve, Jimmy and Shannon sat on the two colts at the top of the slope above the gap. It was a few minutes after ten and two or three stragglers were finishing their exercise. As they came off the track, one of them flashed perfect teeth and called out, "Ah, *Guapa*. Time for me to ride your horse?"

"*En tus suenos*," Shannon replied, eliciting Teg's usual laughter.

"You know that guy?" Jimmy asked.

Shannon shrugged. "He's always after me to let him gallop Acky."

Jimmy grunted. "That ain't what he's after."

Shannon nodded and wondered if Jimmy knew something about Teg that she didn't. She did not tell him she let Teg buy her a beer once in awhile.

While they talked, Good Prospect looked at the activity on the track below with interest. Two tractors pulling wide rakes followed a water truck around the oval, grooming the surface for the afternoon's races. Shannon and Jimmy had jogged the horse path several times and each time Jimmy stopped the horse just above the gap. Now the colt shook his head up and down, stuck his nose out and, on his own, walked down the slope towards the gap. Jimmy felt the colt hesitate just inside the rail, but he decided not to let him think about it, legging him firmly into a jog. They trotted the wrong way around the outside rail with Shannon and Acky alongside. Freddy waited until they had stepped away before he pressed the button on his walkie-talkie. "Hey, Juan, hold up them tractors. And stop that water truck," he said softly.

But the chestnut colt jogged around like a champ.

"Omigod, Jimmy, look at him. How's he feel?"

Jimmy didn't take his eyes off the colt's flickering ears. "Don't say nothing."

Shannon held her tongue but couldn't keep from grinning.

Carl and Lawrence watched the proceedings each day from the picnic tables overlooking the gap. When Good Prospect trotted off as if on a routine workout, Carl nodded in satisfaction. "He's okay now."

"Just like that? Is he going to gallop? Do you think he'll gallop?"

Carl just nodded again, watching the horse trot along, his ears flicking back and forth as he looked around and listened to his rider. The two horses disappeared behind the tote board. The seconds stretched out like a rubber band that finally popped when Good Prospect emerged from the shadow of the tote board. He came cantering around the clubhouse turn at an easy gallop, his training partner at his side. His head was tucked as he floated noiselessly over the loam. As the horses passed them and cantered away, Carl stood up and clapped his hands once in satisfaction.

Back at Barn Four, the good news ripped through the stalls, setting off excited squeals from the groomettes. As they waited for the horses to return, the girls lined up and clapped, a gauntlet of cheerleaders at a game. After weeks of worry throughout the barn, the black mood had lifted like a flock of starlings showing the bright colors of its opposite side.

Lawrence, ever the clown, quickly became infected. By the time Jimmy and Shannon rode up and slid off their horses, Lawrence was clapping with the girls. He whooped and gave a Shannon a high-five, spooking her horse.

"Whoa, Acky," she laughed, grabbing at the reins. "Lawrence, are you insane?"

Carl had a wide grin on his face. He stood at the end of the aisle studying the sweaty chestnut colt, pleased that his protégé had come around, proud that he had managed the horse correctly.

Lawrence pounded Jimmy on the back, oblivious to the exercise rider's awkwardness. "Great ride! Man, you're awesome!"

Lawrence turned back to Shannon. "Let's go to the kitchen. C'mon, Jimmy. You come with us."

Shannon, equally excited by their team triumph, let one of the girls take Acky away for his bath. The ebullient Lawrence hugged her around her shoulders, pulling her away from the barn. "We gotta celebrate."

As they burst into the kitchen, Lawrence called out, "Rodell, your finest hot doughnuts all around!"

Shannon, like everyone in the room, watched the electric handicapper. Caught up in his excitement, she became vivacious and flirty. As he stood in front of the counter, waiting for doughnuts, he suddenly grabbed a bag of potato chips off the rack and tossed it at her. She juggled the bag and felt another one hit her ear.

"Lawrence!" she squealed as he pelted her with potato chips.

Quickly, he turned back to the counter and began counting out payment for the doughnuts. "Rodell, I'd make her pay for them if I were you."

Shannon trailed helplessly after Lawrence, grinning and bumping his shoulder as they settled down in the air-conditioned cool of the kitchen with chips, doughnuts and a couple of beers. But Lawrence turned his attention to Jimmy.

"Okay, tell me everything about the colt. How does he feel?"

Jimmy relaxed a little, staring at the doughnuts but refraining. "He feels good."

"Really good?"

"Really good."

"You ever felt one like him before?"

Jimmy shook his head. Lawrence waited anxiously for more. Finally, the rider tore his eyes away from the doughnuts, looked at Lawrence and said, "Not even close."

"It's good but it's different, right? Kind of like sliding on ice or something."

Jimmy's face opened up. "Yeah. Like that."

Lawrence beamed. Jimmy looked satisfied. They locked eyes and nodded.

Shannon had a vague sense she had missed something.

When Jimmy left, Lawrence and Shannon lingered side by side at the table, still aglow with the memory of Good Prospect galloping around the track.

"Oh man, I'm glad that horse came back," he said.

"I'm happy for Carl. I know it sounds weird, but I'm going to miss jogging on the horse path,'" she said.

"Yeah, well now you can go back to training your own horse. Did you ever pass the trainer's test?"

"I'm afraid to take it again. Lawrence, would you help me, please? I hate to bother Mr. Starling all the time, but I need some help with the condition book. That was the thing the stewards said I needed to work on, and that's the hardest thing to learn by yourself."

"What do you want to know?"

"I need you to sit down with me and go over all the different conditions at each level. I can read what the conditions mean, but I can't tell what kind of horse fits those conditions. Like, how do I know where to start my filly?"

"Yeah, sure." Lawrence inhaled through his teeth. "I really want to see that horse run."

Shannon knew he wasn't talking about Bread 'n Butter. "You're really into this horse, aren't you? It's not just 'cause you like Carl."

"Oh, I like Carl, but that colt is…" Lawrence glanced around at the nearby tables and leaned over to her ear and whispered, "…a freak."

She looked at him quizzically.

"He's got awesome speed. Nobody's seen it yet but me."

"You don't think Carl's seen it?"

"Carl just believes in the colt because he's his. And he's won a couple of allowance races. The colt hasn't shown that speed in a race yet. I think he was getting ready to fire when he got knocked down. I hope he's still got it."

"How come you've seen it and nobody else has?"

Lawrence turned to face her, holding her open, curious gaze. Finally he said, "It's my job to see stuff like that."

She returned his gaze. "Handicapper's sight?"

"Something like that," he said. The clatter of the room fell away as he lingered on her face.

She waited for whatever he might say.

He broke eye contact first, letting out a long sigh and picking up the buzz of the cafeteria again. Suddenly he stood up, bumping the table, and called out, "Hey, Vicki, over here."

The tall office assistant with the long ironed hair and the strappy sandals brought a Coke over to their table. "Hey, Sugar," she said, smiling in a proprietary way at Lawrence.

Shannon, who, in her jeans and paddock boots, normally felt superior to office types, immediately hated Vicki.

"How are things in the secretary's office?" Lawrence asked. "All the races fill?"

"Yeah. Same old thing. What are you doing?"

Shannon spoke up, affecting an ultra-casual tone. "Talking shop about how this horse trained today."

Vicki continued to address Lawrence. "Oh, did that horse of Carl's finally go to the track?"

Lawrence nodded and took a swig of beer.

"I know that makes you happy," said Vicki, smiling at Lawrence.

"Yeah," said Shannon, "it's kind of a project we've been working on together."

Vicki finally looked at Shannon. "Well, I guess the project's over, now that the horse has gone to the track."

As the two women glared at each other, Lawrence took a call on his cell phone. Then he stood up abruptly and without looking at either girl, he left. "See y'all later," he threw out absently.

Shannon and Vicki watched him run out the door, then looked at each other. Finally Shannon drained her beer and said, "He is so weird sometimes."

Chapter 24

As Shannon led Bread 'n Butter to the paddock for the fifth race on a Monday night, she was filled with pride and hope that the culmination of her dreams was at hand. In thirty minutes or so, Shannon would have, she hoped, her first win and—although she hated to sound mercenary—a check.

The race was a $7,500 maiden claimer that Mr. Starling had steered her to. When she voiced her fear that someone would claim the filly, Mr. Starling assured her that, as a first-time starter, the filly was more than likely safe. That was the trouble with claiming races: once you entered a horse for, say, a $7,500 tag, any other trainer could buy the horse out of the race, even if you didn't want to sell. And yet there were no other type races for horses of limited or unproven ability. Shannon fretted about losing Bread 'n Butter, half her stable. How would she be able to make a name for herself with only one horse? She hoped Mr. Starling was right. If she lost this filly to a claim, she'd be in deep trouble.

Adding to her worry was the price of the race. The winner's share was barely $4,000 after the jockey's percentage and the other fees were deducted. It was nothing to sneeze at, of course, but she had learned very quickly that $4,000 didn't go very far when you were supporting yourself and two horses. And your spendthrift mother, her rational side whispered. She wished she had overruled Mr. Starling and run the filly in the eighth race, an allowance race with a bigger purse.

Shannon had groomed Bread 'n Butter to within an inch of her life. The filly's chestnut coat gleamed and her feet were glossy with hoof oil. She had brushed her flaxen tail full of static electricity so that the golden hairs stood out like a fan, floating around her hind legs and making the filly look like some toy store pony for a horse-crazy little girl.

Enhancing the image, the filly was tricked out in a brand new white racing bridle, a purchase Shannon refused to regret. Shannon and the filly fell in line with the other two-year-olds and their grooms strolling along the outside rail to the paddock. Shannon and the other handlers each wore a numbered bib, so that when they got to the paddock, spectators could identify the horses.

As she looked at the grandstand where a few hard-core bettors lingered on the apron for the last race, Shannon's heart swelled with pride. She remembered how excited she had been the first time Acky ran at Calder, seeing his name listed in the program and the listing of her own name, Shannon Hill, as owner and breeder. It was an incredible rush to own a racehorse and it was an added fillip to be the breeder of the animal as well. Implicit in the term "homebred" was the notion that you were a knowledgeable horseman who had been in the business a long—and presumably successful—time. To race a successful homebred was to be the ultimate insider. She stroked the beautiful filly walking beside her and grinned. *Homebred.*

Carl Starling, as the trainer of record, was waiting in the paddock to saddle the filly. The filly was on her toes but not as nervous as several of the other two-year-olds. Shannon had schooled her in the paddock numerous times, and in any event, there wasn't enough of a crowd to scare a goose.

"I think she's ready to run, Mr. Starling."

Carl smiled. "You certainly do have her beautifully turned-out. If looks were speed, it'd be no contest."

Shannon beamed. "Yeah, I hope she's as fast as she is pretty."

She led the filly into the saddling stall, and Carl and Raphine Steele's valet assembled the saddle pad and number cloth, cinching Raphine's purple patent-leather racing saddle on top. The filly was standing quietly but Carl directed her to take the filly around the walking ring some more.

Lawrence and Hank came through the paddock gate to do their standup analysis in the center of the walking ring and Lawrence gave her a salute. She returned the signal with an exquisite sense of belonging.

When the riders came out of the jocks' room, Shannon took the filly back into her stall. She had rehearsed a lengthy exposition for Raphine describing the filly's temperament and every aspect of her personality and track preferences that Shannon had observed leading up to this moment. But Raphine ignored Shannon in her numbered bib and turned to Carl, who said, "This is her first start. She is sensible and willing. Just get her out of the gate and see what she wants to do."

"Got it."

Carl introduced Shannon. "This is the filly's owner."

Raphine gave her a professional smile. "I'll take care of her."

"Thanks," said Shannon, determined to study hard and get her trainer's license as soon as possible. Owners got no respect, even ones who galloped their own horses.

Shannon put two dollars to win on the filly and watched the race with Carl from his box. She was pleased to see her filly trotting obediently alongside the pony in the post parade, and she watched proudly as the filly glided off in a smooth canter under Raphine's quiet hands. There was a large field, twelve two-year-old fillies going four and a half furlongs, most of them first time starters like Bread 'n Butter. Shannon could see through her binoculars that Bread 'n Butter was a little fussy waiting to load in the gate, but she did not give the assistant starters any trouble when it came her turn. The bell rang, the gates clanged and the horses surged forward. Shannon tried to pick out the blue and white silks from the rest.

"She broke well," said Carl. "Looks like she's fourth or fifth there, three wide."

That's good, Shannon thought, she won't be trapped down on the rail when she comes out of the turn into the stretch. The flock of fillies flowed around the turn and the horse to Bread 'n Butter's inside carried her wide coming out of the turn. A horse coming up on the outside squeezed her back toward the rail. There was a moment of chaos as the bunched field sorted itself out. The filly to Bread 'n Butter's inside fired, moving ahead, but as the field galloped down the long Colonial stretch, some fillies were drifting back and others were going forward. Shannon could see Bread 'n Butter's face now, far to the outside of the rest of the field. Her ears pinned, she was digging in and running as hard as she could. Nevertheless, the horses in front of her gradually pulled away, and as they neared the wire, the remaining five or six galloped past, despite Bread 'n Butter's spirited effort. The only reason Bread 'n Butter wasn't left in their dust was because she was out in the middle of the track.

As Shannon watched Bread 'n Butter's finish, she worried that the filly had been hurt in the bumper cars coming out of the turn. It seemed only an injury could have prevented her from blasting past the other two-year-olds. She watched the filly gallop out around the clubhouse turn and was relieved but puzzled to see her jog back sound. She heard Carl say, "Come on, let's go see what Raphine has to say."

They went out onto the track to meet the returning horses. Shannon slipped a halter over the new white racing bridle, now covered with dirt, as Raphine pulled her saddle off to weigh in.

Bewildered, Shannon led Bread 'n Butter to where a track attendant was spraying sweaty horses with a hose. She looked the filly over worriedly. Her nostrils were flared and moist but Shannon couldn't find a fleck of blood. Bread 'n Butter walked in circles around her, but her step was sure and sound. Her ears flickered as she took in the grandstand and the loudspeaker, but her manner was relaxed. The filly seemed depressingly sound and fit.

When Raphine came back from the scales, she and Carl were walking together. "She done everything I asked her to do," said the jockey. "Somebody done a good job breaking her in."

Still stunned by the loss, Shannon hardly registered this compliment. "You think she got hold of the track all right?"

"She felt pretty confident there."

"What about getting dirt in her face? How'd she take that?"

"She sucked back the first time something hit her, but she was pretty game after that. The Two horse carried her wide coming out of the turn, but she was still trying."

Later, watching a replay of the race, Shannon sought Carl's analysis. "She broke well, that's good," he said.

"Now see, right there. She threw her head up. That's where she got dirt in her face. I think that was bothering her. Don't you think?" Shannon asked.

"Could be."

"Raphine said it bothered her."

"It's a surprise to them, the first time," Carl agreed.

"Now, see there. She's got her ears pinned. What do you think that is?"

"Well, she has a look of determination about her. I think she's fighting gamely."

She's full of heart, Shannon thought fondly.

Despite her brave front, deep in the night at the Sta*light Motel, listening to the screaming Pakistani couple in the next room, Shannon felt a crack in her confidence. She stared at the insulation bursting from behind the broken ceiling panel. Would Bread 'n Butter be better next time? How soon could she run again? Could Acky support them in the meantime?

The puzzling question was, Why were both her horses such late bloomers? Was there some training secret she didn't know?

Chapter 25

Jimmy and Shannon jogged past the grandstand the wrong way, hugging the outside rail.

"How'd your horse run yesterday?"

She thought about the race chart. By Bread 'n Butter's name, the chart caller wrote: *broke sharply, raced evenly, no response late.* Shannon thought, It just goes to show that chart callers can't tell what really goes on in a race. The filly had been carried wide and had dirt kicked in her face. She fought gamely in the stretch, as Carl had said, but by then it was too late. "I think she's going to be a grass horse. That's why I brought her to Colonial in the first place."

Jimmy just nodded.

"Are you ready for Tuesday?"

He gave a wide slow smile. "Ready as I'm gonna get."

"Have you got a racing saddle and all that?"

"Jesus is loaning me one of his. And some pants. I bought me some boots, though."

They jogged a few steps before Shannon spoke again. "I'm looking for another race for Acky. Would you ride him for me?"

Jimmy looked over in mild surprise. "Yeah. Sure. Thanks. You don't want to get Raphine or one of them others?"

"No," Shannon said firmly. "I've been watching you and I think you'd get along well with this colt."

"You want me to blow him out one day, sharpen him up?"

Shannon was so pleased that Jimmy had agreed to ride her horse that she didn't hesitate to give up her favorite thing: breezing the colt herself. "That'd be awesome. What do you think? Breeze him Wednesday and hand walk him Thursday?"

"You're the trainer."

Shannon beamed. She felt better than she had since the race. She set her hands in the colt's neck. "You ready?" she asked and they moved off in a synchronized gallop.

The kitchen had emptied out. There was a brief lull before the lunch crowd arrived, and Shannon decided to take advantage of the quiet moment. She struck up a conversation with Rodell, who was scraping the grill and straightening up for the next wave of customers.

Shannon asked about his dog, as she always did. "Chiquito is well?"

Rodell appreciated the fact that Shannon spoke Spanish, and he preened at the mention of his dog. "Excellent," he said, patting the tiny head poking out of his apron pocket.

"I wish I had a dog. The horses are company, but I wish I had someone to go home at night with me."

"A dog is good company." Rodell continued working. "You live alone?"

"At the Sta*light. No dogs. I couldn't afford to feed one anyway."

"If you have a little dog, like Chiquito, it's not a problem."

They both laughed. She leaned on the counter and watched him work some more. "Say, Rodell, you ever need any help? Or do you know anybody?"

He stopped what he was doing, wiped his hands and came over to the counter. He put his thick brown hand on hers. "Are you needing money?"

She smiled. "I'm doing fine but my mom's kind of struggling, and I thought if I could pick up a few extra bucks somewhere, I'd send her something."

"What a good daughter." He opened the cash register and held out a wad of bills. "Here. Send this to your mother."

"No, Rodell. I'm not looking for a loan. You know how it is around the track—"

"Yes, the track is like family."

She laughed. "No, I mean everyone borrows money and never pays it back. I just want a part time job so I can make a little extra money. Just till I can run my horses and earn a little purse money."

He went to the phone on the wall and dialed a number. After a short, animated conversation in rapid Spanish, punctuated by several hisses, he turned back to her. "Go to Maria's. The cafe needs a waitress."

"Gosh, thanks, Rodell. Are you sure?"

"Yes. Today. Four o'clock. Supper and breakfast. Very busy."

Chapter 26

The gate-shy Rondo filly was entered in the sixth race with Jimmy Wiseman on board for his racing debut. Shannon appeared in the paddock early, ready to cheer her morning work partner when he came out of the jockeys' room. She was pleased to find Lawrence sitting in the gazebo gazing across the paddock and scooted onto the bench beside him. "Got all the winners picked?"

"Most of 'em. So what happened to your filly Saturday? She okay?"

"She came back fine. She didn't like having dirt kicked in her face. You know. First time starter. I think I'll look for a grass race for her," Shannon said.

"Never can tell," Lawrence said.

"How do you think Jimmy will do today?"

"The jocks tell me it's a surprise to have so many horses all around them the first time. That and listening to the jocks talk to each other." Lawrence chuckled. "Apparently, they gallop down the backstretch talking about what they did last night or some party they're going to."

"Really?"

Lawrence shrugged. "Just a day at the office."

Jimmy came out of the jocks' room, blinking in the late afternoon sunlight. His red and yellow silks billowed in the light breeze as he scanned the grassy oval, locking in on Mike and Louisa and marching straight to them.

"You ready to ride?" Mike asked him.

Jimmy nodded.

"You'll do fine," said Louisa and Jimmy nodded again.

Shannon and Lawrence gave him their encouragement before Mike led him to the saddling stall.

"Riders up!" called the paddock judge, and Mike tossed Jimmy into the saddle. Jimmy walked the filly onto the track amid cheers and calls of good luck.

"Come on," Louisa said to Shannon. "Let's go up to Mike's box and see how they do."

The filly was washed down in sweat as she paraded before the crowd, but she went along obediently under Jimmy's riding.

Mike muttered, "I hope she didn't leave her race in the paddock."

"Let's just see if she can get out of the gate," said Louisa.

"Shit, let's see if she'll get *in* the gate."

They had a clear view across the infield to the gate. Louisa held binoculars to her face while Shannon watched the video screen above the tote board.

"Uh oh. Uh oh," Louisa said.

The Rondo filly's fight-or-flight instinct redlined in the flight zone as she neared the starting gate. Jimmy managed to keep her moving among the agitated pack of three-year-olds milling around the turf course behind the gate.

In the locker room beforehand, Jimmy had been anxious about riding in his first race. Now that he was on a horse, a horse with a problem, his own nervousness evolved into a soothing cloud of soft murmurs that enveloped the fearful filly. She didn't relax but he could feel her listening to him. The other three-year-olds loaded into the gate one by one, the starter waiting, as planned, to load the Rondo filly last. Two assistant starters positioned themselves on either side of her, running a line through the bit to lead her forward. As she reached the huge metal skeleton, the filly jerked her head around, banging her nose and scooting backwards. Jimmy grimaced but kept up his calm encouragement. The other horses stood restively waiting for the filly and the bell.

"Don't pull. Let her walk," Jimmy hollered at the assistant starters. One man let go and stepped back. The other loosened the lead line. Jimmy gave a little chirp and the filly trustingly walked into the gate.

Amid the noise of the loudspeaker and the shouting of the jockeys and the voices of the assistant starters, each perched on a narrow ledge holding a horse's head, Jimmy heard the man in the stall with him cry, "Hang on!"

He had been sitting back to push the filly forward, and he barely had time to shift his weight and grab a wisp of mane when the bell rang. The gates clanged open, and he felt the filly's hind end sink as she coiled the catapult of her hind legs and hurled her body out of the gate. Jimmy found himself in the middle of a line of eight fillies lunging forward. Almost immediately, they were squeezed by the inside horse bearing out and the outside horses moving left to find a ground-saving path close to the rail. For a few frightening strides, he banged irons and elbows with the jocks on either side. Just as quickly, the pressure was relieved as the surrounding fillies were flushed forward. As the horses shuffled and found their positions, Jimmy and the filly galloped straight down the backstretch.

For twenty-four seconds, during the opening quarter of a mile, Jimmy felt the amazing sensation of sailing across the turf. He had breezed many horses on dirt tracks, at the farm and, in recent weeks, here at Colonial, but he had never blown a horse out on a grass course. There was a wondrous difference. It was just as fast but it seemed smoother, gentler, as though the horse were skimming over the blade tips of grass.

The filly was running easily in the middle of the pack, and, although Jimmy knew they were going fast, the presence of other horses all around made him feel as though they were cruising down the interstate. Supporting this notion, the other riders were having a conversation.

"Hey, bug boy, you doing all right?" the guy on his left called out.

"Yeah," he shouted without taking his eyes off the road ahead.

"Watch out, now. Here comes the turn."

The pace picked up as the horses swept into the turn and the Rondo filly started slipping to the outside. He was shocked at the power of the centrifugal force. Even though he was folded up on the horse's back with irons no more than fourteen inches long, he felt as though his right foot was hanging down the filly's side and he was slipping off. He jammed his foot in the iron and pushed himself to the inside, leaning with the filly as she accelerated around the curve. The stewards had impressed upon him the importance of maintaining a straight line, keeping to his own path during a race, but in the melee of shifting positions coming out of the turn into the stretch, it was impossible to tell where his path was. A horse dropped over in front of him and accelerated. He could feel a horse behind him looking to come around.

When they straightened out in the stretch, he popped the filly with his stick and she switched leads. He began scrubbing his hands up her neck and was rewarded with a perceptible surge of speed. With the horses spread out, Jimmy's sense of the pace became stronger. He could see the rail where stanchions flashed past like ticks on a stopwatch. All around him jocks were shouting and swatting their mounts. Some, like his filly, were going forward. Others were falling back. Adrenalin surged through his body like the shock from a cattle prod. He was riding in rhythm with his horse, driving her forward with hands and legs and voice. They overtook a filly on the inside and Jimmy rode as hard as he could, trying to reach the pair in front. The jocks in front suddenly stood up, letting their horses coast. As the Rondo filly blazed past, Jimmy heard the jocks calling out.

"Hey, bug boy, beep beep. Game over."

They laughed.

He slacked the reins and let the filly coast, at once pumped, embarrassed, amazed and out of breath.

During the gallop out, Louisa focused on the horse's legs. The filly's soundness gave Louisa more than her usual feeling of relief. The filly was okay. The filly had gone in the gate and was okay. She had run a race and was okay. Her new jock had handled her well. Together, they were positioned to win next time.

As Louisa checked off the night's milestones, she tucked the horse into her mental scrapbook. One more problem horse fixed.

"Look at that boy grin. You'd think he won the lottery."

They could, indeed, see Jimmy's teeth as he rode back to the scales to weigh in. He waved his stick at the stewards atop the grandstand and dismounted.

A groom held the horse as he pulled the postage stamp saddle off. After he weighed in, Mike shook his hand. "Nice ride, jock."

"Oh man. Oh man," Jimmy said.

"Lose those last three pounds and you win next time."

"Oh man. Oh man," Jimmy said.

Louisa savored Jimmy's euphoria. These were the highs racetrackers lived for, that otherworldly feeling of coiling up like a copper spring and exploding in a shower of red and yellow sparks. Only jockeys knew the feeling of being one with the wind, but other horsemen could appreciate the tension of a race and feel, beating deep in their own chest, the heart of a good horse. When it was *your* horse, the elation went beyond human happiness, as if God had invented a new emotion just for horsemen. Louisa knew Jimmy would be back, three pounds lighter, ready to ride the next race. If he didn't have racetrack fever before, he had it now.

She watched the boy walk away with Mike, his sweaty silks clinging to his poker-thin arms and ribby body. He was barely touching the earth, she knew, like a ballerina soaring on bruised toes. She didn't know whether to be happy or sad.

Chapter 27

As Wick and Louisa sat on the terrace behind the track kitchen overlooking the track, Wick swirled his coffee dregs around absently but made no move to go refill his cup.

"Go on. I know you have things to do," Louisa said.

"No, tell me the rest."

"We can talk at the pool."

He tossed the dregs on the grass sloping down to the track. "Aw hell, Louisa, I can't go today. I forgot to tell you. We've got a full house tonight for the Fourth, and I've got to make sure the fireworks after the races don't burn the place down."

"That's okay. I can handle Alice by myself."

Wick frowned. "Why don't you take Jimmy? He's good and he'll keep his mouth shut."

She laughed. "Don't you think he's been on enough secret training missions lately?"

"That's why I thought he'd be good."

"I'll find somebody, don't worry."

"Get him trained, 'cause I can't go tomorrow, either."

Louisa smiled. "I don't expect you on Wednesdays."

Wick opened his hands in a helpless gesture. "They're moving her to another room. I don't know what the hell for. They said it had a better view, but I think that's just to make *me* happy. She doesn't look out the window. She doesn't look at TV." He paused. "She doesn't look at me."

Louisa put a hand on his arm.

Wick stared across the track. "Hell, she doesn't even know I'm there."

Louisa rubbed his arm. Watching someone you loved sink towards death had to be painful. People thought Wick was gruff but she found a touching tenderness underneath. And generosity. Lord knows he had been good to her, solicitous of her comfort in the RV park, urging her to sit with him in the Turf Club and of course, the whole deal at the camp with Alice.

Louisa looked forward each day to getting away to the camp in the woods. It was quiet enough to hear the clouds. She imagined the children who stayed there in years past were refreshed by the simplicity of the natural surroundings. She'd spent so many years at the track that she had forgotten what the woods sounded like. Now she was enchanted to hear the cicadas and unseen little animals—birds? chipmunks?—twitching the underbrush and rustling the leaves. Often, she and Wick let Alice and the goat graze for an hour, the two animals tugging them around the clearing on their lead ropes while they talked. Monday had been a glorious day with low humidity and Wick brought a picnic. It was just some fried chicken and a couple of beers, but they spent most of the afternoon eating and talking, then laughing guiltily about their truancy. When they got back to the track just before post time, Wick faced his usual list of crises and she fielded angry questions from Mike, but she went to bed with a smile remembering the stolen afternoon of escape.

What would she have done if Wick had not helped her find the camp and fix it up? She didn't know too many men with that kind of class. Watching him suffer was hard. She longed to put her arms around him and comfort him.

Rodell came out of the track kitchen onto the overlook with a plate of hot doughnuts. "*Madre? Señor* Wick?"

Wick and Louisa both started. Wick recovered first, taking a doughnut. "Rodell, I don't see how any of the jocks around here ever make weight."

Louisa watched Wick in private admiration.

"Ah, *señor*. They only eat them for a little while. Then—" Rodell pretended to stick his finger in his throat.

"Hell of a way to live."

"How is Maria doing?" Louisa asked, turning her eyes away from Wick at last.

"Busy. Very busy."

"And she's happy?" Louisa continued.

"Yes, *Madre*. I am giving her all the money. I want to help people, but you tell me, and this is right, that I should give Maria all the money. So, we are helping people together. We are happy."

Louisa beamed.

"Maria is giving poor *Señorita* Hill a job."

Wick snorted. "Shannon Hill?"

Rodell nodded sadly. "Yes. Her family is very poor."

"Don't let her take you for a ride, Rodell."

"It is true, *Señor* Wick. She is sending money to her mother every time. She is *una buena hija*."

"She's a slick talker is what she is."

"Now, Wick," Louisa said. "She was trying to help Carl with his colt. She can't be all bad."

Rodell continued his defense of Shannon. "She works very hard. In the morning and at night. I am trying to give her some" –he rubbed his fingers together– "but she does not take it. She is a very fine lady. *Habla español*. And she likes the dogs."

"Well. There you have it," said Wick, standing up to leave.

As they walked off, Louisa had an urge to take Wick's hand but instead she said, "She seems all right to me. Jimmy gets along with her and she does a nice job with the two she gallops for us."

"Better than wasting time on those two of hers."

"They haven't done much, have they?"

Wick snorted. "She needs to take them up to Delaware Park and run them in the Arabian races. Then she'd only get beat five or six lengths, instead of thirty."

Louisa sighed. "Do you think the stewards are going to rule her horses off?"

Wick jumped to respond to Louisa's disappointed expression. "Louisa, you know it isn't fair to the public. They go to the betting windows thinking every horse has a chance. We're playing them for a sucker if we take their bet on a horse we know can't run."

"I just wonder what's going to happen to that girl."

"Are you going to take her on, too?"

She gave a tinkling laugh and rubbed his arm. "Nooo. My plate is full."

Louisa was late leaving for the camp, subconsciously waiting for Wick to come into the barn and sweep her away. Driving through the country roads, she turned on the radio in the quiet truck. At the camp, there was no breeze to ruffle the leaves and even the cicadas seemed muted. For the first time, Louisa noticed the brown shingles on the empty lodge folded back by the weather. One of the window sashes had been torn completely out and as she turned off the engine, she was surprised to see a buzzard hop onto the windowsill and fly away with an expansive spread of wings and a warning cry. The old man who lived up the driveway and checked on Alice wasn't home and Louisa had a moment of unease as she looked around the deserted camp. She had never been there without Wick.

Then Alice beckoned her insistently and she went to work. Alone in the little clearing around the pool, Louisa realized she couldn't swim the horse and graze the goat simultaneously, so she tied the goat to a tree with a long line. But by the time she got the horse in the water, the goat had wandered off behind the pool house, causing Alice to neigh anxiously from the pool. Then when his exercise was over, Alice rushed up the ramp, slipping to his knees before lunging out and skating wildly across the apron, jerking Louisa down on the rough concrete. Louisa broke her fall with her bad left hand. Still holding tight to the shank, she felt her knees gouged by the broken concrete before she could get to her feet and control the anxious horse. Fortunately, the gelding stopped the minute the goat reappeared. As the agitated horse paced around her while she caught her breath, Louisa saw a nasty scrape on Alice's big right knee.

Oh God. What if he's hurt? She'd never forgive herself. What was she thinking? Trying to swim a horse in a children's pool? By herself. What an idiot! Why didn't she bring Jimmy, like Wick told her to? Ignoring her own bloody knee and scraped arm, she paid out the line and let Alice jog a few steps. Holding her breath, she watched for the slightest sign of discomfort. Amazingly, the horse seemed fine. She limped to the truck and retrieved bandages and gauze for redoing Alice's knee. Back in his pen, Alice ate his grain and pulled at his hay while Louisa studied his every move. After a long assessment she reluctantly drove away.

That evening, Louisa got Ticket Taker off to the paddock for the third race and limped back to her RV, where she finally soaked and tended her own wounds. As she daubed antibiotic cream on her scraped leg, she thought about having to swim Alice again by herself. What if Alice had gotten loose? She had visions of Alice galloping up the driveway and running down the highway with cars braking— or not. For a horse like Alice's Restaurant, danger covered the ground like oak pollen. Louisa paused in treating her leg and stared at a win photo of the black mare. She felt utterly helpless.

She had thought she would be satisfied to monitor Alice's exercise, change the bandage herself and approve his races, but watching the old horse coming out of the turn last week had almost made her heart stop with fear. His easy win and solid step afterwards left her with mixed feelings, joy at the heart of a horse, fear for the price he—or she—might one day pay. Day after day you bandaged and galloped and stroked a horse and what happened? One wild stormy day he jumped up and outran the wind, bowling you over with his grit and drive as he stood where he had no right to be: in the winner's circle. Then on a lazy boring Tuesday, he pulled up from a gallop and looked at you with pained curiosity as he held up a throbbing ankle. The racetrack was gut-wrenching. It was true what they said: "The highs are really high and the lows are really low." She wasn't sure she could handle being jerked back and forth anymore. The highs were amazing but the lows… Just the fear of the lows was getting to be too much to take.

Louisa looked at another framed photograph on her dresser: a football player in a green and yellow uniform staring out of the shadow of his helmet with a cocky grin. She cheered for the Dolphins and wrapped elbows and knees in the Saints' locker room, but her heart lay with the Green Bay Packers. She had watched with her dad as Bart Starr and the Packers beat Dallas in the first Super Bowl. Years later, she and a couple of exercise riders had stocked the car with beer and driven four hours from Arlington Park to Green

Bay, just to watch a scrimmage. Afterwards, quarterback Brett Favre recognized the accent of a fellow Southerner and hung around the parking lot talking to her. "You need to move on up here, gal. We need some more folks who know what grits are." She could still hear his Mississippi accent caressing her ear.

She often joked about moving to Wisconsin when she retired but lately the idea had taken on the soft beige color of a sensible option. Being close to her beloved Green Bay Packers would be a stable and satisfying way to live after the emotional whiplash of horse racing. Alice's gutsy win was thrilling but it could just as easily have been a replay of the black mare. You never knew what would happen when you sent a horse out onto the track.

With the Packers, she would know.

Chapter 28

Shannon was alone in the paddock when Paco Esteban approached her. She had gotten off work at Maria's a little early and managed to make it to the track for the last two races. She parked in the employees' lot behind the low building housing the jockeys' quarters and walked to the paddock through the forest of satellite dishes that collected races from all over the country. When she got there, she saw a groom she knew from Florida walking a horse around before the eighth race. He waved and she decided to wait until he was done. There were few owners in the paddock, so she sat on the gazebo bench to wait.

"May I join you?" asked the steward.

She smiled. "Sure."

Paco was a good guy. He had helped her with the trainer's test, going over her wrong answers and explaining the subtleties of the condition book. And she suspected he had talked Mr. Keswick into letting her and Jimmy jog on the horse path. "How are you coming with your studying?"

"Working on it." Shannon nodded towards the handicappers in front of the camera nearby. "Lawrence has been helping me with the condition book. And I appreciate the help you gave me," she said.

149

"When you get your license, what are your plans?" he asked her.

She opened her hands. "Run my two… I need to figure them out and make runners out of them so I can pick up an owner with some other horses." That was how you did it, wasn't it? You had some success with whatever horses you had and began to make a name for yourself.

"How's your colt doing?"

"He's training great. Looks good. Feels good. I'm ready to run him as soon as the Turf Festival opens." And as soon as Mr. Starling gives me some advice about getting him to run, she added mentally.

Paco nodded. "You think he'll like the grass better."

"Oh yes. His dam was a grass horse." Shannon's old show horse never came within ten miles of a racetrack but she jumped beautifully in a grass ring.

The ex-jockey brightened. "Sometimes changing the surface they run on makes a big difference. Look at Cigar. Went from grass to dirt and won sixteen races in a row."

"Yeah. That's why I brought him to Colonial in the first place, for the turf racing."

There was a pause before Paco continued gently. "You know he's running out of time."

"Oh I think he's ready to run a big race. He's sharp," Shannon assured him. "Jimmy Wiseman's going to breeze him for me on the turf course."

"Girl, I'm pulling for you but I've got to warn you." He lifted his eyebrows in the direction of the stewards' stand at the top of the grandstand. "The other two are going to rule him off if he doesn't run better next time."

She nodded vigorously, her words spilling out in nervous squirts. "Thank you, Mr. Esteban. Don't worry. Mr. Starling is helping me. My colt'll be ready next time out. Ready to run big."

Shannon excused herself and left the paddock. She wanted to throw up. Every organ in her gut twisted and heaved. She stumbled across the apron nearly blind with nausea. After all her efforts to get this far, the stewards wanted to tell her she couldn't run one of her horses. What a sickening nightmare.

She pawed her way past fans marking their programs or eating hot dogs. She had to get to the café tables on The Green beyond the grandstand. It was always dark and empty there on a Tuesday, but tonight for some reason there were throngs of people all over the place. And children. Why were there so many–

A hand grabbed her arm and stopped her. "Shannon, *mi Corazon. Que' te pasa?* What is wrong?"

"Let go!" she barked, jerking away from him.

Teg followed her through the crowd, dodging fat women in tight shorts and small children with snow cones. At the far end of The Green, which hugged the stretch almost to the quarter pole, the crowd thinned slightly. Beyond The Green lay trampled grass where spectators had spread blankets and arranged lawn chairs to watch the fireworks after the races.

Shannon trotted through the prone bodies like a football player doing agility drills. Teg had already begun his personal celebration of the Fourth of July—even though as a citizen of Mexico the holiday meant nothing to him—so he could not keep up with Shannon. But she would have to stop at the fence, unless she tried to climb over it, which he had seen someone on crack do one time.

He was relieved to see that she did not try to climb the fence. When he reached her, she was facing the fence with her fingers laced through the woven wire.

"*Guapa.*"

When she didn't reply, he leaned on the fence where he could see her face. "*Que' te pasa?*"

She stared through the wire. "They're going to rule my horse off."

"Today? They do it today?"

She turned slightly and looked at him. "No. They're going to give him one more race."

Teg relaxed. "Ah *Guapa*, I tell you. We fix him. He runs like the rabbit." He pulled her hands off the wire and led her back through the crowd. He bought beer from a stand on The Green and they found some empty chairs in the dark behind the drink stand.

"I know he can run," she said over and over. "He pulls like a freight train when I gallop him."

Teg comforted her with a slow caress of her shoulder. "Yes, that is a true sign," he lied.

"He's just had some bad racing luck."

Teg shifted his hand to her thigh as she finished her beer.

"I just need some more time to sort him out."

Teg nodded. "A little more time." He needed a little more time, too. As he consoled Shannon, he repeatedly glanced across the infield towards the backstretch dormitories. He was torn. He felt he was getting this girl close to where she would let him screw her, which he very much wanted to do, but he kept thinking about the molly in his room that he was planning to enjoy while he watched the fireworks. Although his stash was small, he was willing to share with Shannon. But she wouldn't go with him to get it, and if he left her the moment would be lost. He had to get her to go somewhere. The last race was over and the track lights had been doused.

"The time is coming for the flashlights," he said, waving at the sky.

"So what do you think we can do?"

"We can lie down and watch the flashlights here—"

Shannon snorted and smacked his hand away. "With my horse, you bozo."

Teg flashed her his perfect smile. "Lasix. You must ask Dr. Z for the Lasix."

Shannon knew that handicappers thought the first time a horse got the diuretic Lasix that it gave him a hop. It was legal to run on, but a veterinarian had to administer it at a certain time. Fudging on the time would enhance the effect. "You think that'll do it?"

"No, *Guapa*," Teg said, venturing a hand to her leg again, "but we give him the blue juice and then he fly!"

"How do we keep from getting caught?"

"The Lasix make him piss it away."

Shannon had little to say the next morning as she and Jimmy galloped the two colts. She tried to concentrate on Acky's stride and imagine how he would feel if he were hopped up. She knew he could run. She didn't know how to make him do it but she would figure it out one day. It was going to take some more time, but when she finally made something out of Acky, it would make people notice all the more.

The Lasix and the other stuff—What did Teg call it? Blue juice?—that was temporary. A one-time deal to buy some time. Paco said Acky had only one more race. One more chance for everything to come together: good footing, competitive drive, fitness, talent and racing luck. Somehow she had to put it all together or her career at the track was over.

Teg's plan seemed simple enough. She would use the vet he named to give Acky a shot of Lasix as close to race time as possible. And Teg would get her a syringe with the stimulant ready to go. She didn't like the idea of sticking her horse, but the worst part was having to deal with that skeez-ball. He clearly thought his help was a down payment on greater warmth from her but she shot him down without a shred of guilt. Her mother always said about boys Shannon hung out with, "You don't owe him a thing but the pleasure of your company." She laughed to herself. She knew what Teg considered to be the pleasure of a girl's company. She'd have to put up with his harassment until she got the juice, but then she'd tell him *hasta la vista, baby*.

Chapter 29

Louisa tried not to limp into the shed row. Beneath her jeans, her knee was swollen and bruised and her whole body ached as though she had been beaten with a stick. Her t-shirt covered her bruised ribs, but she couldn't hide the raw red scrape that decorated her arm from wrist to elbow. Hobo, the head groom, knew her well enough to ask what happened.

"It was stupid. I tripped on the cat and fell in the driveway," she said.

Hobo nodded but she could tell he didn't believe her. She had disguised her condition at the races the night before, but overnight her body seized up. She could hardly get out of bed. Gingerly, she made her way to her desk and looked at the training plan for the day.

While she allowed herself a smile of relief about the Rondo filly, there was still Ticket Taker. Ticket Taker had raced the night before, but he ran no better than previously. The owners, while upbeat in the paddock before the race, told Mike afterwards that the colt had until Derby week to come around. They couldn't afford to support him anymore. Louisa knew Mike would try to find a home for the colt, but you had to be careful where you let a horse go. At least now with the Thoroughbred Makeover Project, there was a secondary market for horses that couldn't run. Maybe the Thoroughbred Retirement Foundation would take him.

The high school girl who came out to walk hots was leading Ticket Taker around the shed row, but Louisa didn't have time for more than a cursory glance to see that the colt was sound. They had eight sets to get out today, including two workouts that she had to watch, and five horses needed soaking or blistering, plus the guy was coming to tattoo the Jockey Club ID number on the lip of a two-year-old colt that Mike had shipped down from the farm.

And there was Alice, of course. Gone was the anticipation of her daily truancy at the camp, laughing with Wick as she exercised the horse. There would be no Wick to laugh with today, no Wick to help her with Alice and the goat, no Wick to share in the delicious secrecy of the camp with a picnic and easy intimacy. It was Wednesday and Wick was in Norfolk with Claire. She'd have to go by herself. As much as she wanted to get away from the barn, she wasn't looking forward to swimming the horse alone again. Without Wick, the secluded camp had an uncomfortable feeling of danger. The once-joyful task of swimming Alice had devolved into just another chore.

"*Madre?*"

"Yes, Eduardo?"

"The eye of the horse, *diez y siete*, he is—" The groom smacked his head with his hand.

As she followed the groom down the shed row to stall seventeen, Louisa prayed for Alice to win his race on Friday so both of them could retire.

Later, as Louisa watched the vet sew seventeen's eyelid shut, Shannon approached her. "Is he going to be all right?"

"The cornea is scratched. Hopefully, with some magic ointment and a week in the dark, it'll heal all right." That was what she needed, too: a week in the dark.

They contemplated the vet's handiwork. The horse was one of the two Shannon galloped. "Do you still want me to come gallop the other horse?" Shannon asked.

Louisa thought for a minute. "You did a nice job with that bay colt today. I'd like you to keep riding him. Can you come early?"

Shannon shook her head. "I can't get here till after the break, maybe nine. I'm pretty busy first thing."

Louisa remembered Rodell's revelation about Shannon's job at Maria's, but she merely nodded. "What about this afternoon? I've got some work for you if you're interested."

The girl looked surprised. "Sure. What time?"

"Meet me in the parking lot by the racing office around one, all right?"

"As long as I'm done by four."

Chapter 30

Wick pulled into the parking lot at the Norfolk Living Home Health Care Center and found a spot where the Leyland cypress screening the highway cast a narrow shadow. He backed in and cut the engine. But his bouquet of snapdragons lay on the seat as he stared through the glass at the building.

He tried to remember how long he had been driving to Norfolk. Let's see: Last year's meet. And the one before that. Year in, year out. First it was Christmas, then it was racing season, then it was Christmas again. At least at Christmas he could go to Virginia Beach and see Boyd Junior and Sally and the grandkids. The rest of the time the house felt like the receiving barn at the end of the meet.

Wick picked up the snapdragons, cracked the windows and walked to the building. The doors slid smoothly open and the receptionist smiled at him.

"Good morning, Mr. Keswick."

"How are you, Nicole?"

"Fine, thank you. Mrs. Keswick is waiting for you in the sun room."

The hallway to the sun room was empty. His loafers tapped on the smooth tile floor. There were double doors at the end of the hall. He wondered where they went. Out into the sunlight? Deeper into unknown chambers of this human holding pen?

Wick stopped inside the sun room door and stared at the figure in the wheelchair with short straight hair plastered to her skull, an ill-fitting green shift, and thin, slack arms.

He was startled by an attendant speaking to him. "Mr. Keswick? Would you like to see her new room?"

"Not now." The attendant left them alone.

He kissed Claire's cheek first, as he always did. "How's my girl today?"

He put the flower arrangement on a table where she could see it, if she looked, which she didn't. Pulling up a chair, he sat close to her, holding her hand.

But today, Wick could think of nothing to say. He started to tell her about Alice's Restaurant. "He's a gutsy old horse, but he's got this big knee, so they can't gallop him every day. We had to find a pool for him down here." Wick paused, embarrassed. It was like trying to explain to the farmer who towed his car. "He's a gutsy old horse." He paused again, staring at the unresponsive creature next to him. He pictured Louisa's hard arms, her gnarled hands holding the shank when Alice stepped on the ground bees. He saw her soft gray hair flowing in wisps around her face so rich with life. He heard her wind-chime laughter and felt the warmth of her touch when she said *I need your help.*

For a long time he sat there without saying a word. Then he got up and left.

Chapter 31

"Where are we going?" Shannon asked as she climbed into Louisa's truck.

"Mike's got a horse in training nearby and I need some help exercising him," Louisa said as she turned the key.

Shannon opened the truck door. "Wait. I didn't bring my helmet."

"You won't need it," Louisa said, backing out, wincing as she turned the wheel with her scraped arm.

"What'd you do?"

"Fell down."

They drove the back roads of New Kent County with the windows rolled down and the air condition blasting. Shannon decided she liked having the wind rushing in the window and the cool air blowing from the dash. It was too noisy to talk, so Shannon waited until they turned onto the weedy track through the woods.

"Who's farm is this?" she hollered.

"I don't know," Louisa shouted back. "We're just squatting."

They eased past a weathered cottage with asphalt siding sliding off and a porch propped up with rocks. Louisa waved at the elderly black man sitting on a couch on the porch fanning himself.

When they pulled into the deserted campground and Shannon saw the abandoned lodge, a slightly creepy feeling oozed over her. Where was Louisa taking her? Then a piercing neigh overwhelmed the blasting air conditioner and she saw Alice's Restaurant. Alice's bay coat was dark with sweat from the hot humid day. He was pacing around the pen with his chin over the top bar, clearly saying, *Where have you been?*

Shannon, schooled in the nefarious ways of her Florida trainer, instantly grasped the situation. She was amazed that the respected Louisa Ferncliff would be behind such a set-up. No wonder she didn't care about Jimmy's jogging Carl's horse on the horse path.

"You're hiding him so everyone will think he's retired, then you're going to bring him back for a big score! Right?" Shannon grinned at Louisa.

Louisa, her muscles loosened up since the early morning, pulled a lunge line out of the back of the truck. "Well, I hope he's coming back for a big score. Or even a little score."

She looked at his knee. "Is he sound?"

"Maybe," Louisa said, rubbing the horse's face. She opened a plastic bag and offered him some grapefruit sections. The gelding scarfed the fruit up, fleered his upper lip, then nosed around for some more. "Not now, that's enough. You can have the rest after your swim."

Louisa told Shannon to take the goat over near the pool and tie him up while she took the bandage off Alice's leg. Then she let Alice, who marched eagerly out of the pen, browse through the desiccated weeds looking for something edible. She explained to Shannon her role in getting the horse down the ramp into the pool.

Shannon thought the whole thing looked pretty risky, but she took up her post with the racing stick as instructed. She could not imagine that a Thoroughbred racehorse would—or could—get down that steep ramp safely, even with water at the bottom. She was scarcely reassured by the rubber stall mats on the ramp.

"All right, now, don't hit him. Just wave the stick a little and threaten him."

Shannon shook the stick at the old horse, who pinned his ears but gingerly stepped down the ramp. He stopped when he was in up to his chest and thrust his face into the greenish water. Shannon stepped forward, but Alice suddenly exhaled, blasting water in all directions and shaking his head with laughter. Then he stepped forward and began swimming his therapeutic laps.

Shannon grazed the goat while Louisa walked around and around the pool.

"How many laps does he do?"

"I give him about twenty minutes."

Shannon's heart went out to the bay gelding moving methodically around the pool. Horses were so brave. Something about the way Alice held his chin above the water and drove himself around the exercise pool flooded her with emotion. She pictured Bread 'n Butter fighting her way down the stretch despite getting a bad trip. "How does he act when he loses?"

"He gets depressed. He won't even eat his grapefruit."

Awwww, she thought. Then the light bulb went on. *That* was Acky's problem! He was depressed because he was losing! All he needed was to feel the rush of success, the thrill of beating the other horses. Juicing him would spark his confidence and jump-start his career. As Shannon raced through the glorious ramifications of this insight, she realized she was learning to understand her horse. This is what trainers did. *Omigod.*

Shannon heard Louisa talking and picked up the word "retire." Louisa couldn't mean herself. Nobody retired from racing. The racetrack was full of old people who refused to retire, people like Carl Starling who hung on training two or three horses or worked as valets in the jocks' room or galloped a few horses for trainers desperate enough to hire sixty-year-old exercise riders. "You're retiring?"

Louisa laughed. "I keep trying to retire but"—she gestured at the swimming horse—"here I am."

Shannon could not imagine anyone choosing to leave the track, especially someone like Louisa, who was such an insider she practically owned the track. "How could you leave the horses?"

Louisa looked off at the woods. "Sometimes the people make it hard to stay." She increased her steps, marching around the pool, her hair coming loose and Alice struggling to keep up with the taut rope. "Mike keeps talking me into staying to deal with the Rondo filly or Alice or some other horse with an issue. They've all got issues. That's what racetrack life is about, fixing issues. I can't fix everybody's issues. I have my own to deal with."

Was she talking about people or horses? Shannon wondered. "If you left, where would you go?"

Louisa shrugged. "I have friends in Wisconsin."

"Do they have racing there?"

Louisa laughed her tinkling laugh. "I hope not. I can't be a rail bird," she said, "I've tried that. But I can be a football fan." Before Shannon could respond, Louisa said, "So, tell me about your horses."

Shannon brightened. "Oh, they're wonderful. The filly is just like Alice, full of heart. She had her first start Monday and she had a bad trip: dirt in her face, carried wide on the turn, but she dug in and fought all the way down the stretch. I was so proud of her."

"How about your colt?"

"I brought him here to run on the grass, but his training got interrupted because he's been Good Prospect's work partner. Mr. Starling's been so nice to me, I just had to help him. But they're galloping now and I'm going to run him at the Turf Festival. Jimmy's going to ride him."

"That's nice of you to give him the ride. I think Jimmy's going to be a good jockey when he gets some more experience," Louisa said.

"Yeah, he says it's real different from galloping in the morning. He was so pumped about riding that filly, he couldn't stop talking."

"Jimmy? Couldn't stop talking?" Louisa and Shannon laughed together. "I wondered what it would take to get him to open up."

"Oh, we talk a lot in the morning when we're galloping. He knows so much about horses. I've learned a lot."

Louisa smiled. "I'm glad he's got you as a friend."

Something about Shannon's earnest optimism reminded Louisa of herself at that age. Divorced, nineteen-year-old Louisa hung around the clerk of scales office at her first track, absorbing everything about horse racing that the clerk would impart. She remembered one morning when he hung up the phone and said, "You want to help me out?"

Surprised, pleased, she nodded. "Sure. What do you want me to do?"

"How about running over to the secretary's office and asking Tommy for the key to the quarter pole?"

"Back in a minute."

When she got to the secretary's office, Tommy was standing by the counter, talking to one of the stewards. She waited politely until he looked at her. "Adam sent me over to ask you for the key to the quarter pole."

Tommy and the steward smiled at her. "You know," Tommy said, "I'm not sure where it is now."

The steward spoke up. "Last I heard, it was in the film room. Walter's back there. Go ask him. He'll know."

When she found Walter, he was not as helpful as expected. "I don't know why they always send them to me," he groused. "Go ask the stall man, down in the receiving barn."

She had begun to wonder how people could be so careless with something as important as the key to the quarter pole. When she found the stall man and asked him for the key, he started chuckling and rooting around in a drawer. "Do you know what it looks like?" he asked her.

"No. The clerk just sent me to get it."

He pawed around in the drawer some more and finally found a stick of gum. "Well," he said, unwrapping the gum and folding it into his mouth. "It's about as long as from here to there and it's got a hook on the end for pulling your leg."

Louisa gaped at him for a moment. "Why, that jerk."

The stall man chuckled some more. "Don't feel bad. Everybody at the track gets that gag at first. Now you can pull it on somebody else."

"I'm going to get him back."

"Who started you?"

"Adam."

"Go back and tell him you couldn't find the key but you ordered him a saddle stretcher."

"And a sky hook to go with it," said a trainer who walked in.

It seemed like a harmless initiation gag, and Louisa looked back on Adam and the others fondly. But as she considered this reincarnation of her younger self struggling to make runners of two show horses, the pointlessness of the search jumped out at her. Her brow furrowed at the thought of Shannon's impossibly optimistic goals for her horses. She pictured the girl running from office to office, from barn to track, paddock to gap, eagerly, innocently seeking the key to success and happiness at the track. Success at the track was a gamble, a bigger bet than one you made at the mutuel windows, but you had to make your own happiness at the track. Unbidden, Wick's smile and his hand on her arm came to mind.

Louisa turned away from the memory and gazed fondly at Alice's innocent face, picturing the horse fighting to do what horses do: run. She saw him jerking away from the outrider, bolting out of the gate and matching strides with the other horses in the herd as they swept down the stretch, under the wire and out across the wide open plains.

Alice made her happy.

Alice finished swimming and went into his exit routine. But after splashing in the water at the foot of the ramp, he refused to climb out.

"Come on," coaxed Louisa. "He slipped coming out yesterday and I guess he's worried," she said without looking at Shannon.

"What happened?"

"He took a bad step, then lunged up the ramp and slipped on the concrete. It was kind of scary."

Shannon absorbed Louisa's confession without comment.

Louisa jiggled the lead rope a couple of times and whistled to the horse. Shannon leaned over and shook the racing stick at him, but Alice just threw his head around and pawed the water, setting off waves that washed over the side of the pool.

Louisa held up her hand. "Let's let him stand a few minutes. Maybe he'll get bored and come out."

Minutes ticked by under the July sun.

"Maybe he'd rather stay in the water where it's cool."

Alice stood motionless at the foot of the ramp, his body submerged, leaving his rump exposed like a sandbar in the river. His chin was touching the water as though resting on the dark glassy surface. He stared calmly ahead. Occasionally, he exhaled deeply, pushing ripples across the water to the top of the ramp.

"Has he ever done this before?"

Louisa shook her head.

"Do you want me to go get some help? I could go get Mr. Keswick."

Louisa shook her head.

"What are we going to do if we can't get him out?"

Louisa let out a deep breath.

"Does your truck have four-wheel drive? We could winch him out."

"I don't know…"

Finally Shannon said, "Let me get on him and ride him out."

"No, that's too dangerous. What if he slips and falls?"

"He's been doing this for a couple weeks, right? He knows how to do it, he's just having a crisis of confidence. Besides, what else are we going to do?"

"I can't let you do that," Louisa said.

They stared at the horse. Alice stood quietly in the water.

Finally, Louisa said, "You want me to tie the rope to his halter like reins?"

"Yeah, that'd be good." Shannon sat down and took off her paddock boots.

As she eased down the ramp beside the horse, he sniffed her curiously.

"Watch he doesn't suddenly come out and step on you."

Alice sniffed Shannon's hand then lifted his nose to her ear and nuzzled her hair. He went back to her outstretched hand, looking for something.

"He wants his grapefruit."

"Sorry, boy, not till you come out." She tried rubbing his face, but he shook her hand off and butted her. "Okay, I think he's ready to go."

Getting on the wet horse in the water wasn't as easy as Shannon thought it would be. Other than throwing his head around, though, Alice didn't move as she clambered aboard. Louisa handed her the stick, making sure Alice saw it.

"Grab mane."

Alice's thin strands of wet mane didn't give her much handle, but she clutched as much of the crest as she could, then gunned the horse forward. It was hard to kick underwater, but she flailed around, smacked Alice's rump with the stick and hollered. Louisa clucked and waved her arms.

Obediently, Alice leaned into the collar of water around his neck and pulled his twelve hundred pounds out of the grasp of the pool. As he lunged forward, Shannon felt herself slipping backwards on the horse's wet hide. Rather than hold herself with the shank tied to Alice's halter and risk throwing the horse off balance, she tried to wrap her arms around his neck. But she was too far gone. As Alice made one last jump up the ramp onto level ground, Shannon was flipped off the back.

I knew I should have brought my helmet, she thought.

Shannon's head did not hurt nearly as much as her forearm, which had hit the edge of the ramp wall and already had a spectacular bruise. She lay back in Louisa's recliner, her arm resting in a nest of ice, and compared the pounding in her arm with the pounding in her head. The arm was definitely worse.

"How long was I out?"

"Long enough to make me think you were dead."

Shannon smiled weakly.

"How do you feel?"

"Like I've been run over by a horse."

"Are you nauseated?"

Shannon tried to shake her head. "No."

"I wish you'd let me take you to the emergency room," Louisa said.

"I'll be all right."

Louisa held out a glass. "Here. Here's a Coke. And take these ibuprofen."

"Got any bute?"

"Bute will eat a hole in your stomach. Besides, it's hard to chop up a horse pill and judge the dosage."

Louisa's travel trailer was so cozy and nicely appointed that it didn't seem like an RV at all. Comfortably worn leather sofa, walnut side table, tv sitting on a mahogany chest of drawers. Photographs of horses everywhere except the mahogany chest of drawers. There, flanking the television, was an autographed picture of a football player in green and yellow, grinning at the camera. Number four.

"Is that your friend you were talking about?"

Louisa smiled fondly. "He's retired now."

Shannon looked around the RV and back to the incongruous photograph of a professional football player. "What time is it?" she suddenly asked.

"Quarter past four."

Shannon struggled forward. "Man, I gotta go. I'm late."

"Where? Can I help you?"

"Where are my paddock boots? Are they still out at the camp?"

Louisa looked stricken. "Oh, I'm so sorry. By the time I got you in the car and caught Alice, I'd forgotten about your shoes."

Louisa protested, but Shannon insisted on going to work at Maria's. She compromised by letting Louisa drive her to the Sta*light Motel to change and then to the restaurant.

"I'll go get your boots, but you call me if you get to feeling bad," Louisa said as she dropped her off.

"How'd you get that bruise?" Jimmy asked Shannon as they walked the two horses back from the track the next morning.

Shannon's arm was swollen and marbled blue and purple from elbow to wrist. It was all she could do to make a fist around the right rein. "Oh, this horse I was riding for somebody else slammed me."

"You gotta watch whose horses you get on. Some of them bring babies to the track that ain't all broke."

Shannon nodded.

"Whose horse was it slammed you?"

Louisa had sworn her to secrecy. "Uh, actually, it wasn't here. It was somebody's horse they're going to run off the farm." Shannon started fiddling with the stirrup leather under her left leg.

"You sure that was a horse and not that piece of trash in Barn Twelve?" Jimmy said, and Shannon knew he meant Teg.

"Eew, no." Shannon could feel Jimmy's disgust in the airwaves and wondered what he knew. About Teg. About her. About the juice. What would he think if he knew? Would he understand it was just this once, just to help Acky find his confidence? Would he understand that she had to be friends with Teg to get the juice? *The Lasix make him piss it away.* She thought about drinking beer with Teg on the Fourth of July, his hand on her leg as she despaired over the steward's warning that Acky had only one chance left. How'd she get mixed up with that sleazebag? It was his voice, she decided. *Tell me your name, pretty lady.* All those Latino guys had such mesmerizing voices. *We give him the blue juice and then he fly!*

Jimmy was still giving her a skeptical look, so she opened her hands and said, "It was a horse, I swear." Just then her cell phone played a distinctive ring tone. For once, she was grateful to hear from her mother. "Hi, Mom. Can I call you back? I'm on a horse right now." Shannon rolled her eyes at Jimmy as Mrs. Hill talked anyway, dumping her latest financial crisis on Shannon. Her mother's profligacy combined with her financial ignorance was hard to believe sometimes. She had a brief, disloyal thought sharing her father's frustration with Mrs. Hill. "You'll have to cash in one of those CDs," she told her mother. Shannon weighed the impact of sending more of her own meager funds to her mother against the risk of a conversation with her father. "No, I'm not going to call Dad for you…How much are you overdrawn?…Jeez-almighty! Mom! What did you do? Buy the Hope Diamond?"

Shannon felt like she did flipping off the back of Alice's Restaurant, just before she slammed into the concrete. She knew it was going to hurt and she couldn't do anything about it. Here she was a thousand miles away with no money and no way to help her mom. What if something bad happened to her? What if she got evicted? As Shannon listened to her mother prattle on, she went from helplessness to anger. Damn that bimbo who stole her father! It was all *her* fault. If she hadn't lured her father away…

Shannon and Jimmy rode into the shed row of Barn Four and slid off their mounts. As the tinny voice of her mother crackled in her hand, Shannon wanted to throw the phone against the side of the barn, but habit stopped her from spooking the horses. Her self-control wicked the boiling anger out of her skin, leaving her clammy with fear. Shannon remained still, holding the phone and staring down the long dark tunnel of the shed row. Finally she said, "I'm taking care of my skin, Mom, I promise."

Chapter 32

As Louisa turned the gooseneck trailer into the camp driveway, Wick thought to himself that it wasn't strictly necessary for her to keep the horse's whereabouts such a secret. Mike's help thought the horse was back at the farm and nobody else on the backstretch gave a damn. It was probably a good thing to keep it a secret in the community, though.

"If you're trying to keep this quiet, I don't know why you had that gal from Florida out here."

"It goes faster if I have help."

"*Good* help. Not somebody who's going to get herself hurt." Wick felt guilty about Louisa's scrape from Tuesday. Now he had Shannon Hill on his conscience.

"It wasn't her fault. She got the horse out, didn't she?"

"I wish you'd waited for me."

"Wick, you've got a racetrack to run. I can't impose on you every day."

"They can get along without me for an hour. I just can't believe you took her. No telling who she might tell. All those kids who come in Maria's at night," Wick said.

"She's not going to tell anybody. Nobody would believe it anyway."

Wick snorted. "No telling what some young punks might decide to do if they knew there was a racehorse and a goat out here in the woods."

Louisa laughed her wonderful laugh. Something about the way she laughed always made Wick think she should be wearing dangly earrings. As she parked, she turned to look over her shoulder at the horse trailer and a wisp of hair came loose. Wick lifted his hand from the back of the seat, intending to brush it back, then stopped himself.

"Do you think there's such a thing as an *old* punk?" Louisa asked, giving him the full benefit of her warm smile.

Momentarily unsettled, Wick finally said, "That boy who gallops for Max Fox. He's an old punk, with that dyed hair and those tattoos."

"Everybody has tattoos these days," she said.

"Not where he's got them. And he had them before the rest of them were born." Wick wondered how they got on this subject.

Alice's Restaurant was trotting back and forth in the round pen, whinnying. He was always glad to see them, but the appearance of the trailer stirred him up. Patches of dark sweat marked his neck and flanks. His high-pitched whinny startled the goat, who jumped around on his chain.

"Great companion, there. He's supposed to keep the horse calm."

"They'll be okay as soon as I stop." Louisa cut the engine and Alice stood still. He maintained his shrill calls, however, his sides reverberating with each note.

Wick shook his head. "Listen to that girlish whinny. Puts me in mind of Jesse Hasselback. Were you at Croaker's when he was there?"

"I think he came after me," Louisa said as she took some shipping boots out of the trailer.

Wick followed her to the pen. "He's the strongest man I ever saw. He's not that big, maybe five-seven or -eight, but he has a chest like a barrel. I saw him one time back up under the front end of a horse and lift him off the ground. Any time we had one that wouldn't load, Jesse would just shove it up the ramp. Most of the time, he was real easy-going. Never lost his temper with a horse. But he had this soft, high voice like a girl, and when he got mad, his voice went up an octave. Sounded real funny, this little girl's voice coming out of that powerful man."

"That's my Alice," Louisa said, running a chain shank through the horse's halter and rubbing his face. Wick held the sweaty gelding while Louisa Velcroed stained blue shipping boots around his legs. "All right, fella, vacation's over. Time to go back to real life."

Wick thought about that: the racetrack as real life. His only life these days. He had no life at home. Just those weekly drives to Norfolk.

Louisa stood up and stroked the muscular neck and gazed lovingly at Alice's face. "Yes," she said to the horse, combing his wispy mane over to the right side with her fingers, "you can go home. A win tomorrow is a bus ticket to the farm. No more stalls, no more needles, no more bandages. Just a big field to graze in all day long."

"Good luck."

"It'll work this time," Louisa said. She walked the horse up the trailer ramp and snapped the crossties to his halter. Wick dragged the goat in beside him. The exertion made him sweat in the July heat.

Wick was skeptical. He had seen these horses who couldn't adjust to another life. It wasn't just the clank of the starting gate flipping open and the long smooth straightaway they craved. They fed off the bustle of the backside like some people throve on the noise and congestion of a big city. They loved the morning commute of training hours and the electricity in the air when they walked to the paddock in the afternoon. He felt the same way. He was going nuts knocking around that empty house. After he mowed the lawn, what could he do? Take another long drive to Norfolk? Better to come early and work late at the track. And maybe steal off to the woods with Louisa for an hour or so. "This is home for Alice. Just like us," he said as they lifted the ramp and latched the back of the trailer.

Louisa stopped and gave him a long look. "What do you mean, 'us'?"

Embarrassed, Wick swatted a swarm of no-seeums, avoiding her eye. The way Louisa said "us" sounded intimate, even naked and snuggly. A surge of guilt made his face warm and he responded in a testy voice. "All of us. You. Me. Mike." He warmed to the topic. "Eighty-year-old Carl Starling. That coke-head exercise rider Teg. Every hot-walking kid from New Kent High School. This is where we *live*. Anywhere else is just a place to take a shower." Suddenly the black hole of the past two years engulfed him and he burst out, "You don't live in that RV, or your sister's house in Florida, any more than I live at 2215 Grove Avenue. There's no life outside the track. There's no one waiting at the door, no one to cook your dinner or ask you how it went. Any other place you go is dead. This is the only place where you can breathe without an oxygen mask. This is the only place where people understand, where people care. This is home." He paused for breath, head down, waiting for her customary words of comfort.

Throughout his speech, Louisa had looped and unlooped the shank in her hands. "Maybe it's home for you," she said, "but not for me. Not anymore. Horse racing is a disease, but Alice and I are getting over it, aren't we, boy?" She glanced through the slats of the stock trailer. "We're leaving."

Wick looked at her in alarm. "For the farm?"

"Wisconsin."

It sounded like a challenge. Wick snorted. "Louisa—"

"Don't say Louisa in that tone of voice." The dangly earrings were gone.

"Louisa, I don't know what the hell tone of voice this is, but I'm going to use it. If you want to leave the track, leave. Take the horse and go to the farm. Don't let Mike keep talking you into coming back."

Louisa walked around the trailer, the shank swinging in her hand. "It's not Mike." Now she was the one avoiding his eye. "There's always a horse who needs me."

Just a horse? Wick thought, as sweat trickled down his side. Sweat bees buzzed insistently around his face but all he heard was the hollow mausoleum of his house. "There's always going to be somebody who needs you, *Madre*."

"Not in Wisconsin."

Wick threw up his hands. "That's crazy. You think living near a damn football team is going to make you happy? Are they going to come over and drink beer at your house on Friday night? Are they going to help you swim a racehorse in a goddamned pool out in the woods? Are they going to buy you a goat, for Christ's sake?"

"No." Louisa threw the chain shank into the back of the pickup truck. The chain ricocheted off the toolbox, clattering like broken machinery and causing Alice to spook and kick the trailer. The goat bleated in fear. Louisa soothed the animals, her back to Wick as she said softly, "I'm done with goats."

"Louisa, you know what I mean," he pleaded. "You're talking about a bunch of strangers. They won't care about you like…"

Louisa turned slowly and looked directly at Wick. "…like…?"

Wick floundered. Louisa's hair had come loose in two or three long wisps and he desperately wanted to sweep it back up and sweep her up and hold her and crush her to his chest. He imagined them naked, entwined. He wanted to run his hands over every soft curve and hard muscle of her body.

Louisa waited. "Like who, Wick? Who cares? Mike wouldn't care if I broke my leg, as long as I could sit on a bale of hay and run the barn."

He stuttered, stepping back from his fantasy. "Like… everybody at the racetrack."

"Screw the racetrack."

As they drove back to the track in silence broken only by the occasional sound of Alice's stomping in the trailer, Wick struggled to understand what had happened. Did Louisa want to leave or not? Was she serious about Wisconsin? She couldn't leave, not yet. He needed the stolen afternoons in the woods with her and the horse. He thought she did, too. Didn't she thrive on fixing horses, supporting the people around her, even, he conceded, comforting him?

Her angry shot, *Screw the racetrack*, cut him. It felt like a personal slap. *Screw you*. He wanted her to, he admitted, but not like that. Like what? he asked himself, suddenly uncomfortable as a figure in a wheelchair floated into view. He pushed aside the fantasy of Louisa's body next to his with a guilty brush and exhaled sharply. He hoped Alice would win his damn race the next day. Then Louisa could take the horse to Mike's farm…or a condo in Wisconsin, whatever the hell she wanted to do.

Louisa parked the rig at the end of Barn Six and got out quickly, flinching when she landed on her sore leg. Grooms appeared to unload Alice's Restaurant and the goat, and Louisa busied herself giving them unnecessary directions. Wick watched for a moment then said, "Good luck tomorrow," and walked off without waiting for a reply.

Alice's stall was ready and his bandage had already been changed. There was nothing for Louisa to do, but she fussed around the barn until she couldn't stand the ache in her leg anymore. Back at the RV, she iced her knee and tried to put the argument with Wick out of her mind, but his gruff voice caressed her.

There's always going to be somebody who needs you.

She could almost feel his hands on her body. And she had been ready to slide hers under his shirt. What would he have done? she wondered. Would he have kissed her first? Or rubbed her back, slipping a hand under her t-shirt to loosen her bra? Men loved her boobs and she smiled imagining Wick's pleasure. And hers. But he had pulled away, mumbling something about how "everybody at the track" cared about her.

What did she expect him to say? How could she think he would say *he* was the one who cared for her, *he* was the one who needed her? Wick was a busy man. He had a racetrack to run. He had to go see his wife. He had a wife. She was barely conscious but she was his wife. They were married. He was a married man. She had tried that once before, with J. G. Lippincott. See how that worked out.

But that was different. She had let herself fall in love with J. G. The two of them were planning a future together, whereas she and Wick were nothing but old friends. If Wick was lonely and they had a fling, so what? She wasn't expecting a long term deal. She didn't need that.

What if needing each other was how you made it last?

She needed Wick to find her a pool, to hold the goat while she swam Alice. Was that the kind of need to build a relationship on?

Louisa's cat jumped onto the sofa and dug a nest in the cushions next to her legs. Louisa petted her absently.

She was being silly, dangerously silly. She didn't need a man in her life. She didn't need Wick. Even if he wanted her—and her antennae weren't so rusty that she couldn't tell—it was a bad decision. Hadn't she made enough of those? In the morning, she'd buy a ticket to Green Bay and go look for a condo. As soon as the Derby was over, she'd tell Mike she was leaving.

Chapter 33

Louisa ran her hand down Alice's leg feeling for heat.

"Is it okay to tack him up?" Mike asked, half in jest.

Louisa nodded. The horse's leg held her eyes but her ears rang with the sound of the chain shank ricocheting around the bed of the pickup and Alice's hooves scrambling inside the trailer. *Screw the racetrack.*

They were in the saddling stall next to seven other horses and their trainers, preparing for the fifth race. After Mike and the valet cinched Jesus' racing saddle snugly in place, the groom led Alice's Restaurant around the paddock. Louisa analyzed the gelding's walk but to her disappointment his stride passed her inspection. She was torn. Part of her wanted the horse sound enough to run and win; part of her wanted him to be the tiniest bit off so Mike would scratch him and send him home and she would be done with all this madness. The madness of racing and Alice and bad knees and thinking about Wick. Tension cut two rows in her brow as she focused on the horse's legs.

Just when she thought she detected a hitch in Alice's walk, Louisa heard Wick's voice behind her. "You'd think that old horse has been swimming, as good as he looks."

She turned quickly and found the track president, relaxed, a program in his hand, running a professional eye over the horses. She gasped. "Oh Wick. You came." Disarmed by his smile, she ventured half the truth. "I was afraid you'd miss him, after all you've done."

"Not if he's shipping out to a condo in Wisconsin tomorrow. Might be the last time I see him." He smiled and held her eye.

Wick's tone was light but she felt the forgiveness. It was sort of like the way Jimmy communicated about the horses he rode: the words carried much more meaning than it seemed on the surface. She touched his sleeve. "I'm sorry I was such a bitch."

He glanced around the paddock. "I don't know what you're talking about. Have you seen that get-up my handicapper's wearing these days? Are those red and green curlicues supposed to mean something?"

"I'm sure it looks good on TV," Louisa said, relaxing with a rush of tenderness she had felt so often in Wick's presence. Leading him towards the grandstand, she said, "Come on, I need you to prop me up while I watch this race." Vaguely, a little-used sector of her id registered what she had said: *I need you.*

Shannon decided to watch the race from the rail. She liked to be close to the action, to see a dirt-covered closer bearing down on the frontrunners at forty miles an hour, to hear the crowd roaring behind her, the pop of the sticks on sweaty flanks and the muffled hooves in the velvety Colonial loam. Often, she watched with the grooms who led the horses to the paddock as they cheered their charges in accented voices and waved the halters slung over their arms.

But for this race she found a spot on the rail a little further from the finish line, a little removed from the people who knew her. She didn't want anyone to speak to her and break her concentration. As she took up her post, she pulled the humid Virginia night around her like a sort of invisibility cloak. She kept one hand in her jeans pocket, guarding the little sheaf of tickets.

When Alice's Restaurant jigged past her in the post parade, she could see the old war horse jerking to get away from the outrider leading him. She smiled. The horse looked sound, big knee and all. It reminded her of Florida and the rumors her trainer floated about his horse's possible unsoundness. God, she'd been lucky to find another sure thing like that when she needed it.

While Shannon was worried about her mother's situation, she felt panicky about her own. Neither one of her horses had earned a dime since they arrived. Instead, they had chewed up her stake from Florida as casually as a flake of hay. Now she was in a hole. That morning, Bread 'n Butter hobbled out of the stall on three legs, and she feared half her potentially income-producing stock was permanently disabled. Fortunately it was only an abscess in her hoof, painful but not permanent. A few days of soaking the filly's foot in a bucket of hot Epsom salts would clear it up, but the veterinarian left with her coming week's rent. And she still had to come up with the money to pay Teg for Acky's juice.

The horses pranced to the other side of the track where the starting gate awaited them. Shannon watched the horses load on the giant infield screen. Please don't let him stumble out of the gate, she prayed. Alice was in the first stall and it looked to Shannon as though the horse broke through the gate before the bell. But he was out and running and the race was on.

With a fast break and a ground-saving trip along the rail, Alice was in good shape. Shannon watched the gelding gallop down the backstretch with Jesus sitting perfectly still on his back. As they came out of the turn into the long Colonial stretch, the pace picked up and the volume of cheering grew. The bunched horses ran towards her. Alice's heavy legs churned, hurling his chunky brown body towards the finish line. Two horses ranged up alongside him, but Alice had his ears pinned and a fierce look that dared the two to come by him. Just a few dozen yards to go, Alice grinding out the victory.

Then, to Shannon's horror, one of the challengers stuck his head in front. The horses flashed past her and under the finish line. A blanket would have covered all three. Immediately, the word "photo" lit up on the tote board in the infield.

Shannon's mouth, dry from shouting, was now flooded with the sick taste of bile. She watched the replay of the finish on the big screen, praying for Alice to do in the replay what he had not done in the race. It was clear the outside horse had caught Alice at the wire. Alice was beaten. Shannon was stunned. She felt the paper chits in her pocket turning to mush in her sweaty palm. All those straight win tickets were so much trash. Only the ticket betting Alice to finish first or second was any good.

As the finish replayed over and over, Shannon could feel her stomach convulsed by the image. She tried to swallow to get the nasty taste out of her mouth. The stewards seemed to be taking hours to sort out the win photo. At last the cruel numbers were stacked on the tote board.

Alice was third.

Shannon pulled the damp, wrinkled tickets out of her pocket and stared at each one, comparing the numbers to those on the tote board, shuffling through the stack like a deck of cards. Three times she read them through. Three times they mocked her. All her money was in these tickets and they were worthless. They were dry leaves, a handful of gravel, shards of glass, cutting her to the quick.

She was beyond broke. This wasn't about not being able to send money to her mother. This was about feeding her horses. Paying her rent. How would she live until Maria paid her next Friday? And how would she live after that?

Up in the box seats above Shannon, Wick put his arm around an unhappy Louisa and patted her shoulder.

Mike threw up his hands. "I don't know why it's such a big deal. The horse can stay here. Gallop him every other day for a week or two and run him back. What's that? Seven, eight more times to the track? He can handle that."

Louisa looked pained.

Mike relented. "Or you can keep swimming him, if you want to fool with it. It's up to you."

She looked up at Wick, who shrugged. "You've already got the set-up. Might as well take him back. I'll help." He squeezed her shoulder. "Besides, I ain't got my money's worth out of that goat, yet."

Louisa leaned into him with a relieved smile. "Thank you, Wick." He gave her a reassuring hug.

Jack and Mike exchanged glances.

Chapter 34

Shannon watched the last race of the night from the rail. It had been three days since Alice's stunning loss, and Shannon found herself standing in the same spot, reliving the moment with each successive race. She had galloped her horses, worked at Maria's and packed all her stuff from the Sta*light Motel, but she remembered nothing except standing at the rail, watching horses blow by her to the finish line.

The horses came back and Darryl, a friend from Florida, went out to pick up Max Fox's horse who had run second. She slipped out onto the track to walk back to the barns with him.

"He ran good," said Shannon.

"Yeah, that was a tough break at the start."

"What did the jock say? Did he get bumped or did he stumble?"

"The jock said he threw his head just when the gate opened and he got left a step, then he tried to catch up too fast and he stumbled. But he ran a good race."

"I guess Fox was mad."

"Nah. Well, he wanted to win, but he was moving the horse up a class. He showed he could run with them. Isn't that right, boy?" Darryl said, stroking the sweaty neck. "Damn I hate having the last race of the night and you got to sit around the test barn for an hour."

"I'll go with you."

When they got to the post race detention barn, a horse from the previous race was being walked. Darryl bathed Fox's horse and walked him while Shannon sat in the doorway and talked with the security guard. The groom with the other horse called to the catcher, "Hey boss, I think this sumbitch is ready." They took the horse into a box stall and Shannon could hear the catcher whistling. In a moment he emerged and took the cup full of urine to the office to seal and send to the lab for testing. Meanwhile Darryl walked Fox's horse.

"This old boy ought to know the drill. Maybe he won't keep us here all night."

When Darryl saw the horse's back muscles relax, he nodded to the catcher and they retired to the modesty of the stall. The catcher whistled and in a moment emerged from the stall triumphant.

She and Darryl walked the horse to the barn.

"Darryl, did you ever have a horse that didn't test clean?"

"Everyone has an overage once in awhile. If a horse is coming off treatment, sometimes the medication hasn't cleared his system. Bute or Lasix, usually."

"I mean something stronger."

"Not no horse of Fox's. He don't do that."

"Who does?"

Darryl snorted. "Trainers who juice? Barn Twelve. Nicky Renfro's the worst. Nicky the Narc."

"Why doesn't he get caught?"

"They say Lasix will mask it. They load the horse with Lasix and take a chance on the overage." Darryl shrugged. "How the hell do I know?"

He topped off the horse's water bucket and put the hose away. "Come on, I'll give you a ride to your car."

At the upper barns, Shannon got out and leaned in the window to talk. They could hear salsa music and see a fire glowing on one of the grills by the upper dorms.

"You think that's those chickens they keep in the dormitories?"

"Maybe Canada goose," Shannon said.

"Yeah, they could trap some of them geese from the infield pond. I wouldn't put it past them."

"A little Christmas in July goose."

"See you in the morning," Darryl said and Shannon let go of the car.

After Darryl drove off, Shannon walked to her stalls. She checked the water buckets for her two, even though she knew they would both be full. She rubbed the filly's face and lingered in the colt's stall. He had always been a sweet and affectionate horse, but ever since he had been gelded, he seemed to thrive on her attention. It was mutual. She put her arms around his neck, laid her head against his mane and hung there for a long time. The straw knee-deep in his stall looked so inviting she was tempted to bed down there herself. She remembered all the childhood horse stories about grooms who were so attached to their horses they slept in the stall with them. The sensible part of her knew she might get kicked in the head, but the lonesome part yearned to curl up in the corner. The day had been muggy and hot but in the darkness of the stall the humidity seemed like a cozy comforter.

She was too tired to move her gear out of the back seat of the car. She had packed a lot of things in grocery boxes in the trunk, but the back seat was full, too. She wondered how she had accumulated so much stuff in a month. She'd have to take the grocery boxes out of the trunk and put them in the tack room, then move the stuff in the back seat to the trunk. Tomorrow she would get some more boxes. And she'd have to get a pillow. Tonight she'd use the trash bag full of clothes. At least she didn't need a blanket in the Virginia heat. She clung to that thought. One less thing to spend money on. It was all too overwhelming right now. She'd get up in a little bit and deal with it, but right now she just wanted to sit in Acky's stall and be still.

PART V

Chapter 35

Wick went to the racing secretary's office to see which trainers had shipped in for the Turf Festival. It was one of dozens of conversations he had daily with Jack Delaney about track hospitality for the connections of the Derby horses. As they were talking, Luke, the stall man, stuck his head in the door and said, "The French horse is here with a couple of guys and I can't understand a word they say."

Another man appeared and said, "They got a whole string of horses."

Wick said, "I thought he was leaving the others in New York. Isn't he going to Saratoga after here?"

Jack shrugged. "I guess he decided to bring them all down here when he got out of quarantine. Luke, let me see your stall chart. We can't put them all in the stakes barn, but we can't split them up. Just tell them to hang on a minute."

"I can't tell them nothing. I don't parlee-voo."

"How are we going to deal with them for two weeks if they don't speak any English?" Wick said.

"We're in luck. We have a gal who's fluent in French," said Jack. "Luke, tell Vicki to come here a minute."

Wick said, "That's great. Can you assign her to look out for them and relieve her of her other responsibilities?"

"You bet."

Carl Starling invited Shannon to come to the paddock with him for the New Kent stakes and she tried to dress up for the occasion. She noticed as she dressed in the bathhouse that her clothes had that wadded-up-in-a-box look. That was the least of her worries.

After scrouging for food all week in the wake of Alice's devastating defeat, Shannon had finally gotten her Friday paycheck from Maria. It wasn't enough for a room, but she could buy some gas and feed her horses. She would have to make a show of bringing in feed bags; she was afraid Ashley and one of the grooms had seen her taking grain out of Carl's bin one night. They didn't say anything and she went yadda yadda yadda, but it was awkward.

Lawrence and Hank came into the paddock to do their race analysis. Shannon was suddenly glad to be wearing a skirt, however wrinkled. Since Lawrence didn't ride or muck stalls or walk hots, he always looked nice, whereas she never wore anything but jeans, a t-shirt and a bandana. She'd seen a lot of Lawrence for a while, getting lessons on reading the condition book and talking about Good Prospect, and she had long harbored the hope that he would leave Vicki to be with her. She stared at him, willing him to look around and see her in street clothes, but he and Hank were engrossed in conversation.

Carl was talking to her, so she smiled and nodded. "Yes sir, he looks great. He really looks ready to run."

Mr. Keswick came over and shook Carl's hand. "Good luck, Carl."

With him was one of the stewards. Shannon spoke politely to both men.

"Oh, yeah, Shannon Hill," said the steward. "I didn't recognize you for a minute. Got some good news for you: You passed."

Omigod, Shannon thought. *At last.*

She'd passed the test for her trainer's license! The old men at the racetrack had examined her and found her worthy of the ultimate badge of racing professionalism, a trainer's license. She waited to feel the mantle of skill descend on her shoulders. She waited for dissolution of the gut-wrenching fear she slept with in the back of her car and woke up with every morning. Instead she felt only a mild sense of relief, a slight relaxation of the muscle drawing her eyebrows together. She took a long deep breath and slowly exhaled, considering the ramifications of *You passed*. One of her emotions, she was shocked to discover, was surprise. Although she was remarkably determined, her dislike of schoolwork and study and the attendant failures in that area had made her doubt she would ever pass the test. But after weeks of flipping through the condition book and asking every trainer she knew a million questions, she had learned enough about this arcane business to join the ranks of licensed trainers.

She grinned. At last, her hard work was starting to pay off in a tangible way. With a license in her own name, she could open a professional stable, attract clients and build a successful business to show her father and all those who had doubted her. The license was her ticket to becoming an insider at the track. Her heart swelled with pride and the growing conviction that her dark days were behind her.

When Mr. Keswick and the steward moved on, she turned excitedly to Carl. "Mr. Starling, did you hear what he said? I passed the trainers' test!"

He bowed. "Congratulations."

"Oh, thank you. I couldn't have done it without your help."

"I'm happy for you."

She looked around, eager to tell Lawrence of her triumph and thank him for his help but he and Hank were on-camera. She edged closer to hear what he had to say about Good Prospect. He was talking about the colt in that intense way he had. She could tell it annoyed Hank. Oh well, *she* understood that intensity. She had been there with Carl, with Lawrence, when they were worrying over the colt. Hank didn't realize what a milestone it was just getting the horse to the race. No matter how he ran it would be a big deal just because he went into the gate. She and Lawrence could share the triumph. She smiled and waited just outside camera range to go watch the race with him.

But as soon as the camera switched off, Lawrence put his mike down and ran through the crowded paddock. He was gone before she could speak to him. She followed far enough to see him go up the stairs to Jack Delaney's box and start talking to that girl Vicki. She stood a moment and watched them as the crowd jostled her.

"Shannon! Over here!" It was Sarah Anne, one of Carl Starling's groomettes.

Shannon joined her and they elbowed their way to the rail for the race. "Guess what? I got my trainer's license."

Sarah Anne shrieked and threw her arms around Shannon's neck. "Congratulations! That is great news!"

Sarah Anne's unqualified excitement cheered her. She rolled her eyes. "I wasn't sure it would ever happen."

"Oh I knew you could do it," Sarah Anne gushed. "You are so smart and so good with your horses."

Shannon sucked up the praise from a third-rate groom and tried to believe it was true. "Thanks."

After Alice's Restaurant's loss the week before, Wick had assiduously cleared his schedule for an hour or two each day to go to the camp with Louisa. The stolen afternoons in the woods were precious, a lifeline to sanity that he had nearly lost. There was no talk of retirement or where their "real" lives were lived, just easy conversation about horses they had known and laughter over the foibles of racing's human participants.

Comfortable with his own conventionality, Wick had always been amused by the non-conformists who populated the track. But as he and Louisa talked about the hot-walker with a Ph. D. in religion, the exercise rider who rode only fillies, the trainer whose car was spotless while his shed row was filthy, he began to sense undefined opportunities outside the traditional rules that had always governed his actions. A pathway through the woods seemed to be opening up. Observing all around him racetrackers' hope and optimism— optimism that often bordered on delusional—made Wick feel more hopeful about his own life.

Standing in the paddock before the New Kent Stakes, Wick looked at Carl Starling and Shannon Hill and thought they both epitomized the delusion of racing hope. And yet, in Carl's case, hope and optimism had been rewarded, improbably, with a colt with freakish speed who had overcome adversity to reach stakes-level competition. The colt—Good Prospect—walked boldly around the paddock, sucking in the scene through flared nostrils and bleeding a dark patch of sweat in the hollow of his neck. Jogging a few steps, he curled around the groom leading him.

Admiring the well-muscled animal, Wick found himself believing the horse could win, and he wondered if that was due to Lawrence's handicapping analysis or if he had gone soft. Yeah, the old trainer, the green jockey and the obscurely-bred horse deserved to win, but, amazingly, they somehow seemed a reasonable choice to win. It was the sort of racetrack fairy tale that came true often enough to inspire horsemen of all stripes and abilities to get up at five o'clock every morning and fool with horses. Most times a trainer would toil for years in obscurity, taking pleasure and encouragement from small accomplishments by ordinary horses. But sometimes a trainer would catch lightning in a bottle: a Good Prospect would come out of a four-horse barn run by an eighty-year-old trainer who had never won but a few dozen races in his life. It was enough to make every trainer believe, *If his horse, why not mine?*

As the colts queued up and paraded onto the track, Wick and Louisa gravitated towards each other. Mike had two entries in the race, but Louisa had come to cheer Carl's colt, she confided as they made their way towards the stairs to Wick's box.

"And your jock?" he teased.

"And Jimmy, of course." As they watched the horses warm up on the track, she said, "I'll bet he's even more nervous than when he rode his first race."

"Yeah, he's got a chance to win this one." Wick excused himself to go to the windows and place an uncharacteristically sentimental bet.

They watched the horses load into gate uneventfully and burst out the front like a brilliantly colored flock of birds. As in his first race, on the Rondo filly, Jimmy got squeezed on both sides coming out of the gate. This time he gunned his horse forward and established his position among the leaders. The field sorted itself out and slid into the first turn on the wide green turf course. Wick and Louisa had a perfect view of the colt's beautiful way of going as he raced alongside two horses going around the first turn. The horse was running strongly, giving off confident vibes.

With only three or four races under his silks, Jimmy was still learning how to position his horse, but Carl had told him to keep it simple: lay off the leaders a few lengths and wait until they got fully into the stretch before asking the horse for his top gear. The Colonial

185

Downs stretch was long and often fooled riders who moved too soon.

As the horses ran down the backstretch, Wick and Louisa switched their attention to the wide screen above the tote board. They couldn't see Good Prospect for the other horses on the rail, but they could see Jimmy's bright yellow cap lying third. When they hit the turn, Good Prospect was rolling past the other two. "Too soon," Louisa murmured. She pressed her glasses against her face so hard her eyeballs hurt.

Suddenly it seemed as if the colt had rocket boosters. Like the flash of an orange meteor, Good Prospect zipped around the turn and burned up the stretch, leaving the rest of the field in his flaming wake. The crowd screamed approval at the monster move. Louisa dropped her glasses to her chest and watched the horse finish, the outcome settled at the quarter pole. Jimmy was hand riding, holding his stick as an afterthought. They watched the horse skimming over the grass like a prairie wind, happily cheering the colt's brilliant display of speed.

"And it's all Good Prospect at the wire!" called Hank from the announcer's booth.

Louisa threw up her hands and shrieked. Jumping up and down, she turned to hug Wick, her binoculars making an awkward lump between them.

Her wind-chime laughter and wild cheers followed him to the winner's circle for the trophy presentation. Afterwards, he found her waiting for him on the apron.

"That ought to make the crowd happy: the Cinderella horse, the old trainer and the apprentice jockey. What a story."

"Oh Wick, wasn't that wonderful? I don't know when I've had such a happy day at the races."

He permitted himself a satisfied grin. He knew the excitement of watching a beautifully-trained athlete demolish the competition would last for days, bringing him to the track every morning with a broad smile and a hail-fellow attitude. It wasn't his horse but it didn't matter. A horse like that, a performance like that belonged to all who saw it. *My team won* was a glorious feeling.

As he and Louise walked off, he said loud enough for the

crowd to hear, not that he cared, "What time are we going swimming tomorrow, *Madre*?"

"Can you go during the races? We have horses in the first three races, but then I'm okay until the tenth."

"That's a tight squeeze. How are we going to have a picnic when you have to watch the clock?"

"This isn't about having a picnic. It's about exercising a racehorse."

"The hell it is," he said, smiling down at her and sliding his arm around her shoulder.

"Mr. Keswick, may I remind you that you have official duties?"

"I've already handed out the trophy."

"I'm talking about your employment as official goat hotwalker."

"For which I expect to get paid in-kind."

Louisa raised a threatening finger. "Zip your pants up. You are way out of line."

Wick squeezed her shoulder and had a good laugh.

Chapter 36

Getting a leg up on Good Prospect each morning was the height of Jimmy's day. The colt moved like no other horse he'd ever been on.

Now the thrill of riding the horse had been taken to a whole new level. Riding him in a race, ripping around the turn and passing the other horses like they'd been swept off the track by some unseen hand had Jimmy on an adrenalin surge that lasted long past the finish line. He hardly knew what he was doing, galloping out and then cantering back to the winner's circle. Parson, Carl's head groom, grabbed the colt's bridle and posed him for the win picture. Jimmy wanted to keep riding the horse around, but Parson smacked his boot and told him to get off and weigh in. After he carried his saddle to the scales, someone whisked it away and he found himself surrounded by friends.

Jimmy thanked Carl over and over for the chance to ride the horse, even as Carl thanked him for sticking with the horse. Louisa congratulated him and Shannon hugged him. Lawrence was there, and lots of people he didn't know shook hands with him or patted his shoulder or pulled the brim of his cap down. A swell of well-wishers accompanied him back to the jocks' room. As he neared the building, the crowd around him suddenly jumped away leaving him exposed. Out of the door rushed the other jockeys and the valets carrying cups and buckets of water and soda. Before Jimmy could grasp the situation, they had dumped liquid cheer all over him. Those who followed him from the winner's circle joined in, too, tossing their drinks on him. One of the jockeys had a Super Soaker and sprayed him with orange Gatorade. The crowd around him laughed and cheered as he braved the spray, charging headlong for the water-gun-toting jock, chasing him around the paddock. One of the valets hollered at Jimmy and handed him the hose, and the two jockeys had a water battle.

Outside the paddock rail, Shannon looked on the raucous rite with longing. Jimmy had won his first race and a circle of jockeys, valets and racing officials cheerfully welcomed him to the racing fraternity. She watched the exuberant play until horses arrived for the next race and the paddock judge shouted at the jocks, shooing them into the building.

Shannon felt as though she were watching Jimmy's initiation on a theater screen, so far was she from being a part of the picture herself. The whole racetrack experience was pixilating. Now she thought of the steward's news that she had passed the trainer's test with bitterness. She had naively imagined that when she passed the test she would be struck by a bolt of knowledge, privy to the secret skill required to train race horses. Yet all she knew was that Acky had to be hopped up on illegal stimulants to race. The license itself meant nothing. Without a winning horse, she had no way to attract owners. Without owners willing to pay her to train their horses, she would spend her life living out of the trunk of her car.

Every time something good happened, something else undercut her happiness. Yeah, she had a trainer's license but no owners, no friends, no way to survive. She would have to try to get back to Calder. At least she had some friends in Florida. Nobody here gave a damn about her.

Lawrence's distracted response to her news about the trainer's test had disappointed her, but the real blow came when he forgot their bond with Good Prospect. They had so much fun together talking about horses. For awhile she had hoped that he would break up with Vicki and want to be with her. She realized how much she had depended on the friendship of Lawrence and Jimmy and how short-sighted she had been. Lawrence had a girlfriend and now Jimmy had the jockey colony. She had nothing.

She would run Acky tomorrow—in her only race as the trainer of record, she thought ironically—juice him and hopefully pick up a check that would get her back to Florida.

Shannon sat on the hood of her car with her chin in her hands.

"Ah, *mi Corazon. Que' pasa?* What is wrong?"

"Leave me alone," she said.

Teg was uncharacteristically quiet. He sensed this was a golden opportunity and he didn't want to blow it. When she didn't say anything else, he said, "A pretty lady should not be alone when she is sad."

Shannon exhaled, blowing out her lips. "Tell me how the juice thing works. When do I give it to him? Before the Lasix or after?"

"Do you have the money?"

She nodded. She had stooped to borrowing from Rodell. "Do you have the stuff?"

"We go now." He approached the car and touched her arm. "The horse runs. You will see. It will be fine."

She slid off the hood. "Where can we get something to drink?"

Teg's heart leaped. "If you drive, I show you the way."

Shannon sucked deeply on the joint, holding the smoke in her lungs as long as possible and passing the joint back to him with a smile. Teg's bare muscular arm was draped over her shoulder and even in the muggy summer night the warmth of his touch felt good. Yeah he was sketchy but he smelled good, not that gross Dollar Store smell most of them had, just a good man smell.

They sat on a broken picnic table that had been moved away from the dormitories for disposal. A blue farm light shone on them as the last color faded from the sky.

Teg wondered a bit at his extravagance. A pint of bourbon and now a joint. He didn't usually have to work this hard to get a woman. He rubbed the back of her neck and ran his fingers up into her hair. She leaned back encouragingly, giving him a lovely view down the canyon of her shirt. He let out a little laugh when he saw the horseshoe tattooed inside her breast.

"What?" she asked, still enjoying his neck massage.

"*De nada.*"

"Bullshit. You're looking at my boobs."

He never could get over the way American women were so bold. "Ah, *Bonita*, I love you. I could never do such a thing." He grinned. "Unless you want me to." She hadn't objected when he slowly slid the syringe of blue juice into her breast pocket, so now he rubbed her neck some more, sliding his hand around to her collarbone. He put the joint in her mouth as she reached for it with her lips.

"This is good stuff," she said out of the corner of her mouth.

Teg nuzzled her neck and was rewarded again with a view. This time he felt for the outline of her tattoo. She pushed his hand away.

This is really a bad idea, Shannon thought. *I should go home.* Then she remembered she had no home to go to and laughed in relief. The idea of standing up and walking to her car was uninviting. She was comfortable. It was nice to smoke a joint in the evening and have someone call her *mi Corazon*. In her shirt pocket, resting against the horseshoe tattoo, lay the small syringe of insurance for Acky's race the next day. She listened to the tinny sounds of a radio from the far side of the bathhouse and lingered. Teg's hands began wandering in earnest until she finally pushed them off and stood up.

"Where are we going?" Teg asked as he stood up and rearranged his arm on her shoulders.

"I'm going to say goodnight to my horses and to you."

"You are breaking my heart, *Guapa*. The horses first."

They made their way to Barn Four and checked on the horses. In the shadow of the shed row, as Shannon opened her mouth to dismiss him, Teg made a serious move, wrapping his arms around her and kissing her face and neck. After a moment, Shannon realized her shirt was open and Teg's hands were expertly caressing her, the syringe pushed to the side. Then somehow, without interrupting his lovemaking, Teg had the two of them settled on a horse blanket in the hay room. *No. Stop*, Shannon whispered. Or did she think that?

The part of Shannon's brain not swimming in dope knew that Teg was creepy, but the other part of her brain telegraphed impulses of pleasure as he ran his hand up her leg. Even as they grappled on the horse blanket, the rational part of her brain was disengaged, watching, repeating the notion that this was really a bad idea. But it felt good and anyway, it was too much trouble to try to stop him. Too late, regret flooded her gut, spilling out and staining the sheet.

It was no big deal, she told herself. The price of the friendship. Her mother was wrong.

Chapter 37

A few hours' sleep was not enough to shake off the hempen cloud of the night before. Only the fact that Acky was running that night and needed to be hand-walked got Shannon out of her nest in the back seat. She felt around under the seat for a Red Bull, popped the top and took a swig, making a face as the beverage kicked. I wonder if this is how blue juice feels, she thought.

Sarah Anne, one of Carl's groomettes, greeted her as she trudged down the shed row, hot Red Bull in hand, syringe tucked inside her shirt. "Hey, Shannon. Congrats again on your license! Waytogo!" She held up her hand for a high-five, which Shannon belatedly met, feeling the syringe shift

She forced a smile. "Yeah, thanks. Finally."

"Just in time for Acky's race," said Sarah Anne.

Shannon nodded. "Cool."

"You want me to take him to the paddock for you?"

Shannon had not thought about the details of Acky's preparation beyond slipping him the juice. "Uh, thanks. That'd be great," she said, pleasantly surprised at the idea. With Sarah Anne leading the horse, she could make her training debut in street clothes instead of barn clothes. "That's so nice of you."

"No problem. You gotta look good for your first start." Sarah Anne beamed as if she were Bill Mott training Cigar.

As Shannon led her three-year-old around the shed row, the groomettes mucked his stall and filled it with fresh bedding and hay, sparing her a visit to the hay room. Snippets from the night before tugged at her consciousness, but she kicked them aside.

Good Prospect was being hand-walked after his dramatic win the day before, but Jimmy showed up anyway. He hung over the stall webbing as Shannon brushed the double swirl on Acky's bald white face.

"I hope you got him ready to run 'cause I'm ready to ride."

She found herself returning his grin, happy that Jimmy was riding her horse. "Y'all go out there and kick some grass," she said.

"Have you looked at the entries? What do you think?" Jimmy seemed as excited about riding Acky as he was about Good Prospect. His enthusiasm cheered her and the Red Bull kicked in, allowing her to look forward to the evening's race.

"I'm hoping grass will be the magic charm. I hope he runs a good race for you." Shannon thought how cool it would be for Jimmy to have another win and she was tempted to tell him, *We have insurance.* But even as she imagined the thrill of a win, she recalled what Darryl said: *Sometimes it backfires. The horse gets all pumped up and has a heart attack in the middle of the race. Or they flip out in the paddock and never get to the gate.* She quickly dismissed those thoughts. That wouldn't happen with Acky. He was such a sensible horse.

Jimmy's excitement and the enthusiasm of Carl and his groomettes restored some of Shannon's normal early-morning happiness, allowing her to go about her stable chores in a warm

192

pocket of hope. Her hope was short-lived though, turning to anxiety as she sweated out the medication plan in the hot, heavy lull of midafternoon. During a quiet moment after lunch, Shannon slipped the syringe into the bottom of her brush box, brushing away the memory of Teg sliding it into her shirt pocket. She would stick Acky when she put his bridle on to go to the paddock. The empty syringe would have to stay in her brush box until things got quiet again at the end of the night.

The vet came at three to give Acky a shot of Lasix. Mr. Starling seemed surprised that she had asked for that. Lasix was the prescribed treatment for exercise-induced pulmonary hemorrhage.

"Has he bled?" Carl asked.

"He had a little pink in his snot after Jimmy breezed him last time. I just wanted to be safe," she said.

"Did you have the vet scope his lungs?"

"I couldn't afford to."

Carl smiled and patted her shoulder. "Well, it's good to be on the safe side. It won't hurt him and it might help him."

Acky was already shining like a new penny, but Shannon spent most of the afternoon in his stall, running her hands over his rich coat and feeling the cool tendons in his legs. His mane lay over on the right side, the hairs in parallel formation. His bright white face beamed like a locomotive's headlight. She remembered how as a foal his bald face made him stand out in the herd of mares and foals. As Shannon brushed his face one more time, she noticed again what a kind, intelligent eye the horse had. It was almost as if he could speak. "Buy us a ticket back home," she told him and he nodded.

As post time approached, Shannon fitted the white racing bridle to Acky's head. Twice she reached for the syringe, only to have Sarah Anne or Parson stop by the stall to see if she needed help. Go away, she thought. Just give me thirty seconds.

But Sarah Anne just stood by the door of the stall. "Are you ready to go? They're calling us to the paddock."

Shannon's street clothes were soaking wet from nerves and the oppressive July heat. The colt rubbed his handsome face against her shoulder. Suddenly she thought, What I am doing? Acky was her friend, her best friend, maybe her only friend. The horse stood next

193

to her, alert, innocent, ready to go do his job. For what? she thought. He wouldn't get a paycheck or an endorsement contract. He'd get the same tub of oats whether he won or lost. She stroked Acky's muscular neck as he tossed his head up and down. For Acky, it was all about instinct, the generational urge to run, to join the fleeing herd and race across the plains. For him, for all the horses breaking out of the gate around him, racing was pure sport, sport as it was meant to be, the striving of competitors to see whose drive and muscle and heart should be crowned with a laurel wreath. Shannon felt her throat tighten. And she wanted to dirty that with a cheap, dangerous gamble. Even in the heat, she felt herself burning with shame, shame that she had let the worst scum on the racetrack corrupt her. Taking a deep breath, Shannon stuffed a rub rag in her brush box to cover the full syringe and came out of the stall. "Let's do it."

"You want me to take that?" Sarah Anne asked.

Shannon clutched the handle. "No, you take the horse. I'll take the stuff."

Even though Sarah Anne led the colt, Shannon walked with them, not wanting to miss an instant of the experience.

"Sarah Anne, thanks for bringing him over."

"No problem. Thanks for letting me be part of your first start."

Her first start as a trainer. She was a licensed trainer. She let herself smile. Her license with its identifying green stripe was clipped to her belt, and she fingered it as she walked, as though it might be taken away if she didn't hold onto it. It might be, she reminded herself, if anyone looked in her brush box.

The valet who was helping Jimmy helped Shannon tack Acky in the saddling stall. Carl and the groomettes waited for her in the paddock, cheering Acky and Jimmy on. The paddock judge gave her a Colonial Downs hat for luck. She barely registered these little signs of support, focusing her still-wasted brain cells on guarding the brush box and watching her horse. She fretted when Acky got all sweated up, but Parson said, "Hell, it's ninety-four degrees. I'd worry if he didn't sweat."

As Shannon gave Jimmy a leg up, he grinned and said, "Any instructions, boss?"

There were a million things she wanted to tell him. Make sure he breaks well. Don't foul anybody. Don't get boxed in. Find some running room. For God's sake, win the race! But she stroked the colt's neck, looked up at her friend and said, "Y'all come back safe."

Shannon was always proud of her handsome horses in the post parade, but this time she watched Acky prancing next to a lead pony with a tear in her eye. It felt as if she were sending him off to war to fight for a noble cause while she waited at home, alone and lonely.

The starting gate was set at the top of the stretch on the Secretariat Turf Course, so when there was a scuffle behind the gate, Shannon couldn't see anything but plunging equine bodies and flying scraps of silks. Her stomach lurched.

Hank May's voice boomed across the apron. "Ladies and gentlemen, we have a rider off. The Seven horse, Oak Feathers, is giving the starters a bit of trouble."

Now they showed the scene at the gate on the big screen monitor in the infield. Shannon saw Acky, the Six, walk promptly into the gate, followed by the riderless Seven horse. The jockey scrambled up the metal frame and settled onto the horse.

Almost immediately, the bell rang, long and insistent, shocking Acky and the others into a bump-and-run melee like an electric whip. Emerging from the pack, two horses sped off to a big lead on the rail. Shannon wasn't worried about them; they would come back to the pack the next time around.

Next to her, Sarah Anne shrieked, "Go Acky! Look! Shannon! He's third!"

Shannon heard herself screaming, too. Acky, galloping steadily and gracefully, as always, showed his head in front of the rest of the pack. As the horses rounded the clubhouse turn and entered the backstretch, the speedballs were fifteen lengths ahead and Acky was running comfortably with a slight lead over the other five horses. Omigod, Shannon thought, it's coming together, he's running a good race. There in the text box under the live photo on the monitor, listed third, she saw "6 – Acky," with Jimmy's name and a little blue patch to mark her silks. Happy for her horse, happy for herself, she held her hand over her mouth and blinked furiously as tears blurred the sight of Acky and Jimmy leading the main pack down the backstretch.

As the two speedballs ran out of gas around the turn, Acky and the pack raced past them. Acky's number moved to the top. Shannon and the groomettes leaped up and down, screaming and cheering as the crowd on the apron roared its support.

Then the other horses started their stretch run.

Shannon had loaded her horse with blinkers, a tongue-tie, rundown bandages and Lasix. She had switched him to grass and stretched him out to a mile and three-sixteenths, which gave him time to gallop along at a steady pace and catch two speed horses who were spent and wobbly-legged in the stretch. All of that wasn't enough for him to win, but he was at least in the picture. Shannon and her supporters screamed as the field finished in a loose bunch with Acky somewhere in the middle. The horse that finished third was disqualified and placed last, moving Acky up to fifth, his best-ever finish, good enough for a check.

When Jimmy slid off the gelding and took his saddle to weigh out, Shannon gave him a tearful hug. "Thank you, Jimmy! I'm so glad you're okay! Thank you for bringing Acky home safely!"

The check was nice, Shannon thought as she washed bits of dirt and grass off Acky's chest after the race. It was more than nice. Fifth place money of eighty-five dollars would buy her some feed and help dispel Parson's suspicion she was stealing from Carl. But eighty-five dollars wouldn't get them back to Florida. And fifth place probably wasn't enough to keep Acky from being ruled off.

She'd just have to wait and see. The important thing was Acky was okay. He didn't hurt himself. Or Jimmy. How could she think of risking that? What had she been thinking? She combed a damp lock of his mane with her fingers and thought about Louisa Ferncliff doing up the bandage on Alice's Restaurant's knee. Racehorses were so brave, she thought. *And they are at our mercy.* She could have stuck Acky with some foreign substance and gambled on the consequences, consequences that the horse would have had to live with while she went her merry way. She closed her eyes and leaned on Acky's neck, whispering apologies.

Later, after the barn emptied out and Shannon gave Acky one more loving rub, she slipped the syringe out of her brush box and into her pocket. As she made her way to her car, she paused by a trashcan and held the syringe full of liquid up to the light. I wonder what makes it blue, she thought. Rolling the syringe between her finger and thumb, she wondered if she could get her money back from Teg.

She grunted and tossed the syringe. She'd just as soon never see that leering face again.

There are no secrets on the backstretch. Anyone who stood at the gap in the morning or hung around the kitchen when the track closed at ten or stopped to watch action on the basketball court by the dorms could easily hear about the hookups, the boasting, the triumphs, the acts of kindness, the illicit products in use by horses and humans—in general, the decisions good and bad that Colonial horsemen had made that day. Since he didn't talk much, Jimmy had time to absorb all the news about human interaction at the track, just as he did back home at the pool hall or in the Tastee-Freez parking lot. With no family here and few friends, he had no opinion about most of what he learned. But occasionally something came up that rubbed him the wrong way, inspiring him to take the extraordinary step of breaking out of his bubble to do something.

This was one of these times, the sticky night after he had ridden Shannon's horse to the animal's best-ever finish. Shannon had choked up as she thanked him for his ride, leading Jimmy to connect various dots. Now a few hours later, he was feeling amazingly calm. He had made two decisions and it felt good. Both of them involved Alvarez Montegro. He was not concerned with the quality of the decisions, just pleased by his own decisiveness. Jimmy walked confidently into the shadow behind the horse trailer to meet Teg.

Teg was already there, watching for him nervously. Jimmy didn't say anything. He just counted out the bills and handed them to Teg, who handed him a small plastic bag in return. "Good luck, *vaquero.*"

Jimmy nodded and stuffed the bag in his pocket. He noticed the ripped muscles in the exercise rider's upper body but it didn't change his mind. Size never bothered him.

"You been with Shannon Hill?" he asked flatly.

Teg was a lover, not a fighter, and anyway, he didn't want to get crossways with a customer, especially not a *gringo.* "Oh no, *señor. Señorita* Hill is a fine lady. I could not—"

But Jimmy wasn't interested in Teg's protestations of innocence.

Despite having the quick reflexes of a man who worked with large, unpredictable animals, Teg never saw Jimmy move. Jimmy cracked him in the face, knocking loose one of Teg's perfect white teeth and felling him like a tree. As Teg rolled on the ground holding his bloody mouth, Jimmy stood over him and said, "Don't do it no more."

Chapter 38

"I think your exercise rider's sleeping in her car," Wick said as he tied the goat up to Alice's pen. A slight breeze found its way through the trees on a mild overcast afternoon. Wick had brought their customary picnic of fried chicken and beer, which they had consumed while grazing the animals after Alice's swim.

"Who?" Louisa asked, latching the gate.

"That Hill girl."

"Shannon?"

Wick leaned an elbow on the panel next to the gate. "I saw her going into the bathhouse early this morning."

Louisa turned and found herself almost brushing into Wick's chest. She looked up at him with a smile. "Maybe she had to go."

"She works the early shift for Maria. She doesn't get to the track till after the break, eight-thirty or nine." He was looking down at her with the intensity he reserved for screwups. Louisa wondered what the girl had done now.

"Wick, do you really think so? That poor child."

"I don't know why you worry about her. Of course, I don't know why you worry about half the people you do." Wick's gruff voice was almost soft. His hand, where he was leaning on the pen, brushed her loose hair.

Somewhere in the distance, Louisa heard the coy tones of a voice like hers. "Most people aren't as fortunate as I am."

"Yeah, most people don't have a private groom for their goat." Wick slid his arm around her shoulders and pulled her to him, kissing her easily at first, then with more passion as he felt her respond. He had to bend over to reach her and she stood on her toes to meet him halfway, running a hand up to his shoulder to keep her balance.

He kissed her for a long time, until her legs went wobbly and he had to catch her to keep her from falling. They both laughed. It didn't seem necessary to say anything. He brushed her hair back, searching her face. Then he picked her up, spun her around and set her on the running board of the truck where he could kiss her eyes and mouth and neck and press her whole body close to his.

It had been a long time since she'd been kissed, Louisa thought. She was glad to find it came back to her so quickly. He tasted of beer, which made him seem sexier. She leaned into his embrace and enjoyed his nuzzling mouth and searching hands. Men loved her boobs.

Inevitably the *what next?* moment arrived. She didn't want to take off her clothes on the running board of the truck in the woods and it seemed headed that way. When she stopped him and saw the question in his eyes, she said, "I have to go back to work."

"Now?"

She laughed at his directness. "Now."

He shook his head. "You've got a hell of a sense of duty."

He patted her bottom as she climbed into the truck and she held his hand as he drove. Every time he glanced at her and grinned, she squeezed his hand and thought about her plane ticket to Wisconsin. She tried to be glad that she had already bought and paid for it. She didn't want to make another bad decision. *Don't think too much,* she told herself.

Shannon was grazing the goat and Alice was swimming steadily around the pool when Louisa said, "Thanks for helping out this week. Wick is so busy with the Turf Festival, he doesn't have time to breathe."

"I like coming out here," said Shannon. She had avoided Teg ever since the night he gave her the syringe, that gross night when every bit of sense she ever had abandoned her to leering seduction by that scumbag. She'd washed herself but she couldn't wash away the memory of his sweaty body on hers. Even worse was the memory of how close she had come to hurting her beloved Acky. The gentle woods and the green undergrowth were a balm, though. Louisa was easy to be with and she loved Alice. Every afternoon for an hour she gratefully let her mind go blank as the goat tugged her around the clearing.

"I have another favor to ask: After the Derby, I'm flying to Wisconsin to look at a place, and I was wondering if you would look after my RV for me."

"Really?"

"I'm afraid if I leave it dark, some of our friends on the backstretch might move in."

"Well, sure, I'd be glad to help you out."

"I have a cat, too. She doesn't take much attention but she might decide to take off if she's locked outside for a few days."

"That's okay."

"Thank you. Also, I don't want to impose on you," Louisa continued, "but it might be good for you to stay there with me before I leave, so you can learn where things are. So the cat will get used to you."

When Shannon didn't answer, Louisa looked up. The girl's head was down, her eyes closed, her fist on her mouth. Finally, Shannon turned to her and nodded.

"I'm not much of a cook," Louisa said.

"I eat at Maria's," Shannon whispered.

"Oh, that's right. Well, drop your clothes off before you go to work this evening and I'll show you how the sofa-bed works."

"Yes, ma'am. Thank you."

"Don't thank me. You're doing me a favor."

Chapter 39

At quarter to ten, Carl Starling walked into the secretary's office where a small group had gathered to see Jack Delaney take entries for the Virginia Derby. Trainers for the major stables came by to drop their entries in the box. Carl had his entry form neatly filled out and a check for the horsemen's bookkeeper that included a chunk of his colt's winnings that he had saved against this day. Lawrence had been there since nine o'clock, counting the entries. He whispered eagerly to Carl, "You're okay so far."

At ten o'clock, two assistant trainers hurried through the door and put three more slips in the box. One of Jack's assistants added an undetermined number of entry slips called in by trainers from around the country. At five minutes after ten, Jack opened the box, counted the entries and said to nobody in particular, "Eighteen."

Lawrence exhaled in frustration, and Carl smiled philosophically. Four over the capacity of the starting gate. The entries would be ordered by previous earnings, which meant Good Prospect would likely be near the bottom. Carl would have to hope a couple of horses didn't make it. A bruised foot, a missed flight, an elevated temperature. It could happen.

Shannon was on the rail with Darryl and some other grooms from Max Fox's barn watching the horses gallop out after the second race when Wick approached her.

"Shannon?"

"Hi, Mr. Keswick."

"Could I speak to you for a minute?"

Guilt immediately suffused her. Did he know about the grain? Or worse. Did he know about the syringe? Maybe they wouldn't prosecute her, just yank her license and throw her out. "Ah, sure." She cast a look of mock terror at her friends and walked away with the general manager of the racetrack. Pulse racing, she wracked her brain for a way to talk herself out of this jam. After all, she didn't use the juice. Maybe they would let her go if she told them where she got it.

"I need a favor," he said. "Louisa Ferncliff tells me you're friends with Jimmy Wiseman."

Shannon felt her heart rate slow down. "We don't really hang out together, if that's what you mean, but we gallop those two horses together every morning."

"Friday night is the Virginia Derby Gala at the Jefferson Hotel. It's a big event for the track and it's a fundraiser for the Thoroughbred Retirement Foundation. We get a lot of publicity from it. It's a big deal."

"Yeah, sounds like it." She'd been hearing about it since she got to Colonial. A formal dinner dance with open bar, party favors and a steep ticket to raise money for the Thoroughbred Retirement Foundation.

"Are you going?"

"I haven't really decided."

"All the owners and trainers of the horses for the Derby and the Oaks will be there, and we expect the jockeys to attend, too. They are celebrities and that attracts more people," he said.

"Yeah, you need them there. Let me guess. Jimmy won't go."

"Carl's been after him but he's not getting anywhere. Louisa, too. I need your help."

"Does this mean Good Prospect made the field? I thought he was on the also-eligible list."

"It looks like he's going to be in," said Wick. "And we want his connections ready."

"Gosh, I don't know. I'll be glad to talk to Jimmy, but he probably doesn't have a tux. It's black tie, isn't it?"

"We'll get him a tux. And I'll give you a couple of tickets if you can get him there."

Okay, this was sounding good. "Maybe if he knows it's helping the Thoroughbred Retirement Foundation. Are you getting the jocks to pose for pictures with the guests and then selling them the photo?"

Wick smiled. "You know, that's a good idea. I'll have to see if we can line that up. Thank you, Shannon. I'm going to count on you."

"Yes sir, Mr. Keswick." *Omigod,* she thought, *I've got to get a dress.* She hadn't been to a formal dance since the Christmas her parents split up, but the thought of dressing up and looking pretty at a dance with a lot of men was exciting. All she had to do was persuade the most backward guy she'd ever met to do something he'd probably never done before. Compared to her other challenges, this was a piece of cake.

Space was limited in Louisa's RV, so Shannon left most of her things in the trunk of her car. But a few days after talking to Mr. Keswick, she had something to add to her little pile on the sofa bed.

"Lord have mercy, what's in that box?"

Shannon dragged a tall cardboard box through the door of Louisa's RV. "My mother sent me this. I asked her to mail me a dress to wear Friday night because I left all my stuff with her."

"Either that's Lady Diana's wedding dress or she sent you the whole closet."

"Knowing my mother it's probably both."

Shannon opened the box and lifted out a little black dress, a long black and red evening dress and an electric blue chiffon gown with price tags still attached. "This," said Shannon, "is why I'm so poor. My dad gives my mother money to live on and she spends it on clothes, then I have to send her money to pay the phone bill." Shannon held the blue chiffon up to her shoulders.

"She has beautiful taste."

"Oh, there's nothing wrong with her taste. I love this color but I don't think I can wear it. You have to have boobs to wear a neckline like this." She tossed it in the box.

"Jimmy's eyes would be out on sticks if you wore that."

Shannon laughed. "It'd be fun to wear it and see his face."

"You'd have the full attention of every man there."

Chapter 40

Jack Delaney and Wick were in the racing secretary's office discussing entries for the Virginia Derby when the door blew open and a tall, lanky man burst into the room.

"Come on boys, let me buy you a drink!" The disheveled old man's voice was shockingly loud but neither Jack nor Wick seemed to notice.

"Can't right now," said Wick.

"What's the matter? You ain't got no bars open at ten o'clock in the morning around here?"

Wick said, "Come back in an hour, Croak, and we'll go to lunch over at Maria's."

"I tell you, this is a slow damn crowd," the old man muttered as he turned away. "I thought I taught you better'n that, Wick," he said and slammed the door before Wick could reply.

Wick resumed his conversation about the entries in the Derby. "The race still holding up?"

Jack consulted a sheet on his desk. "Well, Sabatini called and confirmed that he's only got the one colt for the Derby, but he has another filly for the Oaks if we have room."

"You've got room for her, don't you?"

"Yeah. The Oak's got two or three slots left."

"So what does that do for Carl?"

"If the Irish horse doesn't get on a flight today, there's a spot for him." Jack looked at his watch. "I was going to check just before we do the draw. Carl might just make it."

There was a long pause.

"Be good to have another local horse in there," said Wick.

"He might be able to run a little bit," said Jack.

"You heard what Lawrence said that day."

Jack snorted. "I used to think that boy knew what he was talking about. Have you seen what he's been picking lately?"

"Oh, he's just having a little cold streak. Give him a break."

Jack looked at Wick hard. "You've gotten mighty easy going here lately. I figured you'd be ready to pull a knot on his head."

Wick stood up to leave.

"You going to be around the rest of the day?" Jack asked.

"Yeah."

"You sure?"

"I'm sure. What do you need?" Wick asked.

"I need to go over some stuff with you about the connections of these other Derby horses."

"Right after lunch?"

Jack waved his assent.

When Wick got back to his office, his secretary looked up in surprise. "Oh, Mr. Keswick, I wasn't expecting you."

"Well, I'm here. Who were you expecting?"

"It's… well… Have you been to lunch already?"

"No, I'm going to Maria's in a few minutes, though. If a real tall old man comes in, just try to keep him from tearing the place apart until I get off the phone."

"Croaker Norge?"

"You got it."

Wick closed the door and picked up the phone. He'd been tied up with Virginia Derby details since six a.m., and he wasn't going to get a break till after the race on Saturday. He hated for Louisa to do Alice's Restaurant without him. He also hated to call her on the phone. He liked to go by and see her, but that wasn't going to happen, either.

"Hey, Louisa," he said when she answered.

"Wick! Good morning."

He smiled at the enthusiasm in her voice. "I'm not going to get out there today. Again. I'm sorry." He suddenly realized just how sorry he was to miss their afternoon tryst.

"I'll miss you, but it's all right. I didn't expect you today anyway."

It occurred to him he wouldn't get to the camp with her the rest of the week, either. "Derby week is rough."

"Shannon can help me for a few more days. Alice is doing fine."

Wick was annoyed at that prospect. Helping Louisa with Alice was *his* job. He forced himself back to his other job. "Has she talked to Jimmy about going to the Derby ball?"

"He said no at first, but she thinks he'll come around. She's a pretty good salesman. I think she'll get the job done."

Wick had to admit, grudgingly, that Louisa was right.

"I'll pick you up at five-thirty. That okay?" he said.

"Wick, you have a lot of people to look after that night. Why don't I meet you there?"

"Damn it, Louisa, if you're going with me, I'm going to pick you up."

"Like a real date."

"Like a real date."

"If I can remember how to do that," she said and he heard her wind-chime laughter over the phone.

He hung up feeling very satisfied with life and looked out the window at the empty parking lot. Empty because it was a dark day. Suddenly, he remembered why everyone seemed surprised to see him today.

It was Wednesday.

He stared at the parking lot a long time. Beyond the lot a fringe of trees screened the interstate. A steady stream of cars rippled through the trees, heading east, towards Norfolk. Yeah, Derby week was rough. It was all rough.

Croaker Norge had consumed an eye-popping amount of Canadian Club without discernible effect when he turned to Wick. "Who's here from the old days?"

"Hell, Croak, nobody's as old as you are," said Wick.

Norge rubbed his right eye ostentatiously with his middle finger.

Norge, Wick and Jack had finished lunch at Maria's and moved on to liquid dessert.

Wick grinned. "I'll tell you who's here. Louisa Ferncliff."

"No shit? She got any good horses?"

"She's not out on her own. She's Mike Lucci's assistant."

"Hell of a horsewoman."

"Did you teach her everything you know?" asked Jack.

"About horses. Nothing else. She was always in love with somebody else. Wick, you remember Dean?"

"He was before my time," Wick said.

"The two of them about burned down the barn."

"Hot romance?" said Jack.

"Firecracker hot. They were in the tack room drinking one night and he dropped a cigarette. They got the fire out but it made enough mess they couldn't hide it."

"I remember hearing about that," said Wick. He had worked for Norge a couple of summers, one of them overlapping briefly with Louisa's employment in the legendary trainer's barn. Back then, she worked hard and she played hard.

Norge rocked his chair back on two legs. "I'm surprised she's working for somebody else. She's a good trainer. She beat all the boys down at the Fairgrounds one year, oh, I reckon it's been thirty years ago."

"She had a falling out with one of her owners, didn't she?" said Wick.

Norge snorted. "She got screwed. She had these owners named Lippincott. J. G. and Annabelle. They had a little string and

Louisa was doing good for them. They went to the sales and Louisa helped them pick out a couple of nice two-year-olds. Then they really got hot. Lippincott was second or third leading owner. Louisa was in the race for leading trainer. By the next season, J. G.'s talking about leaving Annabelle and setting up a separate stable with Louisa, complete with living quarters, you know?" Norge waved his empty glass at the waitress. "You got another one of these?"

Wick shifted in his seat and waited for the rest of the story.

"They tell me one day J. G. and Louisa are going at it in the hay room at the track and Annabelle comes busting in on them. Everybody's hollering and cussing and Annabelle snatches their clothes and throws them in the muck pit. Then she goes down the shed row unsnapping the webbing on every stall door. Had about two million dollars worth of horses running loose in the stable area. J. G.'s sneaking away under a horse blanket and Louisa's in a vest and a couple saddle towels trying to catch the horses. Three fillies got bred before they caught them all."

"What finally happened?"

"Just what you'd expect. Lippincott crawled back to his wife, and they gave all the horses to another trainer who made Lippincott leading owner. Louisa couldn't get any horses after that."

"If she was a man, nobody would have thought anything of it. She'd have a new stable in a week," said Jack.

Norge nodded. "Women get a raw deal in this business. I don't know what happened to Louisa after that. This is the first I've heard of her since then."

Nobody said anything for a minute.

"I guess that's when she went to the Saints," said Jack.

Wick tossed some bills on the table and stood up. "I've got to get back."

"Damn, Wick, I'm just getting caught up here," said Norge.

"Y'all can stay. I've got a racetrack to run."

Chapter 41

As Shannon and Louisa dressed for the Gala, Shannon asked what Louisa was wearing. Louisa showed her a simple, street-length navy blue knit dress with a cardigan.

"Louisa, you have to dress up. This is the Virginia Derby Gala. You have a cute date."

"It's not really a date."

"Yes, it is. And he's really into you, so you have to look hot."

"I'm too old to look hot."

"Here. Try this on. I bet it'll fit you." Shannon held out the blue chiffon dress.

"Oh, no, darling. I can't take your dress. Besides, it won't fit me."

"Yes, it will, as little as you are. It'll look great on you. You've got the boobs for it. Just try it on."

Louisa stepped into the dress and pulled it up. "My bra's going to show…and I haven't had a strapless one since the Kennedy administration."

"Don't wear one. The dress is tight enough to give you support."

"I'll say."

Shannon struggled with the zipper, delicately trying not to pinch Louisa's side. "Stop being so careful," Louisa said. "Just stuff the flab in."

Shannon cracked up. "I'm trying. I'm trying."

Both of them were speechless at how good Louisa looked in the dress. The blue accented her silver hair, and the V-neck showed her impressive cleavage. Fit from years of working in the barn and galloping horses, Louisa had a good figure. The dress was plain enough to suit her age, yet provocative enough to distract from the slack skin on the back of her arms and her gnarled hands.

"Omigod," said Shannon. "Wick is going to flip."

Louisa studied her unfamiliar image in the mirror. What the hell. It had been a long time since she'd been excited about going out.

"We've got to do something about the length," said Shannon. "You're going to trip on the hem unless you have some four-inch heels, which…"

"Which I couldn't walk in if I had them."

"Okay, duct tape."

Louisa found a roll of tape and handed it to Shannon. "You'll have to fix it with me in it. If I take this dress off, I'll never get in it again."

"You look beautiful. I'm not going to leave until Wick gets here. I want to see his face."

Louisa turned around as Shannon worked, imagining herself dancing again. She hoped Wick was a good dancer because she adored dancing. If he wasn't, she'd go find the best dancer in the place. Dancing made her feel sexy, which reminded her of Wick's kiss. She smiled to herself. He was a good kisser. She imagined Wick nuzzling her neck and peeling the blue chiffon dress off.

"He's going to want to get you in bed."

Louisa gave a guilty start. *Oh yes.* She thought about the afternoon at the camp when he kissed her and the other days when he teased her and touched her. But all those Wednesdays were piled up between them. That's why she'd bought the ticket to Wisconsin: She needed a prop for her courage. "I don't know what he'll do," she said, more to herself. "He's…"

"Moody?"

"He's trying to sort things out…but he is a sweet and generous person."

"Well, I'm terrified of him, but he's adorable with you," Shannon said.

"He's a very dear person." Louisa insisted. "Wick is a good man. They don't make them any better."

"Are you in love with him?"

"Oh, heavens no," Louisa said quickly. "We're just good friends. He's been a great help to me this summer with Alice. We go back a long ways."

Shannon gave Louisa a long sideways look. "Are you sure?"

"Shannon, I gave that up a long time ago. I wasn't even in love with my last husband."

"Who was that?"

"Rodell."

After Louisa left with a suitably speechless Wick, Shannon went to pick up Jimmy. He was wearing the tuxedo the track had rented for him, but he didn't have on the tie. As Shannon helped him do the shirt collar and put on the black tie, she couldn't help but notice how gaunt he looked up close. His face was tight and dry and the skin on his neck had crepey folds. Without his muscular forearms showing, his wrists looked bony and brittle.

"How are you doing with your weight?" she asked.

"Good. I'll make it tomorrow."

She had lectured him about how he should reduce, remembering the scary stories she'd heard about jockey weight-reduction gone awry. Now, taking in the visual results of whatever method he used, she was reluctant to say anything. "Just be safe," was all she said.

"That sumbitch Teg ain't bothering you, is he?" Jimmy asked as she fiddled with his tie.

She flushed. It had been over a week since Acky had raced and she had last seen Teg. Ten days in which she had walked in the woods with Alice's goat, trying to forget, and rubbed on Acky, trying to make it up to him. The juice thing and the night with Teg were all rolled up into a big black glop, one of those things in your life so depressing you can't believe it really happened so you just pretend it didn't. She wondered what Jimmy knew. "Did you talk to him?"

"Awhile back."

Jimmy didn't elaborate and she didn't ask.

Lighter now by almost twenty pounds, Jimmy seemed

taller and Shannon walked into the party happily holding his arm. Although most of the horsemen had come in groups, Shannon was glad she had a date, however fake. Among a certain subset of the guests it was cool that she came with one of the Derby jockeys. Serious status. She could cruise around and flirt with whatever guy she saw without looking like a pickup. There was that exercise rider who worked for Max Fox and that young trainer in Barn Six, next to Mike Lucci's string. Plus of course, she looked forward to appearing in front of Lawrence all dressed up, made up and on equal footing with Lawrence's girlfriend.

Chapter 42

Lawrence carried his tuxedo jacket over his arm as he left his apartment to pick up Vicki. It was ninety-two degrees and so humid it felt like you were breathing mashed potatoes. His car was parked in the shade but his shirt was still soaked by the time the air conditioner started cooling the car down. Despite the weather Lawrence liked wearing his tuxedo, possibly because he had happy associations of romantic evenings. He didn't need coaching from his sisters to realize that girls loved a man in formal attire. Girls had demonstrated that to him too many times.

He was looking forward to a fun and romantic evening. For one thing he'd had a good day at the races, picking five winners and a trifecta. This was more than he'd done in weeks. He'd holed up with race replays and past performance data for the past two days prepping for the Oaks card and the Derby card. In the paddock for the Oaks that afternoon he felt cautiously optimistic looking at the three-year-old fillies: He could tell the two who were ready to run a big race. To Lawrence's relief, his picks were coming in again. He smiled remembering the kudos he got for picking a difficult trifecta in the Oaks. He was starting to feel good about his Derby day handicapping.

He'd hardly seen Vicki the last week. He'd memorized past performance data and burned up his computer studying race replays. It was a good thing Jack had Vicki busy babysitting those French guys; she couldn't be mad about his absence. After his triumph today, though, he was ready to celebrate with his hot girlfriend, who, he knew, would have on some sexy outfit that would make him the envy of every man there.

So he was surprised when Vicki texted him that she would meet him at the Gala. He immediately called her.

"Everything okay?" he asked.

"Oh, yeah. But Jack wants me to go with him and his wife to have a drink with Jean Louis before the party. I'm sorry, sweetheart."

"Not a problem. We've got the rest of the night."

Lawrence got a drink and wandered around the rapidly filling ballroom, exchanging greetings with people he knew.

"Hamner!" It was Hank May, accompanied by a woman who had the most amazing breasts Lawrence had ever seen. These large perfect melons were racked at the top of her low cut green dress, which barely covered the protruding nipples. This marvelous visual effect was somewhat diminished by her dyed red spiky hair and her gum-baring grin, which Lawrence eventually noticed. He assumed Hank had a light switch in his bedroom.

"Good day today, partner."

"Yeah," said Hank, "I was glad you finally decided to come back to work."

"Oh, I was just giving you a chance to shine for awhile," Lawrence said, looking around the ballroom.

"So where's the lovely lady Vicki?"

"I don't know. Jack's got her screwing around with the connections of that French horse."

"You sure it's Jack?"

Lawrence flipped him a finger.

"No, really. You seen that guy? Looks like he blew in from *Casablanca* or something."

Lawrence shrugged. "Are any of the jocks here yet? I want to ask Florent Geroux about that colt."

"They're all over at the bar sucking down free whiskey."

Lawrence drifted in that direction, keeping an eye on the door. He saw a familiar-looking couple come in. Horsemen looked so different when they took off their jeans and put on evening clothes, the women especially. They all wore bandanas or helmets around the barn and it was a surprise to see them with hair.

He realized the guy walking towards him was Jimmy and his good-looking date was…Shannon.

"Hi, guys."

"Lawrence, hey, do you know where they're taking pictures of the jocks? We've got to get over there."

Jimmy stood there with a drink, looking, Lawrence thought, remarkably at ease. He gestured towards a backdrop at the end of the room. They departed and he checked the flow of guests through the door again. In a few moments, Shannon was back.

"Jimmy's over there with all these groupies who want to get their picture taken with him. Isn't that cool?"

"How'd you get him to come?" Lawrence said.

"I told him he'd have a hot date in a sexy dress."

Lawrence looked her over. "Nice, but you'd better not leave him with the groupies too long. You might not get him back."

"He's cute, isn't he?" Shannon said.

"In a short, penguin-looking way."

She punched him in the shoulder. "That was mean."

"Ow. Look, I don't usually notice whether guys are 'cute' or not."

"Okay, why don't you buy me a drink, since I've lost my date. By the way, where's yours?"

"Spicking Frawnch." When Shannon looked confused, he added, "Jack had her spend the week with the trainer of the French horse to help translate for him."

"The really hot guy with the cap and the aviators?"

"Once again, I can't personally comment on a guy's 'hotness,' but, yes, I think that's your man." He put his arm around her shoulder and they sauntered towards the bar. "What would you like?" he said, rubbing her shoulder lightly. She smiled back in a very encouraging way. Vicki was hot, he thought, but getting to be sort of high maintenance.

Chapter 43

"That filly of yours ran a helluva race today," Wick said, raising his glass to Norge.

"One more jump and she'd have caught that other filly," said Jack. "She was flying at the end."

At six-foot-five, Croaker Norge had to hunch over the dinner table to get anywhere near his plate. He was hunched over now, shoveling prime rib into his mouth and washing it down with Canadian Club. The blended whiskey was the only thing smooth about him. "Gotta get her cranked a little sooner," he said between mouthfuls.

"You need to get a consultant like you had for that Harborman horse," said Wick.

"What was that about?" Jack asked.

"I had this owner one time who believed in all this Indian mystic crap," said Norge. "She had a horse that was moody. Run one day and wouldn't do shit the next. So she had this guy come do an astrological reading on the horse. The guy said the horse needed a jock who was the right sign to get along with him. Had to be Libra."

Wick laughed. "So Norge is going around the jocks' room asking them, 'What sign are you?' They had this bug boy in there from Nebraska or somewhere, and he thought Norge was hitting on him."

Norge held his glass up to a passing waitress. "I didn't give a shit what they thought, long as one of them could get this horse to run."

"Did it work?"

"He won one race but then I lost him."

"Claimed?"

"Tell them what happened, Croaker," said Wick.

"The horse was entered in a little state-bred stakes and the consultant says don't run him, it's a bad day, stars all wrong. Well, the horse is training good, the race makes up nice and it looks like he can get the win, so I tell the owner I'm running the horse."

The waitress brought his drink and he said, "Thank you, darling."

Everyone at the table was waiting for the punch line. "Did he win?"

"Nah. Didn't even get to the gate. Walked out on the track and dropped dead."

Wick hooted. "The consultant was right. It was a bad day."

Wick was in his element, sitting around the table swapping lies about the old days over a glass of Jack Daniels. He hadn't seen him in years, but Norge never changed. Always good for a story. And a drink or three. Wick wondered if he was still running women as hard as he did thirty years ago. The guy had to be way up in his seventies but it hadn't slowed him down. Wick leaned back and draped his arm over the back of Louisa's chair.

"Louisa, what kind of wine is that you're drinking with ice in it?" Norge asked.

"Cranberry."

"Cranberry wine? What the hell kind of wine is that?"

Louisa laughed her little sparkling laugh, which ordinarily made Wick smile. "It makes me sleep like a baby."

Norge gave a little snort. "I remember when you could drink every man here under the table."

"I had to give that up." She shook her head in mock sadness.

"Hard to gallop the next morning?"

"Hard to have fun with all the men passed out."

Norge sat up to his full height, threw his head back and let out a great honking guffaw. Just watching him laugh was humorous in itself, and Jack and Nora, Louisa, and Norge's owners joined in. Wick sucked on his coffee and ordered another Jack Daniels as Norge continued his flirtation. "By God, Louisa, you're still as sharp as you are pretty. And you look prettier than a speckled pup under a red wagon tonight. Damn, girl, you clean up good."

"She looks good in her jeans," Wick said mildly.

Louisa beamed. She was having a wonderful evening, fully aware of the growing tension between Wick and Norge over *her*. She felt like Cinderella in the beautiful ball gown Shannon had loaned her. She had been torn about wearing it, but Shannon insisted, and, what the hell, it *did* make her look good and feel young. Wearing Cinderella's ball gown with the deep neckline had the expected effect on the men at her table. Wick's mouth fell open when he came to pick her up and Shannon winked behind his back. Wick, always a gentleman, became positively courtly, sweeping the door open, helping her into his car, making sure her duct-taped hem was tucked inside before closing the door. At the gala, he was not only attentive but proprietary, keeping his hand on her back as they walked through the crowd, always touching her. His attention felt good. She found herself thinking about kissing him again, somewhere more comfortable than the woods. That made her think about maybe having a glass of champagne, too.

"Drinking seriously affected my judgment," Louisa said, glancing from Wick to Norge.

"Speaking of that, you ever see Dean after he got out of jail?" Norge asked.

She shook her head.

"I wonder what he's doing," said Norge.

"He ran the Thoroughbred Retirement Foundation rehab program at the prison in South Carolina for awhile," she said.

"I thought you hadn't seen him," Wick said.

"I haven't, but I keep up with all my old husbands."

Norge guffawed again, to the amusement of everyone at the table except Wick.

"I hear he's got some horses down at El Commandante," said Jack.

"The Caribbean ought to suit him. He always was easy-come, easy-go," Louisa said.

"There's an easy-go song I can dance to," said Norge. "Come on, Louisa, let me push you around the dance floor."

Jack and Nora got up to dance, too, leaving Wick at the table to brood.

Lawrence and Hank made such a good pair on camera because they were genuine friends who fed off each other's humor. At the gala, they had a good time bantering with a couple of jockeys' agents about the Derby owners and trainers who danced and drank in a circle around them.

"By the way, have you seen Louisa Ferncliff?" Hank whistled.

"Have you seen Wick with his tongue hanging out?"

They both laughed, and Hank said, "Man, I've got a claiming race for older fillies and mares that she can enter any time."

"I don't think she's looking for a race. Wick's put a halter on her."

"Maybe not. Who's that tall old geezer? He's bird-dogging her pretty good. Wick better watch out."

"Croaker Norge?"

"That's Croaker Norge?! I thought he was dead!"

"If he's dead, he's so well embalmed with alcohol he doesn't know it yet."

"Three to five, if he doesn't stop running his hands all over Louisa, Wick's going to make sure he's dead."

Lawrence had almost forgotten that he had a date until Vicki appeared in a lime green strapless dress that drew everyone's eye as she passed. *That's my date,* he thought smugly. When he stood up to greet her with a kiss, she gave him her cheek.

"I'm sorry it took me so long—" she began.

"Hey, don't worry. Have a seat. We'll get the waiter to bring you a plate."

"Oh, I'm okay. I had…a bite at their table."

Despite the number of drinks in his system, Lawrence noted the fact that Vicki had been at the gala long enough to eat dinner but had not joined him for some reason. He deduced the reason. He sat down.

"Uh, Lawrence, Sugar—" She glanced over the table of Lawrence's friends. "Why don't we dance?"

"My feet hurt. I've been dancing all night."

She stood there uncertainly.

Lawrence turned to the rest of the table. "Hey, Hank! Has that race for fillies and mares closed? I've got a filly I want to enter."

"You putting a tag on her?" Hank hollered over the music.

"Cheap. I've run her as hard as I can. I'm hoping somebody will claim her," Lawrence called back as Hank and the rest of the table laughed broadly.

"Lawrence," said Vicki sharply. "I came over here because I thought we should talk."

Lawrence remained seated with his friends. "What do you want to talk about?" he said innocently.

"What a jerk you are," she said and spun around to leave.

"You know, I can speak French, too," he called after her. "Voulez-vous coucher avec moi?" She left in a huff, walking as fast as her four-inch heels would allow, her satin-coated butt sashaying in such an alluring way that Lawrence had brief pangs of regret.

Louisa sipped from her champagne glass and leaned over to Wick. "Are you going to dance with me or not?"

"I'm not much of a dancer," he said.

"I don't care. You're my date, and I want to dance with you."

He got up and held her chair. It was a slow song, and he was able to put his arm around her and walk around the floor more or less in time to the music. His arm felt good and she smiled up at him. "This isn't so hard, is it?"

"I've done harder things."

"Like what?"

"Finding a swimming pool in the middle of nowhere."

"Huh. That was nothing. I'll tell you something hard: getting this dress on."

Wick clutched her waist a little tighter. "How hard would it be for me to take it off?"

"Are you any good with zippers?"

Wick grinned and opened his mouth to speak but Louisa interrupted him. "No, wait! Don't answer that!" She burst into wind chime laughter.

Norge and Jack watched them dance. "How's long's that been going on?" Norge asked.

"Ever since he bought her a goat."

Norge threw his head back and guffawed.

"Let's get out of here," Wick said.

As they approached the door, the Thoroughbred Retirement Foundation director rushed up to Wick. "Oh, Mr. Keswick, I want to thank you for another wonderful gala."

"You all did the work," he said.

"Everybody loved having their picture taken with the jockeys. That was a great idea!"

"Thank you. I'm glad it worked out." He ushered Louisa out.

When they got to his car, he kissed her, just to see. She kissed him back, sliding her muscled arms up his. "Where are we going?" she asked. "Some place with more champagne, I hope."

"That rules out the Sta*light Motel."

Her laughter this time was a soft, throaty chuckle. She pulled him down where she could nuzzle his jaw and whispered, "My place?"

"You've got a boarder, remember?" He slid a scrap of blue chiffon off her shoulder and ran his tongue down her breast.

"Hmm," she said.

"There's probably some champagne at my house. You okay with that?"

She leaned back and searched his face. "You want to talk about it?"

"No." He pushed her strap back up and opened the car door. "You're off duty, Madre. Get in the car."

Chapter 44

To Lawrence's delight, Shannon slid into the chair next to him. She immediately asked the question *du jour*: "Who's going to win tomorrow?"

"It's pretty wide open. The French horse looks really good, but it's hard to evaluate him without a race on this side of the pond," said Lawrence.

"With all this rain the turf course ought to come up like a European course, so that'll help him," said Hank.

"What about Good Prospect?" asked Shannon

"I know Lawrence loves that horse, but this is a huge step up in class for him," said Hank. "Plus, you're going to put a guy on the horse who's ridden—what?—four? five races? Ortiz and Castellano and Mike Smith—the top jocks in the country—they're not going to open any holes for him."

"It's going to be tough," Lawrence agreed. "Come on, Shannon, let's dance."

Slightly buzzed, they danced several songs.

"Where is Vicki?"

"Apparently she is not only spicking Frawnch, she is, ah, doing Frawnch."

"Oh, I'm sorry."

"Shot down in the prime of my youth." He held her a little closer, ready to whisper something in her ear, when she said, "Omigod. Is that Hank's date? Do you think—?"

"He swears they're real," he said without letting her go.

Shannon leaned back and looked at him quizzically. "Oh!" She laughed an inebriated sort of laugh.

"What were you going to ask?"

"Nothing. Nothing."

He pulled her close again and continued dancing. "Tell me," he said, rubbing her back.

"She doesn't really look like his type."

"Which is?"

"She looks like a guy in drag."

Lawrence choked. It was getting hard to maintain his seductive approach. "I think Hank knows what equipment she has on board."

She shrugged, a delicious wiggle in his arms. "I thought he was gay anyway."

Lawrence cracked up. "Hank? Gay?" He swung her around. "Hank! Hey, come here! You gotta hear this."

Shannon gasped. "No! Lawrence! No! Don't tell him I said that." She squeezed his hand, hard, with a horseman's grip. "Please."

He paused. She was holding his eyes with a look of deep pleading. He found himself attracted to her, not in the usual ironed-hair, big boobs sort of way, but in a slightly different way. There was definitely a carnal element to it: He wanted to kiss her and hold her and, for some reason, touch her face, but there was a strange need to protect her that he was unaccustomed to feeling. They were standing in the middle of the dance floor, still in position. He brushed her cheek with the back of his hand. "Okay."

Hank and his date, laughing and squealing, danced up beside them. "Okay! What's happening?"

"Nothing," said Lawrence. "We're going to leave."

"Ooooo," said Hank and his date in unison.

"No, we're not," said Shannon.

"Ooooo," said Hank and his date again.

"Good night, Hank," said Lawrence and he danced Shannon off in another direction. The vulnerable look was gone, but he still wanted her. "Come on, Shannon. Let's get out of here."

"I can't leave with you. I came with Jimmy. He's my friend and I'm not going to treat him like that."

"Give me a break. He's got jockey groupies all over him."

"Lawrence, I'm not going to be another scalp on your belt. Go get Ashley. She'll sleep with you."

He had, sometime earlier, been thinking of making a run on Ashley, but now that didn't seem like such an attractive option. "That's not what I'm thinking," he protested.

"Right."

Okay, it *was* what he was thinking, but it was different this time. He didn't know what to say. He wanted her every bit as badly as he had wanted, say, Vicki, at one time, but the dynamics were different. He felt a strange sense of desperation. "Let's just go somewhere and talk," he said. "My place is just a few blocks from here…?"

Shannon laughed at him.

He took a deep breath. "Now it's my turn: Please?" He could tell she was wavering. "We can go to your place and you can kick me out whenever you want."

"I'm staying at Louisa's this week."

He paused. "Okay, we'll sit on the doorstep."

"We might have to. We can't keep Louisa up."

Lawrence had a vision of Wick's hand sliding down Louisa's back on the dance floor. "I'll leave whenever she gets home, okay?"

On their way out, Lawrence detoured past the bar and picked up a refill. In the elevator, he said, "Here. Hold this." And when her hand was occupied with the drink, he leaned over to kiss her, holding her gently until the elevator bumped on the ground floor and Virginia Derby rum sloshed down his side.

He swept his jacket, laughing at her. "Nice job."

"I'm sorry!" she snorted, spilling more of the drink.

"I should have known that would be a mistake," he said, taking the glass as they grinned and laughed at each other. "Did you save me any?" He drank most of the remainder and offered the glass back to her.

She finished it and said, "Let's go to the track."

Lawrence looked at his watch. "Freddy's not going to open the gap for training for a few more hours."

"I just like looking at it at night," she said, holding onto his arm and smiling up at him.

He parked behind the paddock and left his jacket in the car. She took off her shoes and they slipped through the forest of satellite dishes to the sandy oval. They were both momentarily distracted from their mutual attraction by the unearthly sight of the racetrack under the nearly-full moon. Floating like an oval halo in the dark, the moonlit silver rail hovered over the hallowed ground. On the far side, the starting gate gave off a luminescent glow. Behind them, the massive grandstand loomed in backlit grandeur.

"It looks like a cathedral for horses, doesn't it?" Shannon said.

Lawrence nodded. As a handicapper, he focused on the mechanics of a horse's performance and tried to compare one horse to another objectively. Despite his success at parsing the Beyer speed numbers and Ragozin sheets and Dosage Index reports, it was factor X, the unquantifiable heart of an athlete, that so often made his parsing useless, but that drew him back to the track each day. Which horse would show that heart tomorrow? Which horse would make him lower his binoculars and forget about his betting tickets, just to watch an amazing display of beauty and talent and heart? It annoyed him the way some handicappers reduced racehorses to a number. "The Six horse." He always knew the names of the horses he picked. It was almost holy what they did on the track and they deserved to have names.

"And you're praying for Good Prospect, right?" he said.

"Yes, aren't you?"

"I'm praying for him but I'm betting the French horse. Come on, let's go get on the tote board," he said.

"We can do that?"

"Best seat in the house." He took her hand and they ran, laughing and stumbling in the sand, across the track to the infield.

Shannon's long dress dragged in the dirt, picking up a sandy edge, the grains shaking off into Lawrence's face as they climbed the ladder to the fenced terrace. On top, she turned all around to peer through the night, and he grabbed her to keep her from tripping and falling, taking the opportunity to kiss her again. She kissed him back eagerly, and he maneuvered her to the fuse box where he could sit and pull her on his knee. It wasn't as comfortable as his apartment, which was air-conditioned and equipped with a bed and a couch, but he decided coming out to the track was okay.

Then Shannon gently pulled away from his mouth, leaned back and said, "Stop. I have to go home now."

Chapter 45

The sun seemed brighter than Shannon had seen it in a long time when she looked out the window of Louisa's RV Derby morning. She had had a wonderful evening at the Derby gala and couldn't wait to savor being in the middle of all the Derby Day excitement.

Jimmy had given her an entrée to meeting the big time jockeys in town for the weekend. Joel Rosario was really hot. They all were. Jimmy was adorably protective of her around the jockeys, but he drifted off with a couple of groupies after dinner. She also enjoyed the attention of several guys she knew on the backstretch, but the best part was being the one Lawrence hung out with after his public break-up with Vicki.

She wasn't sure now why she didn't let him come into the RV after the party. She was surprised to find she had mixed feelings about him. When they were talking about Good Prospect, they were buds, but dancing with Lawrence made her feel different. And kissing him. She closed her eyes at the memory. He was so sexy that it kind of unsettled her. She could handle him in her paddock boots but not an evening dress. And definitely not on top of the tote board. She hoped he wasn't too mad at her.

He'll get over it, she thought, stuffing Lawrence under her pillow along with the fears and worries she went to bed with every night. *Today is Derby Day!*

She fed off the buzz of the big day. The backstretch crackled with anticipation of the race to be run that afternoon. Horsemen lined the rail by the track kitchen, clogged the gap and even milled around the apron with the rail birds on the grandstand side, hoping for a glimpse of the big horses as they came out for a look around or a jog the morning of the race. With her green-striped trainer's license clipped to her belt, Shannon floated around the track as if she owned it, rubbing shoulders with celebrity owners and trainers.

She was taking Acky out with Good Prospect later, but she had a sudden urge to take Bread 'n Butter out now. She combed the straw out of the filly's mane and tail and tacked her up quickly. Bread 'n Butter was used to going out with Carl's filly and balked at leaving the barn alone. Shannon kicked her on and the docile filly relented.

As they jigged up the horse path to the gap, Shannon nodded to returning riders along the way. Walking down the slope to the track, she felt the eyes of the spectators sizing up her and her mount. Bread 'n Butter was a handsome, eye-catching filly and it always gave Shannon a wave of pride to ride out on her.

She heard a wolf whistle and turned to see Darryl and some boys grinning at her. "Hey, you looked hot last night."

She laughed.

"If we take up a collection, will you gallop a horse in that dress?"

"Sorry. It doesn't match my flak jacket."

The rail birds joined the laughter and she jogged off.

She trotted along the outside rail the wrong way, keeping an eye on the horses galloping and breezing the other direction. Their flying hooves made a rhythmic *shu-shu-shush* in the loamy track. After weeks of oppressive heat, the humidity had dropped out overnight and the fresh morning air felt brisk on her bare arms. She jogged standing up, although the filly barely took the bit. Along the filly's sides, her legs sank into grooves, absorbing the gentle shock of each stride.

At the finish line, she stopped and gazed down the long, wide stretch, taking in the rolling scene of dozens of horses galloping towards her in staggered paths of two and three. She eyed a break in the traffic, turned her filly and joined in. As she cantered around the first turn out in the middle of the track, she reveled in the filly's long, smooth stride. What a good mover. She let the filly pick up some speed passing the gap and moved a few paths closer to the rail. Her face was split with a grin and her chest was straining at the flak jacket. God, she loved the track. She loved the sand and the smell of leather and sweet feed and the motion of hundreds of slender legs and the rhythmic nodding of beautiful heads. She loved the horses. Not just her two, but Alice and Good Prospect and every head hanging over the webbing down the shed row. She loved the people, like Rodell and Paco Esteban. Jimmy. She didn't know what he said to Teg, but she felt grateful somehow. And Louisa. Wonderful Louisa. And Lawrence. She had probably screwed things up with him but she dismissed the idea for the time being, remembering how kind he was when she said "no".

This was heaven. How could she be any happier? And how could she bear to leave?

Shannon closed her eyes for a few strides, feeling the energy stoked in the filly's engine. When she opened her eyes, tears poured out of the corners and her chest heaved with sobs. Glancing over her left shoulder for an opening, she steered the filly to the rail and hollered at her. "Go! Go! Go!" Bread 'n Butter broke into a run, racing along the rail as Shannon waved her stick and scrubbed her hands up the filly's neck. Kicking and driving, Shannon drove the filly as hard as she could around the turn and into the stretch. They flashed past horses on the outside working a more leisurely pace. Bread 'n Butter dug in, flattened out and ran as fast as her show ring legs would take her, through the stretch, past the tote board and under the wire.

At some point past the wire, Shannon stopped shouting and let the filly coast. They galloped out past the gap and pulled up halfway down the backstretch. Limp and shaking, tears snaking down her face, Shannon rode to the outside rail and walked the filly to the lower gap, away from the kitchen and the spectators.

Louisa was humming in time with her champagne headache as she fixed keepers and legged Gabriela up on a horse. "Jog one, gallop one," she said. "Manny? You ready?"

Mike joined her as the horses circled the shed row. "You're mighty fresh this morning. What time'd you get in last night?"

"None of your business."

"Just making sure your love life doesn't interfere with your work."

"When my personal life interferes with work, you'll know about it, because I'll be short-coupled and long gone."

"Get back." Mike laughed.

Louisa's cell phone rang and she grabbed it.

"There's your lover-boy."

Louisa walked away, speaking to the hay man. "Yes, we'll need two more loads to get through the meet."

She had finished her second cup of thick black coffee and desperately needed another. Mike would rib her, she knew, but she was going to take the golf cart and go back to the RV for a refill. After all these years she had earned a ten-minute coffee break. To hell with Mike.

Back at the RV, as she waited for the coffee to perk, she looked at the blue chiffon dress tossed on the chair and remembered the magical evening. She tried to chide herself for being so silly at her age, but she gave up and indulged in the pleasant feelings of romance. It wasn't often you got to turn back the clock to your wild and youthful days. Being at the party knowing she looked good and having two men spar over her was a heady feeling. Although she harbored a lifelong attraction to the rough and gritty Croaker Norge, Wick overwhelmed her with his commanding presence and possessive sexuality. She floated away, happy to be possessed. When Wick had unlocked the door and turned on the light, Louisa hesitated to enter Claire's house. But Wick whisked her into the kitchen, found a bottle of champagne in the back of the liquor cabinet and popped it open. Pouring it into some mismatched glasses, he handed her one. They were both buzzed enough that they didn't notice the golden color of the old spoiled champagne, but the taste was unmistakable. Louisa chuckled at the memory of Wick's sour expression. Turned out they didn't need any more champagne anyway.

Girlishly, she poured her coffee and thought about what to wear to the Derby that afternoon.

Life was good.

The horses were doing well. The Rondo filly had run twice and, while she would probably always be antsy about the gate, the situation was manageable. Two three-year-old colts had come to hand, filled out and had a win apiece. Most remarkably, that morning when Louisa looked Ticket Taker deep in his eye, she thought she saw a response, a flicker of understanding about the racetrack and racing. And finally, Alice's Restaurant had had his last swim in the handicapped children's pool; he was coming back to run on Sunday. Louisa was confident Alice would run into the books as a hundred-thousand-dollar-winner and retire more or less sound.

Now that the horses were settling out the way she wanted, leaving her path to retirement clear, she didn't feel the same sense of desperation. The cottage on Mike's farm in Maryland was homey. She thought about her grandmother's mahogany highboy with its hand-carved drawer panels. Scarred from neglect and Louisa's peripatetic lifestyle, the chest was stuffed with fine table linens, tarnished silver trays and bowls and memories of Louisa's social upbringing. It would be hard to find a condominium with ceilings high enough for such a piece. Maybe, Louisa thought, she'd see if she could get a refund on her ticket to Wisconsin.

When Wick dropped Louisa off at her RV at four that morning, the two of them laughed about sneaking around like kids, and he carried her wind-chime laughter with him the rest of the morning. He went home and showered, put on a sports shirt and went back to the track, wondering when pulling an all-nighter would catch up with him. He felt a little hungover but otherwise very very contented. He cruised the track kitchen terrace, Rodell's coffee in hand, greeting horsemen like long-lost friends.

When he saw Mike on his pony, he scanned the area for Louisa. She was not there and he suddenly worried something had happened to her. It took him twenty or thirty minutes to break free from his role as host of the backstretch, but when he strolled into Barn Six, he could see Louisa wasn't there, either.

Mike walked out of the tack room. "You just missed her. She went home for a coffee break."

Wick was embarrassed at being so transparent. "I'm going down to the stakes barn," he said, annoyed that he needed to explain himself to Mike.

"Yeah, right. I'll tell her you came by."

"Thanks," Wick said, since there wasn't anything else to say.

At the stakes barn, he spoke to Graham Motion and Bill Mott, asking what else the track could do for them and their horses. As he was leaving, Jack drove up in a golf cart and said, "Wick, I need you for a minute."

They drove off and Jack said, "The TVG guys and the network guys are fighting over the scaffolding."

"Where are they now?"

"On the frontside. I'll take you over there. Whatever you do, keep TVG happy. They're our day-to-day. We don't see the network but once a year."

"But the network gets us into forty million homes. Gotta keep them both happy."

By the time Wick had the TV crews sorted out, the Turf Club manager was calling him to decide which dignitaries were to be assigned to the ballroom and which ones to the track owner's suite. The Breeders' Cup president and a couple of board members were in attendance, scouting the track as a possible location for the World Championships. Wick needed to make sure they were well taken care of.

When the track closed for training, Wick made a dash back home to dress for the afternoon. He dialed Louisa but got no answer.

Back at the track, Wick made another trip to the Turf Club to check the seating. Then he decided to make a run up to the stewards' stand on top of the grandstand. As he stepped into the stairwell, he heard footsteps and a voice above him echoing down the stairs. "Aw, give the guy a break. His wife's in the hospital three years and don't know him from Adam. Why shouldn't he have some fun?"

The door at the top closed, cutting off the reply.

Wick stood at the bottom of the stairwell, contemplating the overheard remark. *Fun?* he thought. Was that what he had with Louisa? Somehow it seemed more than the transient frivolity implied by the word "fun." And people thought he deserved "fun" because Claire didn't know him? It was a shock to hear someone say that out loud. Claire knew him, she knew he was there, she had to know he was there. Wick stared at the blank wall. Did Claire know about Louisa? He tried not to think about Louisa's taut body entwined with his, her wind-chime laughter muffled as he nuzzled her neck. He had a woman in his bed for the first time in years and he was deliciously, guiltily reliving the sweaty night when his cell phone went off.

Automatically, he answered it. "Yeah?"

"Mr. Keswick, the mutuels manager needs you."

"Be right there."

Chapter 46

The backstretch of a racetrack runs on hope, but the jocks' room runs on testosterone. The jockeys' locker room at a racetrack is like the caged arena where tigers are collected just offstage. Fifteen or twenty fit, strong athletes spend the afternoon confined to a large room, each with his own perch in view of the others, each with his own barely contained competitive streak, the tension broken every thirty minutes as half of them leave to perform on the big stage. The atmosphere today was charged but restrained as the Colonial Downs jockey colony reacted with both bravado and deference to the presence of half a dozen big name jockeys. Some of the older riders quietly went about their routine while the younger ones sparred and bantered.

After riding a handful of races the previous two weeks, Jimmy had just barely learned the routine. He was still amazed to find himself in the rarified atmosphere of the professional jockeys' locker room. Now he was sitting on the bench next to the nation's leading jockey, Irad Ortiz, their attenuated legs identically bandaged with a safety pin high up on the outside, their feet identically shod in black shower slippers. Earlier he shot a game of pool with Edgar Prado, who had gotten his start at Colonial years before. These guys were the best in the game. Some, like Mike Smith, were considered among the best ever, and he, Jimmy Wiseman, was fixing to walk out on the track and ride with them.

Against them, he reminded himself.

Ortiz made small talk. Mostly Jimmy just nodded and smiled. He was still kind of light-headed from the night before. He didn't know what happened to Shannon, but he ended up in a motel room in Richmond with two or three girls and another guy, who had some coke. He was already pretty buzzed from the open bar, but the coke really wired him. He finally got back to his room after daylight, but he was too spun up to sleep. He couldn't remember whether he vomited up his dinner the night before or not, and he was worried about his weight. He had worked hard to shed twenty pounds in the past three weeks—with a little help from Teg's drug store—and he was anxious that he might have blown it at the last minute. When he got to the track in the early afternoon, he went straight to the scales. Two pounds over. He'd have to sit in the sauna and sweat it off. He could sip a little water, nothing more, till after the race. Fortunately, he wasn't hungry. He was pumped. He smiled and nodded at Ortiz, not really listening.

The paddock before the Virginia Derby was crowded and festive. Shannon left Carl with his entourage of family, friends and grooms and drifted towards the handicappers' table, wanting to see Lawrence but uncertain what his reaction would be. Did he think she had been a tease? Too bad if he did, because she couldn't take the nasty feeling she had after Teg again. But Teg was a sleaze and Lawrence was…kind. She decided to avoid him after all and was sidling through the crowd towards the gate when he called her name. As she looked around, he waved her over.

"What are you looking so mad about? Hungover?" he asked.

Relieved by his teasing tone, she leaned happily on the edge of their table under the awning. "I've felt better. But what a great party."

"How's your roomie? What time'd she get in?"

Shannon grinned. "She tiptoed in about four."

Both men whooped. "Didn't know the old guy had it in him."

"Probably took him all night to get it up."

Shannon punched Lawrence's shoulder. "Y'all are so bad!"

Hank nodded at Lawrence. "He's just jealous, since he didn't score last night."

Lawrence made an obscene gesture behind his hand.

Amidst the banter, Shannon felt a rush of affection for Lawrence.

"Talk about old guys… That guy Croaker Norge was unbelievable."

"I about peed in my pants when he dropped trou."

"What?!" Shannon's mouth fell open.

"Yeah, Hank's date was showing him her tattoo. It's on the back of her thigh, and she hiked her dress up."

"And Norge thought she was mooning him, so he said, 'Check this out,' and dropped trou."

"He has a tattoo on his thigh of a rearing stallion."

"Well, it's kind of a droopy looking gelding now," said Hank, and the three of them doubled over laughing.

The camera man walked by and signaled them.

"Ready?" Hank said.

Lawrence nodded and grabbed Shannon's hand. "Don't go away. This won't take long."

She stepped back to watch. The cameras closed in and Hank said, "Good afternoon, ladies and gentlemen. I'm Hank May here at Colonial Downs with handicapper Lawrence Hamner. We're here to talk about this talented field for the Virginia Derby. Lawrence, you're hot today. You've had five winners and two trifectas. Everyone wants to know: Who do you like in the Derby?"

Jimmy didn't know how these other jocks stood the sauna. It had taken him forever to sweat off a pound and a half. When he opened the door, his legs were so shaky he couldn't stand up. Ricky, one of the valets, gave him a hand as he stumbled out.

"Whoa, Wiseman. How long you been in there?"

"Two hours," he mumbled.

"Man, you can't do that kind of time till you get used to it. Be careful."

He sat quietly off to the side, sipping ice water until he recovered some semblance of energy. It was tough, but it would be worth it when he made the weight. The only thing worse than agonizing over his weight was the pressure of waiting for post time. The other riders had mounts in some of the earlier races, but Jimmy had nothing to do but worry and daydream until the Derby.

The clerk stuck his head in the locker room and called, "Ninth race, gentlemen," startling Jimmy from his reverie. He trudged to the front of the building, where Ricky handed him his saddle for the weigh-out. The clerk of scales barely let the needle settle before waving him along. When he stepped off the scales, Ricky took his saddle and handed him a cup of Red Bull. "Drink this or you're gonna be too weak to ride."

Jimmy tried to refuse it, but Ricky insisted. "Hey, man. You already crossed the scales."

He took a few sips and was surprised at how much better he felt right away.

Jimmy joined the other Derby riders in their blues and reds and greens as they filed out of the door to the paddock. He found Mr. Starling and met his family and a lot of other people. Then they stood on the edge of the grassy oval, watching the horses parade around under tack. He slapped his stick against his hand as Mr. Starling spoke about race strategy and how he wanted Good Prospect ridden. Jimmy heard none of it. Although he was concerned about riding a good race on a talented horse, he was too excited to absorb any instructions. He, Jimmy Wiseman, was riding in the Virginia Derby, a million-dollar race, with the likes of Edgar Prado and Irad Ortiz. He had weighed out at the proper weight and dressed out in Carl Starling's brilliant red and yellow silks. And, he had a fast horse who was a contender.

He practically floated up to the saddle when the paddock judge called, "Riders up!"

Across the paddock, Wick chatted with trainer Ferris Allen. He was running out of steam. Jack had given him some energy drink that jazzed him up but didn't make him feel any better. He hoped Bill Mott's horse won because his owner was getting on a plane and leaving immediately afterwards. He planned on being right behind him.

Wick worked his way around the grassy oval, trying to speak to each owner. He shook Carl's hand and wished him luck. Carl's horse looked good. It'd be a hell of a story if that colt beat all the big boys.

As Wick made his way through the packed paddock, he kept an eye out always for Louisa. She was so little, though, that it was hard to find her in a crowd. As the bugler blew "Call to the Post" and the horses filed onto the track, he was swept out of the paddock with Mott and his owner. Wick ushered them to their table in the Turf Club and stepped away to the men's room. As he exited the men's room, he heard a voice from a nearby office say, "If you want to see the boss, you gotta catch him early, because he leaves at two for his afternoon delight."

Wick frowned and hurried back to his guests in time to see the horses approaching the gate.

Chapter 47

Settling onto Good Prospect's back yanked Jimmy back to reality. As the pony person led the colt, Jimmy knotted his reins, then adjusted his irons, standing up and making sure his legs were tight along the horse's sides.

It felt good to have something to do at last.

The colt jigged through the post parade and then the pony person said, "Okay, jock, now what?"

"Easy," Jimmy said.

They cantered away. Good Prospect felt fresh. Carl had done a good job getting him ready despite the detour in his training schedule. The race two weeks ago had sharpened him up, and Jimmy could tell he was bursting to run. He was bursting to run, himself. As they gathered behind the gate on the turf course, Jimmy was so excited he wanted to pee, even though he knew there wasn't an excess drop of moisture anywhere in his body.

Good Prospect, breaking from the second stall, entered calmly. There was an agonizing wait while the others loaded, then the Three horse, next to him, started acting up. Finally, there was a split second of stillness all down the line and the starter rang the bell. The gates slammed open. Fourteen sets of hindquarters sank down as hooves dug into the ground and twenty-eight hind legs coiled and uncoiled, hurling seven tons of horseflesh onto the race course.

"And they're off!" Hank May shouted from the announcer's booth.

The One and the Ten, the speed horses, shot to the front and Jimmy slid over for a ground-saving trip along the rail. With his position established early, Jimmy let the colt run easily through the first turn. They rolled down the backstretch with Jimmy marveling at the colt's amazing, oiled movement. The smooth undulation of his stride nearly rocked Jimmy to sleep. The shouting of the other riders and the hoof beats of the horses seemed like so much highway traffic outside his window at night. He enjoyed the ride.

Then, there was a detectable change in the noise and the feel of his horse as they swung around the turn at the head of the stretch.

Jimmy could not figure out what was happening. The horses around and in front of him seemed like a pile of rubber duckies bobbing on the water. He was floating in the midst of a large mat of brightly colored water toys that was drifting along in front of the grandstand. Now the mat was breaking up and the pod he was in drifted backwards.

The roar of the crowd in the grandstand shook him out of this dreamy sequence and he was startled to realize he was on a horse running thirty-five miles an hour, a horse who felt ready to explode. Jimmy took back slightly to keep from clipping the heels of the horse directly in front. He desperately looked for an opening in the wall of horses slowing up in front of him. It was solid. However, the horse to his right had fallen back and he moved Good Prospect to the outside, looking for a way around the herd in front. Finally, far out in the middle of the track, seven or eight paths off the rail, Jimmy and Good Prospect found daylight.

The chestnut colt responded to his jockey's urging, leaping through the stretch with awesome acceleration.

Up in the boxes, Lawrence watched the journeymen jockeys keep the apprentice trapped between and behind horses throughout the race. Now that Jimmy finally had running room, Lawrence lowered his glasses and watched Good Prospect make his monster move, admiring the raw speed. *This might be the best horse that's ever been on this track.* It was the most beautiful thing he'd ever seen, better even than watching the legendary Rembrandt's Paint. One box over, Louisa held her fist to her mouth. Behind her, Shannon and Carl's groomettes jumped up and down screaming, "*Go! Go!*" Even Carl abandoned his reserved demeanor and shook his rolled-up program in encouragement.

Jimmy had never ridden so fast in his life. When Good Prospect won the New Kent Stakes, Jimmy felt as though they were skimming over the surface of the grass. But now the horse was working so hard, driving forward with every muscle and tendon, that Jimmy was afraid he'd outrun his feet. With instinctive skill, Jimmy balanced himself and his horse. Sensing that Good Prospect was giving his utmost, he merely waved his whip.

Two bay horses had hooked up in a stretch duel along the rail, but Good Prospect and Jimmy were gaining on them as though they were tied to the ground. He crouched over the chestnut neck, chirping and shoving as the colt's mane flapped in his face.

Screams issued from every throat in the grandstand as the spectators urged the horses to try harder, reach farther, run faster. The run down the long Colonial stretch seemed to be off the clock, the horses galloping in place, racing furiously but never reaching the finish line. The pair on the rail were galloping stride for stride, but out in the middle of the track, Good Prospect seemed to be traveling on a laser beam.

From the Turf Club to the apron, fans were out of their seats, shouting and stomping their feet. The pandemonium of fifteen thousand screaming fans blew across the track like a hurricane, then suddenly dropped out as the horses crossed the line. The riders stood up and coasted around the turn in silence.

The infield tote board blinked "photo".

Shannon leaned past several people and grabbed Lawrence's shoulder. "Did he make it?"

Lawrence, watching the replay on the infield screen, shook his head. "I don't think so."

Shannon joined the rest of the murmuring crowd, watching the replay yet again, waiting for the official results. *Oh please,* she prayed, *let Jimmy and Carl win.* She had ventured two dollars across the board with the racetracker's belief that such tangible support would genuinely help the horse. After all they had been through, Shannon felt they deserved to win. It was probably as good a reason to bet as any other.

As the horses galloped out, Louisa watched not the replay but the horse and rider. She was proud of her laconic exercise rider-turned-jockey. Win, place or show, it was an incredible accomplishment. Less than a month ago, Jimmy had never ridden a race and Good Prospect wouldn't even go to the track to train. And here they were in a photo finish at the Virginia Derby. It was a glorious day for all the people and horses in her life. Louisa's eyes were on the pair as they glided around the turn. Curiously, the horse was drifting to the outside rail. Then he threw his head up as though the bit had been yanked in his mouth. Louisa saw Jimmy slumped on the horse's neck and then sliding off head first. Jimmy's soft boot hung briefly in the stirrup, spooking the horse. The colt's reflexive jerk loosened Jimmy's foot and he crumpled to the turf.

Watching the stretch drive from the balcony of the Turf Club, Wick, who had money on several horses in various combinations, shouted "Go!" with the rest of the crowd and privately hoped the 4-6-2 trifecta would come in. As the horses surged under the wire, the "photo" light came on immediately, but to Wick's practiced eye Graham Motion's horse beat Bill Mott's by a nose. Good Prospect was a fast-closing third. Damn, Wick thought, Carl nearly pulled it off. He leaned over to the next table and congratulated Motion's owners and prepared to guide them down to the winner's circle for the trophy presentation. As he did, he heard the collective gasp of the crowd and looked to see a jockey down and a loose horse. It was a chestnut with the white saddlecloth of the Two horse. Good Prospect. *Not again,* Wick thought.

The ambulance that followed the field all through the race was already there and attendants rushed to the fallen jockey. Wick noted he was not moving. He looked for the horse and saw one of the outriders pick him up. Down below him, several people ducked under the rail and ran out onto the track. Wick recognized among them the figure of Louisa Ferncliff.

PART VI

Chapter 48

The paramedics with the New Kent volunteer rescue squad had a pretty good idea what they were dealing with, and they had IVs with fluids ready to attach to both of Jimmy's arms as soon as they got him in the ambulance. They rolled the limp body carefully onto a board and immobilized the spinal column. Too many paraplegic jockeys out there.

"Probably hasn't had anything to eat in a week," grunted one of the medics as he helped load the board into the back.

Louisa was hovering around. "Can I come with you?"

"Sit over there," said one medic without looking up. The two men continued to work over Jimmy with practiced efficiency, securing the board, attaching monitors.

"Can I go?" the driver called out.

"Lemme get a vein," the medic called back.

Jimmy, semi-conscious, made painful breathing sounds while the medics probed his arms for a vein.

"You got anything?"

"Nope. Get the gun."

Ripping the garish yellow silks open, the medic set a nail gun against Jimmy's breastbone and pulled the trigger. There was a muffled pneumatic thump, Jimmy's body jerked and Louisa gasped. Quickly the medic attached a tube to the needle in Jimmy's chest.

"Ready?"

"Now!"

Louisa saw fluid flowing through the tube. She could see Jimmy's face, his sunken cheeks a grotesque gray. She laid a hand on his leg. It was cold. The monitor above showed an irregular heartbeat.

"All right, Marty, drive."

The ambulance spun away on the sandy track, heading for the gap. One of the medics radioed the emergency room. "This is New Kent. We're fifteen minutes away with heat stroke, collapsed veins, arrhythmia."

"This your kid?" asked one of the medics, raising his voice above the siren.

Louisa nodded. He was one of *la Madre's* charges. She had encouraged him to follow his dream and now he had come to grief. She had ignored Jimmy as he wasted away each day before her eyes, as he took more and more desperate measures to shed the weight. How many riders had she seen wrestle with the sirens of the racetrack? *Come ride these glorious steeds. Feel the rush of speed, the nobility of heart, the zeitgeist of victory. But you must be diaphanous. Airy. Light as an angel's wing.*

And they sell, not their souls, but their bodies to do it. She knew even the greatest riders, the hall-of-famers, had not so much avoided the demons as survived and renounced them.

Looking at Jimmy's deathly appearance, Louisa thought of the irony that everyone envied jockeys. Everyone who worked around racehorses wanted to feel the thrill of riding a brilliant horse in a race but everyone ignored the price of the ride.

This part of racing she wouldn't miss.

Unbidden, the thought of missing Wick leaped into her tired mind. She already missed him. They hadn't spoken since he dropped her off at four that morning, a thousand years ago, and she missed him. She wanted to feel his reassuring arm around her. She needed his shoulder to lean on. She let herself drift into memories of moments with Wick. For all his gruffness and short temper around the track, he was full of kindness. A smile tried to move the corners of her mouth as she remembered Wick ranting about goats before going out to buy her one. Or Wick telling her he was holding a table in the Turf Club and then becoming angry when she politely turned him down. Or his insistence on picking her up for the gala. *Like a real date*. He was so kind to her she didn't know what to make of it. She'd never had a man treat her like that.

By the time the tote board flashed the official order of finish, Shannon and Lawrence were both out on the track, asking Freddy and Bones about Jimmy. Good Prospect was safely in the hands of Parson the groom, and Carl was walking back to the barn with his horse. He alternated between worry over Jimmy and stunned joy at dead-heating for second with a horse trained by his idol, Bill Mott.

Shannon and Lawrence walked back to the paddock. "I want to go to the hospital, but I don't know where it is," she said.

"Let me get Hank to do the last race by himself and I'll take you."

"My car's right here."

Shannon tossed stuff in the back seat to make room for a passenger. As they drove off, Lawrence said, "Man, I thought my car was bad. Do you live in this thing?"

"It's my mobile home," Shannon said lightly.

"Where *do* you live? With Louisa?"

"I'm just staying with Louisa while I look for another place. I was, uh, staying at the Sta*light."

"Pretty rough place."

"You do what you gotta do."

When Shannon and Lawrence walked into the emergency room, they found Louisa holding a clipboard and expecting Wick to show up. "Oh thank heavens," she said.

"How bad is it?" Shannon asked, taking both of Louisa's hands in hers.

"Concussion…collarbone… His heart is what they're worried about. Very irregular. And his kidneys are trying to shut down. They nearly lost him in the ambulance."

"I begged him to be careful," said Shannon, near tears.

"Me, too," said Louisa. The two women shared their anguish.

"I knew when I looked at him last night he had to be flipping or doing drugs."

"Pretty hard to lose twenty pounds in three weeks any other way," Lawrence said.

Louisa sighed and held out the clipboard. "You'll have to help me fill this out."

They sat and worked on the forms. "What about insurance?" Shannon asked.

"Mike has some on everybody, but I don't think it will cover this, because he wasn't riding for Mike when he got hurt," Louisa said.

"Let's put it down anyway."

As they sat and waited for word, Lawrence noticed how old Louisa looked. He had never thought of her as old. The racetrack has no hierarchy based on age, just skill. But her hair was coming loose in long white locks, her face was lined and tired and her eyes had a sunken, aged look. Her copper bracelet looked too big.

"Louisa," he said, "we might be here awhile. I'm going to get us a drink and some chips or something. Is there anything special you want?"

She was too tired to speak, just shaking her head and waving her hand.

He and Shannon exchanged looks. "I'll go with you."

Outside, Shannon said, "Good thing we're at a hospital."

"Don't you think she ought to go home? If you take her, I'll stay here."

"If we can make her leave."

When they got back with a milkshake, orange juice, a Coke, hot dogs and fries, Mike and Carl were sitting on each side of Louisa. She took the Coke and a few fries.

"Any word?"

"No."

They sat and waited, talking about the day. They congratulated Carl on Good Prospect's race, but he seemed embarrassed to talk about it. "Jimmy worked so hard on that horse. He stuck with him. He took a chance jogging on the horse path. Then he promised me he'd make the weight for the race." Carl shook his head.

"It's not your fault," said Louisa.

"Yeah," said Mike. "He was already riding races for me."

"The lure of the races is irresistible," said Carl.

"All them jocks, they do anything to ride," said Mike.

A nurse approached them. "Jimmy Wiseman's family?"

Mike stood up. "We're it."

Chapter 49

When Wick woke up, it took him a few minutes to figure out where he was. He recalled the day's events: the night with Louisa, the press of issues on Derby day, Good Prospect's monster move in the race, Louisa in the ambulance with Jimmy Wiseman, Motion's owners in the winner's circle. He had finally gotten free about seven-thirty or eight. He stopped by the house, intending to go on to the hospital, but the toll of the all-nighter finally caught up with him. He sat down in his den for a moment, looking for a replay of the Derby, and the next thing he knew, it was four a.m. and he was waking up in the easy chair while TVG showed races from Australia.

After a moment, he turned off the TV and went into the bedroom. He lay down on the bed, the covers disheveled from the night before, and stared at the ceiling.

What was he doing? He had been unfaithful to his wife. Claire, his beloved Claire, the mother of their children. It seemed unthinkable, and yet he did not feel guilty. The evening at the gala and the night at home in bed with Louisa had been exciting, but also, at the time, natural. How did that happen? When did it start? When they found the swimming pool and she told him the day would come when he would have to let go? Or when they kissed and letting go became a reality?

Louisa was right, as she was about so many things. Wick understood why people leaned on *la Madre*. He had, too. But lately there had been a change in her. Ever since their fight over her talk of moving to Wisconsin to be near the Green Bay Packers—Wick shook his head at the idea—she had softened in ways he couldn't describe. As angry and hurt as he had been that day, the argument had focused his desire to have her, to take care of her, to love her. Norge's revelations about her past had intensified his feelings. But how did Louisa feel?

And what, exactly, was he prepared to do?

Claire was his wife, for better or worse, and he would not treat her with disrespect. He wrestled with terms to describe his feelings for Louisa. Like? Lust? Respect? He kept coming back to "love," but then he would reject it because that word applied to Claire. He had always been contemptuous of anybody's claim to love two women at the same time. And yet here he was in that box. It was frustrating. Frustrating because he didn't know the rules.

Sometimes you gotta forget the rules and look at the people.

As the light began to seep into the room, Wick made up his mind. He got up, showered and dressed and went to his car. Pausing, he went back inside the house and got a jacket and a tie. As he drove away, he hit speed dial on his phone.

"Yes, I know it's early. Don't get her up. I'll go to her room."

It felt strange walking through the sliding doors at the Norfolk Living Home Health Care Center without a bouquet of fresh flowers. The Sunday receptionist was strange, too.

"May I help you, sir?"

"I'm Boyd Keswick. I called earlier."

The receptionist smiled. "Of course. Mrs. Keswick is in her room."

It occurred to Wick that he didn't know her room number. They always brought her to the sunroom for his visits. "Uh…"

The receptionist continued to smile with professional compassion. "Room 312. The elevators are to your left."

The chunk of the elevator doors and the whirr of the motor reminded Wick of a TV documentary about robots and artificial intelligence. When asked why he had given his robot a human name, one of the scientists said, "Well, he's half alive."

When Wick reached room 312, he found the door open. Standing in the doorway, he watched his wife sleep, her hair matted against her head, light puffs of mortality making her lips tremble rhythmically. He stood there until an attendant came by and said, "You can go in."

He looked at the attendant and back at his wife. "I was just leaving."

At nine, when Wick knocked on the kitchen door in Virginia Beach, two small children looked up and squealed, "Pop-Pop!"

Boyd Junior opened the door. "Dad! What are you doing here?"

He walked in and hugged the grandchildren. "I needed a break and thought I'd come down and go to church and spend the day with you all."

"You want some coffee? Have you had breakfast?"

"That'd be great, but don't go to any trouble." He sat down and let them fuss over him.

"Everything the same with Mom?" Boyd Junior's voice had a studied casualness.

Wick adopted the same tone. "More or less."

Boyd Junior's wife set a mug of coffee in front of him. He looked at the plates with cold eggs and toast crust, the sippy cup on the floor, the cat rubbing his leg, the earnest little face of his granddaughter. He smiled a little sadly. "She's gone."

"Gone?" Boyd asked with surprise. "When?"

Wick looked at his son curiously. "I'm not sure."

Chapter 50

Jimmy's accident cast a pall over the entire racetrack. On Sunday morning the barns were a little quieter, the joshing restrained. Horsemen discussed the uncertainty of the rider's condition in hushed tones. No place was more subdued, however, than the jocks' room. Normally a mood of high spirits prevailed, with one or two jockeys talking trash, someone throwing cards in the air and a couple of valets teaming up for a practical joke on some apprentice or newcomer. But when Marjorie, the track chaplain, arrived for pre-post prayers at eleven, she was pleasantly surprised to find every rider and every valet in attendance. Even the ones who normally read the Racing Form or played pool at that hour bowed their heads and joined the petition for heavenly protection. She accepted the participation of everyone without questioning whether the service was simply one of a range of possible ways to satisfy the overwhelming, superstitious urge racetrackers had to ward off bad luck. She adhered firmly to the practical notion that deeper feelings often developed from the repetition of rites, and she welcomed notorious non-believers and lapsed Catholics.

Louisa and Shannon made a quick trip to the hospital to check on Jimmy. He slept tethered by tubes and wires to a blinking battery of mechanical nurses. The floor nurse translated Jimmy's chart, telling them how near to death he had come overnight. "He seems stabilized now," she said. "The doctor can tell you more when he gets here."

The two horsewomen stared helplessly at the pale figure beneath the sheet.

"He's a pretty strong guy," Shannon said.

Louisa shook her head, wondering what was going to happen to him.

Driving back, Shannon chattered about Jimmy and his future as a jockey while Louisa brooded. She said little as they took Mike's truck and trailer out to the camp to get Alice's Restaurant and the goat. They packed all the equipment, leaving only the round pen for a second trip. "Last trip, boy," Louisa said as Alice loaded expectantly. She gave him some grapefruit. "See? He knows he's going to race."

She thought about everyone who needed her care. Maybe Wisconsin was a foolish idea. She had to stay and take care of Alice, Jimmy and all the rest. Did that include Wick? She didn't know. She hadn't seen or heard from him since the night of the gala. When she left the track, what would happen to her relationship with Wick?

She jerked herself up. What relationship? The man was married. It was just a fling, a night of escape for two lonely people. You could never win against a wife. The fact that his wife was sick and dying made it even harder. He wouldn't leave Claire—and to be honest, she wouldn't like him if he did. He would just keep screwing her and feeling guilty. If she let him.

Louisa rubbed her face with both hands. It was another one of her bad decisions. Drinking did it every time.

Alice was on his toes in the paddock and Louisa smiled at him fondly. Jesus was riding in Delaware that day, so Raphine Steele had the ride.

"I remember this old boy," Raphine said to Mike. "Breaks fast."

"You got it."

"Thanks for riding me," she said.

"Just bring him home," Mike said.

Louisa found herself studying Raphine's face. Was she drawn? Had she reduced too hard? Would she be all right? Would Alice be in good hands?

Watching Alice warm up, trying to jerk free from the pony person and bolt down the track, Louisa smiled to herself. *Enjoy yourself, boy. One last time.*

It was a bittersweet moment and Louisa kept herself dwelling on the sweet part. Alice was leaving the races today. This was the end of his career. He was going into retirement, where he belonged. And he would be happy this time, she told herself forcefully.

She looked across the track to the starting gate, where the horses milled around. Suddenly, she had a horrible premonition. This was the moment she had feared for months. The knee was going to blow. This was the race.

"Mike, you've got to stop him!"

"What?"

"Scratch Alice!"

"Louisa, have you lost your mind? The horses are in the gate."

The bell rang, ominously, it seemed to Louisa. She bit her lip and watched helplessly.

Alice, as usual, seemed to burst from the gate a step early. He barreled down the backstretch as the other horses settled into position beside and behind him. Louisa watched Alice's green blinkers on the huge infield screen with a sense of doom.

Why had she let Mike run the horse again? His knee was going to blow out. He would stumble and fall, perhaps injuring Raphine. He would get up and hobble around on three legs in adrenaline-fueled determination until someone caught the reins. The horse ambulance would trundle around to the fatal spot, the crew quickly erecting a screen. And after a few minutes, the ambulance would trundle away and the track would be empty. Her life would have another gaping wound just like the one left by the black mare.

The horses were nearing the quarter pole at the top of the stretch and Louisa could see Alice's legs now, churning, reaching and grabbing the dirt. She felt the jarring of each stride, the concussion to every joint: ankle, knee, shoulder. The pounding became heavier as the horses neared the wire. Alice pinned his ears as he fought off a challenge on the outside. Then a horse ranged up beside him on the rail. Alice dug in and pumped out every drop of blood in his fourteen-year-old heart. At the wire, he lunged ahead, sticking out his skinny neck as though he knew it would take a head bob to win.

Mike threw up his arms and cheered, then pounded Louisa on the back. "Did you see that son of a gun stick his nose out at the wire? Who says horses are dumb?"

Mike started to leave the box and go to the winner's circle, but Louisa was still watching the horse gallop out. Over in front of the track kitchen on the far side, Raphine eased Alice to a stop, turned him around and let him lope back to the grandstand. Louisa waited, breathless, until they came around the turn and she had a clear view of the old gelding's legs. He slowed to a jog. Every leg stepped in precise synchronization.

She finally heard Mike's voice. "Louisa? Are you coming with me or are you just going to stand there and cry?"

Louisa looked out over the racetrack, tears snaking down her face. All the emotion she had lavished on racing for years came pouring out of her eyes. She wept for the courage and class of the horse. She wept for the grace of the god who bound the tissues of Alice's knee together. She wept for Alice's heart and the joy of victory.

But then she wept for her own heart.

She would take Alice to the farm and then what? She could go to Wisconsin but it wouldn't make any difference. Wick was right. *You think a goddam football team cares about you?* She was alone. The Packers couldn't fill the void and neither could Alice. *There's no life outside the track.* Wick was right about that, too.

On his way to the winner's circle, Mike waved to Shannon. "Come on, girl. You earned a piece of this." She joined Mike, Louisa, Alice, Raphine and all of the barn help in the win photo. Mike's farm manager, the actual owner of the horse, had driven down from Maryland. The racing office surprised them with a celebration of Alice's triumph. Jack Delaney opened a bottle of champagne, and Hank May and Lawrence held up a pre-printed banner that read: Alice's Restaurant, $100,000 winner, 139 starts, 32 wins, new track records at Colonial Downs, Charles Towne and Mountaineer Park. Several photographers recorded the festive scene, which included a crowd of horsemen and fans who had followed Alice's career and cheered the old campaigner at multiple tracks.

At last, the groom led the horse away to the post-race test barn, while his admirers lingered in the afterglow of victory.

Mike, who was always excited about a win, became unusually animated about this one. He circled the paddock, shaking hands, accepting kudos, thanking grooms. When he got to Louisa, he said, "Whatever you and Wick did to that horse out in the woods sure as hell worked."

Louisa looked nostalgically after the horse being led away. "You wouldn't believe what he did."

"Wick or Alice?"

"Alice."

Mike looked around. "Where the hell *is* Wick?"

Louisa looked uncomfortable and Shannon jumped in, "What happens to Alice now? Will he go back to the farm right away?"

"Yeah, next time we've got a trailer going that way. Coupla days," said Mike, staring at Louisa.

"What would you think if I took him home tomorrow?" Louisa asked. "I'd like to get him settled myself."

"Sure." Without turning, Mike reached out and patted Raphine as she walked past. "Thanks, girl," he said, still watching Louisa. "You coming back?"

She looked across the infield to the long line of stable roofs showing through the fringe of trees along the horse path. Somewhere on the backstretch waited a trailer rig that would take her and Alice away from the racetrack and end the life they both loved. "I'm not sure."

Chapter 51

Shannon had bet on Alice with caution this time, and she was happy to cash a small ticket. Lawrence left the winner's circle with her and suggested they go to the hospital and then dinner together. Shannon immediately expanded the invitation to include Louisa.

"Thanks, but I need sleep more than anything," Louisa said. "Tell Jimmy I'll be in to see him tomorrow."

Lawrence was relieved.

He wanted to put his arm around Shannon as they walked to the car but it didn't seem to be quite the moment. Having her in the car next to him, though, gave him a sense of accomplishment. That, plus the solid handicapping advice he had provided bettors that day: six out of ten winners, the daily double and two trifectas. He practically burned up his laptop reviewing old races the last week but he proved he could handicap with the best of them.

"I can't believe you didn't pick Alice for his last race," Shannon chided him, punching his arm.

He stopped himself from grabbing her and pulling her closer. "That's why girls don't make good handicappers."

"Why?"

"Because you bet with your heart."

"I did not! I knew Alice could beat those nags."

"Because of what? His bullet workouts?" he teased.

She was insistent. "I knew he wouldn't let Louisa down."

"And the horse knew she wanted him to hit a hundred thousand?"

Shannon shook her head. "No, because of Wick."

"What do you mean? It looked like they were having a pretty good time Friday night."

"That's what she's worried about."

Lawrence laughed. "Aren't they kind of old to worry about 'Will you respect me in the morning?'"

"It's more than that. I don't think she thought she would care so much."

Lawrence glanced at her. "Sometimes that happens."

Shannon smoothed her khaki skirt and studied the highway signs. "Is this a date?"

"It's whatever you want it to be."

She didn't respond. He took the exit for the hospital. "I just hope Jimmy's all right," she said. "I'm really worried about him."

"You've got a full time job worrying about your friends. What about you?"

"Oh, I'm fine," she said lightly. "I don't have a broken heart or a broken collarbone."

That's a pretty low standard, he thought.

At the hospital, they learned Jimmy had improved enough to move out of the ICU into a regular room. When they found him, Jimmy was propped up in bed staring out the window.

"Hey, guy, how're you doing?" Shannon said with hospital-voice cheeriness.

"Hi, Shannon," the patient whispered. "Lawrence."

Shannon sat on the edge of the bed. "I sure am glad to see you sitting up talking. We were so worried."

"I'm okay."

"What does the doc say?"

Jimmy looked out the window. "I'm okay."

"You gotta get back soon. Bread 'n Butter's ready to run again, and I want you to ride her."

As Shannon ran off at the mouth, Jimmy warmed up a little. Lawrence leaned against the wall, watching the two of them: Shannon, dealing with her own problems, trying to cheer that poor busted-up jockey. A jock's life was hard and then he did stupid things to make it harder. Lawrence had always shrugged off the self-destructiveness of race riders, but he'd never seen the results close up. Jockeys walked big but they looked small under a hospital blanket. Diuretics and aggressive weight loss had made the skin on Jimmy's skull and neck look like parchment. It seemed like the tubes in his arms were sucking the strength out of his slack muscles. He was the poster boy for big dreams and bad decisions.

"Hey, Lawrence," Jimmy said, forcing his voice above a hoarse whisper.

"Yeah, man."

"I'm sorry I screwed up."

"Shoot, Jimmy, you didn't do anything."

"I know you wanted to see that horse win."

Lawrence smiled easily. "Listen, Wiseman, you did a hell of a job getting that horse to the race in the first place. You know he dead-heated for second with Bill Mott's horse?"

Jimmy smiled weakly.

"Carl hasn't come down off the cloud yet. You're a star, man."

Jimmy looked out the window again.

Shannon patted his arm. "You hurry up and get well. Everybody's thinking about you."

"Yeah," said Lawrence, "you can eat all the hospital food you want. No way you'll gain weight on that stuff."

Jimmy smiled again and raised one tube-festooned hand.

At the City Bar, proprietor David Napier seated Lawrence and his date at Lawrence's usual pre-seduction table. They had cocktails and then a very nice cabernet with dinner. David brought them Lawrence's signature after-dinner drink. David did his part, but Lawrence was having a hard time executing his normal seductive routine.

For one thing, he couldn't get hold of Shannon's hand to stroke it sensuously. For another, he kept being distracted by the conversation. He related to her college dropout-racetrack runaway story, but, where he had coasted along skimming the cream with his knack for picking horses, she had worked her butt off to support a couple of horses in addition to herself. And she had moved them from Florida to Virginia, where she didn't know a living soul. And she couldn't be more than twenty-one, twenty-two.

"I thought your folks were into horses."

She rolled her eyes. "They sent me on the show circuit, but they never came to watch."

"But they're supporting you at the track?"

She stared at the wine glass, running her finger around the rim and making it sing. "Can we talk about something else?"

"Sure. None of my business." He signaled David for the check.

She continued anyway. "My dad called and he's coming to see me next week," she said, still playing with the wine glass.

"Is that good?"

"He doesn't give a shit about me but he's going to find out I conned him out of three years of tuition at the University of Miami."

Lawrence whistled. "What can he do?"

She shrugged. "Yell at me. I can't be any worse off than I am right now."

"Bad?"

She gave a short laugh. "I wanted to keep that win ticket on Alice for a souvenir but I couldn't afford to." Lawrence started to say something but Shannon plunged ahead. "No big deal. I'll figure something out." She spoke rapidly, in control again. "Jimmy's the one with problems. No insurance."

This was definitely not going in the direction Lawrence wanted. "I think the Jockey's Guild has some insurance for injured riders."

"He's only ridden six or eight races. He's not even a member."

"The track will probably help him."

"I know!" Shannon slapped the table. "Let's have a party and raise money for him!"

It was the custom at racetracks everywhere for the jockey colony and the backstretch to have a golf tournament or a fundraiser of some kind when a rider got hurt. Lawrence remembered the thin jockey dwarfed by the hospital equipment, apologizing to him. "We could do it at Rodell and Maria's."

"And we could get those guys from Barn Nine who play salsa to do the music."

"How about a wet t-shirt contest?" Lawrence suggested.

Shannon rolled her eyes. "Men. You're always thinking about boobs. How about tight jeans? I think we can get more people to enter."

"Are you going to enter?"

"I have to manage the party. Ask your girlfriend."

"You'll have to ask her. I don't think she's talking to me anymore."

Shannon laughed. "Get Jack Delaney to do it."

Lawrence looked at his watch. "Hey. The races are coming on in Australia. Want to come watch?" He locked eyes with her and managed to slide his hand onto hers. He began making lazy circles around her knuckle.

She broke eye contact and looked at their hands. "What is this? Come see my etchings?"

"I'm not ready to go in yet," he said honestly. "We can watch a movie if you're tired of racing."

"I never get tired of racing. But no wrestling match, okay?" She was suddenly serious.

"What's the fun in that?"

She drew back her fist and he laughed. "Okay! Okay!"

Shannon wasn't sure she trusted Lawrence but she wanted to. She kept her guard up even as she flopped on Lawrence's plush sofa in front of the big screen TV. "Omigod this is decadent," she said, leaning back against the downy pillows.

"This is where I spend many a late and lonely night."

She laughed. "I bet."

"No, really, I sit here and watch race replays and do my handicapping. Want to see?" He opened a laptop and punched a few keys. The screen lit up with a montage of slow-motion and close-up clips of horses racing, set to the theme from "Chariots of Fire". Horses' legs, bandaged in pink or white or blue, trotting to the post. A horse's bay head in yellow blinkers, nodding in time with his galloping stride. A dozen horses racing on the turf, tightly bunched, with a flock of seagulls taking flight in the infield beside them. Parti-colored jockeys mingling in front of a dark green hedge.

"Wow," she said.

When he sat down beside her and handed her a drink, she looked at him with happy amazement. "This is so good. Did you make it?"

"The drink or the video?"

"The video."

He nodded. "I have to take a break from race replays once in awhile."

"It makes me fall in love with horses—" She fluttered her fingers on her chest.

"It's supposed to make you fall in love with me."

She laughed and punched him in the arm. "You should give this to Colonial Downs. I'm serious. Have you seen those lame ads they have on TV? If they ran this, they'd have ten thousand people in the grandstand every day. You know, they're always complaining because they can't get enough people to come to the track, but they're going about it wrong."

Lawrence leaned back and listened to her rattle on.

Chapter 52

Louisa didn't need to pack much to take Alice back to the farm. Shannon sat on the sofa bed and watched her. "You're going to take the goat over to the stakes barn for me?"

"I'll do it after you leave," said Shannon.

"It's not the trip to Wisconsin but I still need you to look out for the cat for a couple of days."

"Sure. I'll try to find a place so I can move out when you get back."

"No hurry."

"The meet's almost over. I have to figure out what I'm going to do anyway."

"Are you going back to Florida?" Louisa asked.

"I don't know."

Louisa stopped packing and looked Shannon in the eye. "Are you in trouble there?"

"Not with the law, if that's what you mean." Shannon stood up and toured the little room. "Are you moving to Wisconsin?"

Louisa resumed her packing with a little laugh. "I'm in the same boat with you: I don't know what I'm doing."

On impulse, Shannon hugged the older woman. "He'll be back, Louisa. He loves you. I know he does."

Louisa patted her back. "It's all right. This is what happens when I start drinking. I make bad decisions."

"Going out with Mr. Keswick was not a bad decision."

Louisa smiled. She straightened up. "You're right!" she said. "I've made lots worse. Did I ever tell you about my first husband? Dimitri? I ran off with him when I was seventeen and he turned out to be a first class con artist. But he had a body like a Greek god."

Wick went to the paddock every time Mike had a horse in on Monday and Tuesday. He drove past Barn Six numerous times. He haunted the track kitchen. He even looked for lights in her RV.

Not that he knew what he would say if he found her.

Finally, on Wednesday morning, he strolled into the barn and looked around.

"She's not here," Mike said, without looking up.

"Any idea when she'll be back?"

"No."

Wick waited, uncertain what to say next. Finally, he asked, "Did she go to Wisconsin?"

"Nah. She give up on that."

"Really?" Wick didn't know whether to be encouraged or not.

"Louisa's going back to Maryland with me. She doesn't trust me to take care of Alice," Mike said, smiling smugly. "Who'd have thought that old cripple would be good for something?"

Wick bristled. "Damn it, Mike. Let her go. Don't guilt her into staying around over that old horse."

Mike laughed shortly. "It's better than letting her move to Wisconsin to be near a goddamn football team."

"Better for who? For her or for you?" Wick challenged.

Now it was Mike's turn to get his back up. "You think I'm using Louisa?"

"Hell yeah. You don't give a damn about her. You're thinking about how much you need her and how hard it'd be for you to have to do without her."

If it had been anybody but Wick, Mike probably would have slugged him. Instead, he studied the older man. He was red in the face and swelled up like a toad, ready to scrap. Mike exhaled through his nose and smiled wryly. "Maybe you'd better look in the mirror."

Chapter 53

Lawrence's internal clock awakened him at five. He had never really accepted the racetrack schedule of early morning work, and although he woke up early from habit, his first thought usually was a mental groan. Sometimes on dark days he let himself sleep in, unless he knew some trainer was going to work a horse he was particularly interested in. This morning he didn't care if Lucien Lauren had come back to work Secretariat. He lay there contentedly, in no hurry to get up.

He became aware of the familiar arrangement of windows in his room, a pair of rectangles with a thin line of blue from the Fan District streetlights glowing around the drawn shades. Next he became aware of the regular breathing next to him and he smiled. He turned his head to look at her but he couldn't see much in the dark. Still, he watched her sleep.

After a few minutes, he slipped out of bed and went to the bathroom. As he relieved himself, he thought about waking her up and then going back to sleep together for a couple more hours.

But when he returned to the bedroom, she was sitting on a chair putting on her paddock boots.

"Oh hi," she said, as though he had surprised her in the tack room instead of in the bedroom where they had spent the previous five or six hours in naked intimacy.

He sat down on the edge of the bed in front of her. "Whatcha doing?"

She exhaled briskly. "Gotta go to work. Horses to feed, horses to gallop."

He leaned forward and rubbed her thighs. "Aw, don't go. Carl's girls'll feed your two nags with the rest of them."

She looked down at his hands and he felt for a moment as though he were invading her privacy.

"I still have to gallop them."

Her voice startled him with her determination. She was dissolving underneath his hands. He squeezed her legs. "No, you don't."

"Oh yes," she insisted. "You saw how short Acky was last Monday, he needs work. And Bread 'n Butter—"

He was grinning at her. "You don't give up, do you?"

"You don't, either."

He shook his head. "I mean about the horses."

She tied her boot and picked up the other one.

"Relax. You're not going to lose anything skipping a day with those two."

"What do you mean?" she said.

He tried to sooth her by rubbing her legs again but she shook him off. "Come on, Shannon. You can't run twenty-thirty lengths behind every time. The stewards are going to rule Acky off. The horse can't run."

She leaped to her feet. "Maybe I'm not the best trainer in the world," she blazed, "but don't you *dare* say my horse can't run!" She swung her boot and clipped him in the jaw.

Lawrence's vision of a leisurely morning cuddling in bed with Shannon was split as neatly as his lip. He touched his mouth and looked at his fingers to see if they were bloody. This was definitely not a prelude to more seductive behavior.

She was standing over him cussing and waving the boot around, and he held out a hand to ward off further blows. "You know, just because you're such a hotshot handicapper doesn't mean you know everything. You make mistakes, too!"

He stood up and grabbed the arm with the boot, whereupon she began to punch him with her other hand and call him unladylike names.

"Hey. Hey. Hey!" He held both her arms and she tried to stomp on his bare feet with her one shod foot. "Shannon! Stop it! Okay! They can run like trained pigs!"

Suddenly she burst into tears. The anger drained out of her like oil out of a crankcase and was replaced by such a welter of tears that they ran down her cheeks and dripped off her chin.

It was way too early in the morning for Lawrence to be able to understand what was going on, and part of him felt that even later in the afternoon he would have no idea what was going on. He did not know why girls cried but his sisters had long ago trained him to respond quickly and correctly when a girl burst into tears, so now he wrapped his arms around Shannon and let her cry on his bare chest until his chest hairs tickled her nose and she needed a tissue. He got her some toilet paper and she wiped her nose. After awhile she sighed deeply and said, "I don't want to leave."

"Here, let's get comfortable," he said. He propped up some pillows and they lay on the bed together, he in his shorts, she in her jeans with one boot on. "You don't have to leave. We can stay here all day, if you want."

"That's not what I meant," she said and cried again.

Lawrence hoped that maybe soon Shannon would just come out and tell him why she was crying. Maybe he shouldn't have said that about her horses. But it was true. She wasn't dumb. She knew they couldn't run. Why was she so upset?

"I don't want to leave the racetrack," she said and screwed up her face again.

Oh, thank God that's all it was. "Hey, Sweetheart, everybody's sad when the meet's over. But there's lots of other racetracks."

"What good would that do?" she asked hopelessly. "Acky won't be able to run any faster at Pimlico than he can at Colonial."

Lawrence almost laughed but he said nothing. He held her and combed her hair with his fingers. He thought about Jimmy throwing his guts up three times a day just to stay at the racetrack. He kissed her hair. "Hey."

"What?"

"Let's go out to the track."

"You got me back in bed and now you want to go to the track?"

"Hurry up or we'll miss Carl's colt."

Lawrence took her up on top of the tote board. Narrow steps on the back led up to a terrace with a railing. Above them in the fresh clear morning, high cirrus clouds made pink-gold streaks over the treetops at the far end of the track.

"Wow. What a great view."

"Yeah. You can really see how long the stretch is from here."

Around the rail, twenty-foot high painted posts marked the furlongs. She tried to count them. "I don't see how the jocks keep the poles straight."

"I guess you learn your way around the track after awhile," he said.

"I want to stay at the racetrack," Shannon told Lawrence. "I don't know why. It makes me miserable half the time."

"It makes everybody miserable half the time. It's the other half that keeps us around."

"You're not miserable."

He brushed her hair back, rubbing her cheek. "Prime example of racetrack misery: The first summer I'm here, I'm learning about handicapping. There's three horses in this race that are a lock for the money. It looks like a trifecta, but I'm afraid to bet an exotic like that, so I go for the exacta. It comes in and I'm jumping around the apron screaming like a crazy person. It's three hundred dollars, the biggest ticket I ever cashed."

"What's so miserable about that?"

"I enjoyed the win for about ten minutes. Then I realized I had the trifecta, which I was chicken to bet. The tri paid four thousand. So I couldn't enjoy the biggest day I ever had at the windows."

She nodded. They watched a set of horses breezing past. "But at least you have a job. You belong here. I don't belong. I want to be a trainer, but I suck at that. I can't even recognize horses with no talent. I don't have a job. I'm homeless. I don't know how I'm going to feed those two worthless horses."

"Go talk to Wick."

"I'm terrified of him."

"Aw, his bark is worse than his bite."

"It's the bark I'm afraid of."

"I used to be afraid of him, too. He'll find something for you."

"Why would he help me?"

"Because you're a racetracker. Everybody who loves the racetrack can find a niche for himself. You're smart. You can talk to people. You know everybody. The fundraiser for Jimmy tomorrow? You planned the whole thing. Look at all that money you got the trainers and everybody to put up. Wick'll find a place for you. He did for me."

"But you know how to do something."

"That's day to day," he said with a laugh.

"No, really, you're good."

"You are the eternal optimist, aren't you?"

She laughed for the first time that morning. "I must be, if I thought Acky could run."

He pulled her over and kissed her forehead. She leaned against him with her arms around his waist. He rubbed her shoulder with one hand and picked up his glasses to watch some horses in the turn. Below them, horses galloped softly in the loam. Shannon felt the sun as it crept over the treetops and hit the toteboard. She wanted to stay there the rest of the day. Lawrence had called her a racetracker. Maybe there was a place for her somewhere, somewhere besides hanging around the apron with the rail birds, the outsiders, the wannabes. She'd screw up her courage and go see Mr. Keswick.

Lawrence whistled. "Hey. Do you know that bay filly with Mike's saddle cloth?"

Shannon roused herself. "No, but he's got so many." She looked down at the horse. "She's a nice mover."

"Fast, too. Let's go down to the gap."

They climbed down and walked across the dew-soaked infield, leaving a dark path behind them.

At the gap, Shannon said, "I'm going to get us a doughnut."

Lawrence saw Mike sitting on a pony waiting for the filly to finish galloping.

"Saw your filly work."

Mike nodded.

"She new?"

Mike nodded again. "You like her?"

Lawrence looked down the track to watch the filly loping towards them, the air bouncing off her shoulders in tiny sparkling pieces and swirling like a comet's tail in her wake. He grinned. "Yeah, man. She can run like Rembrandt's Paint."

In the kitchen, Shannon waited for Rodell to pull a pan of fresh doughnuts out of the oven.

"Omigod, Rodell, these are so good it's insane."

"*Gracias*, Shannon."

"Here"—she gave him some money—"Give me a bunch."

When she got back to the gap, Lawrence was talking to Freddy and Bones. She shared her doughnuts with them.

"Freddy says there's a barbecue at Max Fox's barn tonight. Darryl was up here talking about it," said Lawrence.

"Yeah," Freddy said, "they got one of them pit cookers on wheels."

"Are they cleaning out the dorms for the end of the meet and roasting the chickens?" Lawrence asked.

"Darryl said some trainer was gonna give 'em a goat and they turned him down," said Freddy.

"Why?" said Lawrence.

"Because they're tough as shoe leather," said Freddy.

"No. Why'd the guy want to give them a goat?" Lawrence asked.

"It was Croaker Norge," said Bones. "He got this old goat for one of his horses, and the damn thing got loose and ate up a bunch of tack. So he offered to donate it to the cause."

Shannon started laughing and coughing, blowing doughnut crumbs all over Lawrence's sleeve. "Hey!"

"I'm sorry! Listen, don't tell Louisa Ferncliff about that."

"She partial to goats or something?"

"Omigod! You mean I know something you guys don't? You're not going to believe this." Shannon climbed up on the fence and got comfortable. "This is a great story."

Chapter 54

Rodell refilled the platters on the table while Wick made himself a sandwich. "This is a hell of a party you and Maria put on," he said. "That's mighty nice of you."

"It is not me and Maria. *Señorita* Hill is making the party."

"Really?"

"Every day she is calling the people, making the…" He waved at the crepe paper streamers. "…*fiesta*. She work very hard. *Señor* Ham is working, too."

"It looks like everybody on the backstretch is here. The track must be empty."

"*Sí.* She is telling me to cook for two hundred people."

Wick whistled. He wondered how much money they'd raised for that jock.

Mike Lucci joined him at the table.

"Did you know Shannon Hill organized this whole thing?" said Wick, still amazed.

"No shit. She hit me up for six hundred dollars. Said all the trainers had to put in a hundred bucks for every winner they had since the Derby. And I'm having my best week of the meet."

Wick wandered through the noisy, crowded restaurant, taking note of who was there and looking, always looking for Louisa. He knew his own mind now but how did Louisa feel? Was that new softness still there or had her self-sufficient veneer crept back into place? He would have to be careful what he said.

There were two long tables near the bar with silent auction items. He skimmed the line, put down a bid for a round of golf. The live music blasted his ears but he felt obliged to stay. He refilled his drink at the bar and stood in the back, watching the band. He felt curiously alone.

Scanning the crowd, he felt a quiet pride at the sight of so many horsemen, many of them struggling themselves, throwing money in the pot for a guy they hardly knew. As frustrated as he got over firecrackers in the bathhouse and chickens in the dormitories, Wick was often humbled by the sight of some less-than-minimum wage groom pulling fifty or a hundred dollars out of his pocket to help pay for broken bones suffered by an uninsured exercise rider or to buy impractical gifts for a child living illegally in the backstretch dormitories.

Lawrence slid along the wall and jostled Wick, clinking his glass. "So? What do you think? Good party?"

Wick couldn't decide if Lawrence was buzzed or not. It was hard to tell with that boy. "Rodell says you and Shannon organized this."

"Yeah. It was mostly Shannon. She had about a million ideas. We couldn't even do them all."

Wick nodded, looking at the bodies crowding the dance floor, thinking about the Virginia Derby gala. "Hell of a party. You think she could do one of these for me?"

Lawrence laughed. "She can do anything but train horses."

Wick eyed his ace handicapper. "What are you going to do next?"

Lawrence shrugged and took a drink.

"I know you had a little cold streak," said Wick, "but you've been hot since the Turf Festival started. You're too good to stay here. There's no money in this. You need to be a jock's agent or a bloodstock agent."

Lawrence looked at the ceiling, digesting this notion. "Thanks, Wick."

Wick clapped Lawrence on the shoulder. "You let me know when you want to go to one of the sales. I'll get you together with Bill Graves. He'll help you get started."

Wick moved off through the crowd. Then he saw her. He worked his way through the gyrating dancers and touched her shoulder. "Louisa."

She was startled, then forced a smile. "Hi."

He hesitated then plunged in, leaning towards her ear so she could hear him over the music. "I had some business to take care of out of town. Personal business."

"I hope it went well for you," she said without looking at him.

"I got some things settled."

Louisa smiled and waved at someone across the room.

"I'm sorry," he said, fumbling for words.

"You don't owe me an apology."

Wick did not know what to say next. He was trying to make up but she was being frustrating. "Louisa, stop being like that."

She finally looked at him, her eyes ablaze, her hair coming loose. "Don't–"

"—call me Louisa in that tone of voice," he finished and was rewarded with a small smile. Okay, maybe he could handle this.

Just then, Hank May came to the microphone, announcing the tight jeans contest. "Folks, you have to decide which filly fills out her jeans the best. We're gonna take a vote. Get out your wallet, because you're going to have to vote with dollars."

"It's too loud," shouted Wick. "Let's get out of here."

"I can't, Wick." She shook her head.

He looked into her eyes, trying to read the *why*. She looked back at him steadily. Okay, he thought, I've got to earn my way back. "Well, can I buy a lady a drink?"

"Get me a Jack Black on the rocks."

Wick exhaled. "O-kay."

"And hurry up. I've got to be in this damned contest and I need some courage."

"This thing?" said Wick, pointing incredulously to the stage where exercise girls and one or two girl jockeys in jeans were lining up.

"It was Shannon's idea. Croak said he'd put up five hundred dollars if I'd do it…and we're here to raise money." She threw up her hands.

"You said drinking made you make bad decisions. Well, this is one of your worst."

"Don't be such a stick in the mud. It's for a good cause."

"You just want to show off," he said.

"What if I do?"

As Louisa strolled across the stage, Croaker Norge sidled up to Wick and said, "Damn if you ain't right, Wick. She looks as good in them jeans as she did in that dress."

"Yeah," Wick said and nodded.

"I'd put up another five hundred if I thought it'd do me any good."

Wick hummed.

"I mean, she's still got the tits *and* the ass."

Wick, who was not quite six feet, had to sort of jump up to punch Norge, but he got in a good lick nevertheless. The crowd kept the towering older man from falling down. He reeled back a few steps, felt his jaw, then charged Wick, who crouched and waited. Norge had his fist outstretched and, rather than throwing a punch, he simply ran into Wick. The two men clenched each other and fell to the floor, kicking and swearing. A cheering crowd surrounded them.

Hank, who watched the whole thing from the stage, continued his patter on the microphone, pausing only to say, "Will somebody stop those two old roosters? One of them's liable to peck the other one to death."

Two off-duty track security officials pulled the men apart and hauled them out to the café tables in front of the restaurant. "Mr. Keswick, I never thought I'd have to pull you out of a fight."

"Me neither, George," said Wick, as he touched his bloody nose and looked at his bloody hand.

Louisa followed them outside and fluttered back and forth between them.

"Louisa, get the hell out of here," said Wick. "Norge, you apologize to her or I'll bust you back to Monday."

"Keswick, you couldn't—"

The security guards stepped in again. "Now, gentlemen."

Norge slumped in a chair and shook his head. "Louisa, I'm sorry for telling your boyfriend I want to get in your britches."

"It's all right, Croak. I haven't had drunk men fighting over me in years. It feels good."

Wick glowered at both of them.

Norge struggled to his feet and the guards immediately surrounded him. He waved them off. "It's all right. I'm just going to take a leak. Joe Frazier over there ain't knocked all the piss out of me yet." He threw his head back in a honking guffaw and staggered back inside the building. The guards, after a moment, followed him.

Louisa sat at the café table and pulled napkins out of the holder, dipping them in an abandoned cup of beer. "Here."

Wick dabbed at his face and waited for the pounding in his temples to slow down. Neither one spoke. Finally, he said, "Look, Louisa, I can't do everything I want to do now. It's a matter of respect, for you and for her. Just give it some time. Don't leave. You told me I had to let go one day, but I'm gonna need you to help me pick up the pieces."

"Somebody'll be around to do that."

"I don't want 'somebody.' I want you. I need you." He paused. "I'm not J. G. Lippincott."

She looked away and sighed. "J. G. was a bastard but he never let any of his horses go to slaughter. He claimed them all back and retired them."

"Louisa." He waited for her to look at him. "I'm not going to be one of your bad decisions."

She gave him the barest of smiles. "I hope you're right." But in her head she was replaying that strange phrase, *I need you*. He said, *I need you*. She would have to think about that.

He nodded, carefully, seriously. Finally, he reached out to her shoulder. "Here. You're about to lose this pin."

"Thank you." She took it and fixed her hair.

"What'd you do with my buddy the goat?" he asked.

"I gave him to Croak."

"He won't take as good care of him as I did."

"I thought you were done with him."

"Well, he was pretty ornery and God knows he was stubborn, but I had gotten right attached to him." He caught her eye and tested a smile. "What do you think I'd have to do to get him back?"

She matched him look for look. "You know how goats are: hard to catch. You'll probably have to chase him around."

"I can still run pretty fast for an old man."

"Good. You're going to need to."

BOOK CLUB DISCUSSION TOPICS

Several of the characters in *The Key to the Quarter Pole* face serious moral dilemmas. Boyd "Wick" Keswick struggles with what he owes his dying wife and what he owes himself. Shannon Hill has to decide what price she would pay to win a race with one of her horses. Jimmy Wiseman vacillates between the joy of riding Good Prospect and guilt for breaking track rules.

1. Which character has the toughest choice? How would you have handled the situation?

2. What moral dilemma does Louisa Ferncliff face?

3. Shannon and Jimmy have fairly conventional choices. What about Wick? How would you characterize his determination to honor his marriage to a woman who has been absent for so long? What would you have done? Would your attitude be the same if the situation were reversed, if the husband were the one in the institution and the wife the one who wanted companionship?

4. How do you interpret the title of the book?

5. Why do you think Louisa finds pro football a good escape from racing? What keeps drawing her back to racing? Will she ever move to Wisconsin?

ACKNOWLEDGEMENTS

As a writer, when you finally get the published book in your hands, you feel like a triathlete falling prostrate across the finish line, your clothes in tatters, your muscles flaccid, your mouth too dry to drool, your body wrung out of all moisture, eyes crossed, tongue lolling on the pavement, brain cells reduced to single digits. You are, briefly, too tired to appreciate the achievement.

But after that first kind word by a reader, you are all plumped up, muscles flexed, eyes uncrossed and brain cells firing on all cylinders.

Now revived, I want to thank all the people who inspired me, pushed me, handed me bottled water and cheered me on. Foremost among those people are my family. For many years Cricket patiently accepted my daily disappearance — "I'm going to the back room" — and applauded my progress. Moreover, by giving me a lifetime fellowship at "Long Run," he enabled me to write this and other books. Katie Bo is my best editor, and she read several drafts, saving me from making several big mistakes in the plot. Her racing contacts, which by now far outstrip mine, have kept me in touch with the magical world of racing.

And I could never thank my mother, Flo Neher Traywick, enough for giving me all kinds of support. Mom, you're the best!

Right behind my family comes Rita Mae Brown, who has been a great booster and mentor for years. Endless thanks to her for her generous recommendations of my work to her agents and for her admonition to "write on!" She always perks me up at times when I most need encouragement.

Author Mary Kay Zuravleff is a terrific writing instructor, and I would advise any aspiring novelist to work with her. She led an inspirational and practical year-long class in "revising your novel manuscript" that helped me transform a manuscript containing at least three novels into one coherent story. In analyzing the large cast of the book, my fellow classmates generously slogged through my too-long manuscript and then provided the great service of helping me decide whom to vote off the island. Good luck to them with their own manuscripts, all of which I found to be fascinating reading: Liza Taylor, Charles Heiner, Ron Harris, Linda Hewitt, Ray Nedzel, and Catherine Conner (RIP).

I am indebted to WriterHouse in Charlottesville for offering the aforementioned class. This is a wonderful place for writers to connect and learn and grow. The range of courses they offer is terrific, and the instructors are of high caliber.

As a direct result of my work in Mary Kay's class, the manuscript won the James River Writers and *Richmond Magazine's* biennial Best Unpublished Novel contest. This was an absolutely stunning event and something that kept me going through further revisions of the ms. My thanks to Maya Smart, who judged the final round and gave me good feedback.

James River Writers has played a valuable role in my development as a writer, particularly in my understanding of the publishing industry. Their annual conference in October is one of the best. The founders did a great service to writers and readers alike by creating such a wonderful community for networking, learning and, perhaps the most important influence, cheering each other on.

Brent Anthony Johnston is a brilliant writer who can convey his approach to fiction writing in a wonderfully accessible way. His guidance at the *Virginia Quarterly Review's* annual workshop helped me refine the writing of this book. I reread my notes from that class often and they continue to be useful.

All of my readers and "blurbers" gave me great encouragement and to them I am indebted, especially Leila Christenbury, who read the first (horrible) draft and made tactful suggestions.

Dianne and Wayne Dementi and their team have done a beautiful job with the book. Wayne is always a joy to deal with.

Based entirely on Wayne's enthusiasm, I have become convinced this book will be a best-seller.

Many racetracks inspired me to write this book, and it is a thrill to have Todd Marks' gorgeous photograph of sunrise at Saratoga on the cover.

My thanks to George Allen, who, as governor of Virginia, appointed me to the Virginia Racing Commission, thus opening up the whole fascinating world of racing to me and, ultimately, to my daughter.

Anyone who spends any time at the racetrack comes away captivated by the horses, the people and the entire esoteric environment. Anyone with the least inclination to write wants to write the definitive racetrack novel. But of course, fiction pales beside the true stories of the track. And so my thanks go to all the horsemen who live in that amazing world for inspiring me and for enabling those magical creatures, Thoroughbred racehorses, to do what they love to do.

Many of the folks who made Colonial Downs run before the shut-down in 2014 supplied me with colorful stories and technical details necessary to the authenticity that I was determined to capture. My thanks to the stewards, who indulged me as I roamed around the backside long past the time when I held a valid license as a racing commissioner. Some of my many helpful friends and teachers have gone on to greener pastures, but I will name as many as I can (and apologies for those I somehow overlooked): jockey and clerk of the scales Adam Campola, racetrack executive John Mooney (who needs to write his own book), VRC executive secretary Don Price (who broke me in to the regulatory side of pari-mutuel racing), VRC executive secretary Stan Bowker (who continued my education), jockey and steward Bill Passmore (who rode with Red Pollard and had hilarious stories to tell), perennial leading trainer Ferris Allen, former HBPA-VA president Woodberry Payne, legendary racing secretary Lenny Hale, handicapper "Derby Bill" Watson, turf writer Nick Hahn, paddock steward Denver Beckner, valet Richard Ramkhelawan, announcer Dave Rodman.

Plus all the grooms and hot walkers and exercise riders without whom there would be no racing. I've always thought the backstretch was like family, a few black sheep but mostly a mixed bag of personalities and horse-lovers who, when the chips are down, look out for each other.

Additionally, Mindy Coleman, Esquire, of the Jockeys Guild, made important contributions to my peace of mind about several details.

And finally, thanks to Marilynn Ware, who dragged me away from the computer from time to time for the mental refreshment of an exhilarating fox hunt through the Virginia countryside on a talented horse.

ABOUT THE AUTHOR

Robin Williams is a humor writer and speaker.

She earned an M.A. from the prestigious creative writing program at Hollins University and spent five years as a feature writer for the *Richmond Times-Dispatch*, where she won frequent statewide recognition for her writing, including as finalist for UPI's Journalist of the Year.

The manuscript for this book received the sixth biennial Best Unpublished Novel award sponsored by *Richmond Magazine* and James River Writers.

Robin's next book, *The Last Romantic War*, a bio-memoir of her family in World War II, will be published in 2019. Robin has published two collections of humorous newspaper columns, *Chivalry, Thy Name Is Bubba*, drawn from the *Times-Dispatch*, *The Goochland Free Press* and other sources, and *Bush Hogs and Other Swine*, which includes a foreword by Earl Hamner, creator of "The Waltons."

Mystery writer Rita Mae Brown calls Robin "the country Seinfeld."

Robin served six years as chairman of the Virginia Racing Commission during the early years of racing in Virginia. She also served on the boards of both trade associations for racing regulators, the North American Pari-mutuel Racing Association and the Association of Racing Commissioners International, where she was the driving force behind the development of the National Racing License.

Following two terms on the VRC, Robin became instrumental in founding a chapter of the Thoroughbred Retirement Foundation and later served as president of the national organization. The James River chapter of the TRF operates a rehabilitation program for prison inmates using rescued ex-racehorses.

Robin lives on a farmette in Virginia with her husband and the usual cats, dogs and horses. She is a recovering craftaholic.